I

Working Smart

Working Smart

*How to Use Microcomputers
to Do Useful Work*

Colin K. Mick
with the assistance of
Stefan T. Possony

MACMILLAN PUBLISHING COMPANY
A Division of Macmillan, Inc.
NEW YORK

Collier Macmillan Publishers
LONDON

Macmillan Publishing Company
866 Third Avenue, New York, N.Y. 10022

Collier Macmillan Canada, Inc.

Printed in the United States of America

printing number
1   2   3   4   5   6   7   8   9   10

Library of Congress Cataloging in Publication Data

Mick, Colin K.
    Working smart.

    Includes index.
    1. Microcomputers.   2. Microcomputers—Programming.
3. Computer literacy.   I. Possony, Stefan T.   II. Title.
QA76.5.M5213   1984   001.64   83-43009
ISBN 0-02-949580-6

Contents

copyw 71984 V.

001.64
mic

7-84

copyr 7 1984

VII

Acknowledgments

This book would not have been possible without the assistance and support of Ulla Mick and Betyar Mick, who hung in there through the learning pains of personal computers and the birthing pains of this book. Gerald Papke and Eileen DeWald of Macmillan provided considerable emotional and technical support throughout the extensive process of getting the manuscript published.

Introduction

I saw my first computer in the early 1960s when I was an under-
graduate at the University of Alaska. Actually I didn't *see* it; I
peeked at it through an open door to an electrical engineering lab-
oratory. I vaguely knew what it was, and that one had to be an
engineer to play with it. I experienced a brief pang of regret that I
had abandoned engineering and physics for anthropology and
journalism. But it was too late for me to change my major once
again.

I encountered my next computer several years later while a
graduate student in communication at Stanford. Things weren't
going so hot. The faculty at the Institute for Communication Research and I were having disagreements over whether I was going to remain a graduate student. And then, during the third
quarter I took a required class on data analysis. It involved learning to run statistical programs on Stanford's new IBM 360/67.
Having stronger mathematics skills than the rest of the class, and
being less intimidated by machines, I ended up as the star of the
data-analysis class. The professor's final report read: ''You spent
more money than the rest of the class combined. We winced, but
we paid it.'' Little did ''we'' know.

The Institute had an unofficial policy of designating one student as the computer expert—to run analyses for the faculty and help the other students cope with IBM 360/67. The current "consultant" was getting ready to graduate, and I was soon drafted to help input and edit papers for advanced graduate students and faculty members. My future at the Institute began to seem more secure. I got the job because of my text-processing skills—a cinch for someone who had supported himself as a journalist.

During the following summer I received novitiate instruction. The IBM 360/67 sat in a sealed room. You could look at it through the windows, but you couldn't touch. Most instruction was by trial and error. I learned computers can't spell, and are intolerant of poor typing ability. I had to learn FORTRAN to conduct a computer analysis of educational television programming. I also had to learn about arrays, control language, and loops. And, I learned to write a special purpose program to generate all the tables we wanted in one pass. I rewrote the program three times. In final form there was a respectable stack of boxes full of computer cards, 1500 cards for the program alone and another 10,000 cards for the data, which I hauled to the machine on a hand truck. The program printout measured three feet high—we used the hand truck to haul it back to the office. My future as a graduate student was secure!

Power corrupts. As the only computer expert in a group professionally committed to data analysis, I was easily corrupted. In two years I was the department's consultant, controlling one of the largest academic computer budgets on campus.

In 1970 I designed a course called "Computers for Duffers," to teach people how to make computers work for them, particularly in their writing and data-analysis work. At this time academic computing was divided into two camps: the computer scientists, who viewed the computer as a big toy and invented creative, but generally unproductive things for it to do; and the number crunchers, who saw the computer as an enormous calculator. Both approaches emphasized using the computer for specialized tasks. I was showing people how to use the computer as a general-purpose tool to make their work and life easier and a little less tedious. Students took the course and went through the motions, but few seemed to get the message. One student summed it all up by saying, "I don't give a damn how the computer works, just so it gives me a significant F." Who could argue with a conceptual framework like that?

After graduate school I began research in the field of information behavior—how people create and use information and how new technologies influence those processes. I had been writing with and studying about computers since 1967, but their benefits were still unavailable to the masses. Then, the December 1975 issue of *Popular Electronics* heralded the new age. Featured on the magazine cover was the Altair 8008—the first commercially available microcomputer.

I immediately began following the development of microcomputers. I already had a word processor—a full-screen VYDEC 1146. (This may not impress you, but to me it was like a Rolls convertible parked in the driveway.) I awaited the time when the micros would bring the advantages of computers to those who needed them most—information workers.

You have to understand that to a user of big, macho IBM mainframes, a micro looks the way a rubber duck does to the captain of a cruise ship. It's an interesting toy, appealing to the uninitiated, perhaps, but hardly suitable for my needs. I mean, I once ran a statistical analysis that required a 750 by 750 matrix. It took every bit of memory we could squeeze out of the Stanford 360/67, and tied up the damn machine for forty minutes. There's no way I can do my work on a little bitty 64K machine, I thought.

The reality was, however, that I had run that giant program only once. I did large scale statistical analysis once a year. Most of what I did was writing, processing simple calculations, preparing budgets, federal research grant proposals, and keeping track of my growing collection of articles, books, journals, loose information, and appointments. I was writing on my word processor (a big, pretty, but very dumb micro). I was budgeting on an electronic calculator (a small, very dumb micro). I was filing, indexing, and scheduling by making piles on my desk and occasionally throwing them into file cabinets and boxes by myself (a slightly overweight, dumb contract researcher and consultant).

Finally, in the summer of 1980, I became convinced that the microcomputer was mature and I should buy one. Feeling insecure, I talked to a few colleagues, and we all started investigating the field. We bought magazines—*Byte, Interface Age*, and *Kilobaud*—to read the microcomputer reviews, not just the ads. (This is difficult because it seems that 75 percent of the column inches in these magazines are filled with ads promising everything.) It was clear an incredible treasure existed for the taking. The only problem was deciding what to select from this tremendous pile of goodies. The magazines were no help at all. The writers were all from the indiscriminate, high-fidelity school of reviewing.

We decided to go out into the world and see for ourselves. We went to computer shows and visited computer stores. We talked to people. We learned a number of great truths and a few GREAT TRUTHS. We learned that a lot of salesmen don't know very much about computers. Remember now, we are pros. I can talk BASIC, FORTRAN, ALGOL W, PL/1, and smatterings of SNOBOL and LISP. My hunting companion Jesse Caton could talk assembly language, knew the difference between a compiler and an interpreter, had even written his own language, and was director of computing at a small research company. Between us we destroyed the egos of many sales representatives. We learned by not talking with them. Instead, we played with the machines.

After months of indecision, we finally moved. We agreed to bite the bullet and build three S-100-based systems. We decided to buy the components separately and integrate them ourselves, trusting our own abilities. Jesse could handle the software, and I could solder and puzzle through the instructions and assembly. The third member of our group, Bob Mason, was an honest-to-God Ph.D. engineer. There was no way we could fail.

Our logic went like this: By building the system ourselves we would save money and learn more about microcomputers. We had minimum dollars to spend and we wanted to get the most computing power we could. We were buying three systems at once, so we started negotiating with the mail-order house that advertised the lowest prices. We kept at it until we finally got a full S-100 system—CPU board, memory board, disk controller, and mainframe—two disk drives, and cabinets for just over $2,600. We made the buy.

Then we learned another great truth: A mail-order house advertisement does not guarantee that a component is in stock. Over the next two months equipment arrived sporadically, interspersed with frequent calls to discuss FTC regulations, nonperformance, and return of equipment with mail-order house representatives.

When all the components finally arrived, Jesse and I assembled them and got them working. To our surprise, the machine actually came up quickly. But as we became more sophisticated (we pros "sophisticate" rapidly) we realized our systems were performing at less than optimal levels. While we puzzled over performance, fate stepped in and dealt me an ace named John Mason—my sister's fiancée. While fumbling through the social amenities of our first meeting, I interjected my experience with the new computer. John assumed a somewhat amused expression.

As it happened, he is a computer designer—not just any computer designer—but the cofounder of the company that had manufactured our computer equipment. And he had designed all of it.

John put my equipment through one of the most drastic transformations in the history of computers, and I embarked on a learning curve that would shame 99 percent of the world's students. I got exactly what I needed. I already knew computing from the user end. What I learned from John was the business end of the computer industry: how they are designed, made, and priced; what distinguishes good and bad products. He gave me an inside view of the industry—one that few people ever get.

During this learning process, I was using my new micro increasingly in my work. I transferred my writing from the word processor to the micro the first week it was up. I initiated the filing operations a few weeks later. But the most mindboggling advance was in budgeting, which is, after all, just an exercise in basic mathematics: adding, subtracting, multiplying, and dividing. For a research proposal you usually prepare both a summary budget on a standardized form and a breakdown that details costs by category and task. The goal is to arrive at matching totals on the rows and columns of the detail budget, and have them equal the final total on the summary budget. In ten years of proposal writing my totals agreed only once, and that was when I had made fortuitous mistakes in both budgets, discovered by someone who checked my figures.

For my first budgeting exercise with the computer I used a program called Forecaster, which allowed me to create basic budget worksheets and then vary the data that went into them. It was amazing. I could change an estimate and push a button, and out popped a new set of budgets. The row and column totals were equal. The final total of the detail budget matched that of the summary budget. Two hours of work and fifteen feet of calculator tape were replaced by one minute and a few strokes of the key. Far out! I was hooked. I started thinking about information behavior and the new micros. I started working my theories into my lectures. I bought a second micro for my home, so I didn't have to go into the office whenever the creative urge struck.

All this background brings me finally to this book. In the midst of all this enthusiasm I was talking with Jerry Pournelle, who writes a personal computer column for *Byte* and is a fellow enthusiast on the subject. He asked if I would be willing to assemble a machine like mine for his friend Steve Possony, and help him learn to use it. Nothing to it, I thought. I'll whip this one off in nothing flat, save Jerry some bucks, make a few myself, and also do him a favor. Little did I know.

Jerry, Steve, his wife Regina, and I got together a few weeks later for a test drive on the computer. Steve got interested, and the great undertaking lurched into motion. Assembling the system took longer than I planned. (It always does.) Even with John's help it took time to acquire the components.

Thoroughly intimidated by his test drive, Steve wisely decided to pick up some pointers before he got his machine. He agreed to come by my office occasionally for an hour or so of instruction. After the first few sessions, Steve got hooked. That's not unusual—it happens to everyone who isn't a latent Luddite. Steve quickly discovered that he had found a tool for cutting his workload by a high order of magnitude. He had been writing by dictating to Regina, irritating her by returning totally obscured edited texts and demanding retyped copies. The thought of generating documents by keyboard instead of by dictation didn't thrill him—he was used to giving dictation. What got him hooked to the computer was that it made editing so much easier. He could revise the text, move blocks of it around, and go through permutations in a matter of minutes.

The problem was that Steve didn't behave the way I expected. I had been living with computer technology for so long that its jargon was part of my vocabulary. I was used to working with people who, as information professionals, interact with computers on a regular basis. To Steve I was talking in a foreign language whose vocabulary he had never heard before.

Steve represents a generation that did not grow up with electronic technology. The computer to him was an abstract concept, as it had been to me when I saw the machine in the engineering lab twenty years ago. His self-assurance, however, allowed him to tell me abruptly when he didn't understand what I was saying. His Germanic stubbornness and attention to detail forced him to persist in asking questions.

Steve initially tried the traditional approach to learning. I was teaching him WordStar, a word processing program. He read the entire manual. From cover to cover. He must be the only person in the world to accomplish that thankless task without being paid for it. It didn't help. Bad as our communication problems were, they were nothing compared to penetrating the obscurities of the WordStar manual (much less any other microcomputer manual).

In frustration Steve starting writing down his perceptions of what I was telling him and of what the manual said. He also listed what he didn't understand. (Naturally, he wrote all this as part of his WordStar practice exercises.) His text confirmed that I had fallen victim to jargonitis—the dread disease of the technical communicator. I also began to understand Steve's frustration as that of any novice encountering the computer world for the first time.

I began writing responses to Steve's questions, formulating instructions and tutorials on what I thought he should know to use his system effectively. Jerry Pournelle (Remember him? Steve's friend, the microcomputer writer) monitored all this through telephone conversations with Steve and me. With characteristic entrepreneurial spirit he suggested we expand the lessons into a book.

Most of the material in this book is based on dialogues between Steve and me. Some has roots in the computer-literacy course I taught at Stanford. Some comes from the seminars and workshops I have taught on micros, information behavior, and the use of computers to support information work. All of it has been thrown at Steve, who listened, interpreted, inquired persistently, and synthesized. I shouldn't forget Regina. Steve is a classic European intellectual—left-brain dominant—who likes his concepts broken down so he can understand them. In . . . small . . . digestible . . . pieces. Regina is right-brain dominant. She works with gestalts and feelings. She learned to use the system along with Steve, but she saw it very differently. I have tried to preserve some of her insights here as well.

This book is organized in seven sections:

Section I: A discourse on the usefulness of personal computers.

Section II: Personal-computer applications at work, in education, and in the home.

Section III: Personal-computer hardware. A description of the physical components of a personal computer system and an explanation of how they work and interact.

Section IV: Personal-computer software—the instructions that tell the computer what to do. Description of types of software— operating systems, utilities, languages, and applications programs—and what they do. Emphasis on practical applications.

Section V: How to get started in personal computing. Suggestions on buying hardware and software.

Section VI: How to put a system together and use it. Guide to developing good computer work habits and avoiding problems. Preventive maintenance and trouble-shooting.

Section VII: Working smart: a philosophical discourse on the impact of personal computers on society.

Because the seven sections and their chapters are somewhat independent of each other, it is unnecessary to read them in sequential order. When writing about a technical topic it is difficult to entirely avoid using jargon. I've tried to purge the text of as many undefined terms as possible, but sometimes there just aren't any appropriate synonyms. Since one purpose of this book is to advance your computer literacy, I've included an extensive glossary, which should accelerate your fluency in ''computerese.''

SECTION I

INTRODUCTION

This section provides a philosophical introduction to personal computing and a discussion of how best to use personal computers for business and professional support. It includes guidelines to help you decide if you should invest time and money in acquiring a personal computer and, if you do, to learn how to use it productively.

1

Welcome to the Information Revolution

The computer revolution has been sweeping the country for the past two decades. We hear about it every day. We all receive computer-generated letters and bills. We see movies that show rotating computer tapes, punch cards dropping into sorting bins, and lots of flashing lights. Future-oriented films portray computers as rational beings—talking to people, controlling their environments, providing answers to impenetrable problems, and occasionally running amok. But what do computers mean to you?

If you are like most people, you probably have had very little contact with computers. Perhaps you have played some of the new computer games or you have tried a new personal computer in a store. Maybe you have worked with a word processor or a time-shared computing system at the office. But you probably know little about what computers are, how they work, what they can do for you, and what they will be doing for you in the future.

My purpose is not to tell you about computers, although I do. It's not to tell you about software, although I do that, too. My basic purpose is to help you become information literate: I will show you how the computer can make your information-processing skills more effective and give you the information tools you will need to reach this goal.

The computer is primarily an electronic information processor that is rapidly changing the way we acquire, organize, recall, access, analyze, synthesize, and apply information. The computer revolution is just one aspect of a larger, more pervasive information revolution that has been sweeping the world for the last century. If we take a close look at our high technology society we find that more than 50 percent of our Gross National Product is devoted to the production, movement, and use of information. This statement assumes a broad definition of information, encompassing traditional white-collar work in the communications, publishing, and computer industries, as well as in activities related to inventory, shipping, materials control, government, and the programming and maintenance of automated equipment. A cursory glance at labor statistics reveals that our economy is becoming more information intensive every year. Additionally, a large percentage of our imports are based on information technologies that we have developed.

Japan's industrial base, for example, is built on information and technologies that they have imported from us. The Japanese acknowledge that their industrial emphasis is on development; little is spent on research. They get the information from us and apply it better than we do ourselves. Initially they even learned how to apply it from us.

What do the Japanese do that we don't? Well, for one, they have a much greater respect for information than we do, and, two, they are much more adept at applying information. We have little respect for information and don't know how to use it properly. The management of "information work" isn't just a lost art, it's an art most organizations—public and private—have yet to discover.

We are engaged in an information revolution that will eventually send shockwaves through our entire society. This revolution so far has been technology-driven. That is, management has acquired the new technology to support existing practices and situations. What we need, instead, is a user-driven management approach that selects technologies that augment the workers' performance and productivity and their enjoyment of life.

Because information work and the management of it are so poorly understood, we often have to talk in analogies to make the subject comprehendible to the layman. Here are a couple of analogies we have used.

Parallels Between the Computer and the Industrial Revolution

The best example we have for projecting the course of the information revolution is the industrial revolution. Mechanization of labor began in the late 18th century, yet it has only been in the last few decades that we have learned how to use machines well. Let's look at the mechanization of manual labor and see what guidelines we can apply to the computerization of white-collar (head) work.

Before mechanization, individual artisans created products from start to finish. With specialization craftsmen contributed their skills to different parts of the production process. In the manufacture of cloth, for example, one person might spin the thread, another weave the cloth, and yet another dye it. Because people supplied their own power, they selected their own work sites. The market determined the movement of materials between sites. As work became more organized, managers moved materials between the craftsmen, directed production, and handled the economics.

The industrial revolution substituted machines for craft labor. Machines required power, so factories evolved near natural power sources. Through all of the 19th century and well into the 20th, factories required central power sources. At first mechanization was limited to a few large power-intensive machines. Soon, however, the development of mechanical couplings allowed a large number of machines to share this power. In old factories machines were lined up in nice straight rows, not for appearances, but to receive power from driveshafts along the ceiling that were connected at one end to a central power source.

Soon industrial cities sprang up near water or coal power sources. But dependence on a central power source also meant that the entire system was vulnerable to the actions of a single individual. With a loss of power all machines shut down and production ceased. One stupid mistake or accident could idle an entire production line. The industrial revolution was confined largely to factories, since there was no way to economically transmit power to small businesses, offices, and homes. It took the invention of the fractional horsepower motor, electric power, and wire transmission to finally extend the industrial revolution beyond the factory.

The computerization of society is following exactly the same pattern as did the mechanization of society. When first introduced, the computer was a large machine that could be applied only to centralized tasks. (We called this a batch-process machine.) During the 1960s we finally found out how to extend computing power to multiple work stations through timesharing—a technique by which the mainframe computer is available to each of several users for a small fraction of every second. Because computers execute hundreds of millions of instructions per second, this fraction of time is sufficient to provide relatively continuous support to each user. Timesharing activities, however, had to take place in close proximity to the computer.

Today timesharing requires expensive, specialized telecommunications links for high-speed data communications to take place between remote user locations and the centralized computer. A cheaper alternative is connection by telephone line, which is very slow. Timesharing repeats all the problems of centralized mechanization. When the mainframe goes down, all computer work ceases. The timeshared computer is vulnerable to software crashes and misuse.

Microcomputers are to the information revolution what the fractional horsepower motor was to the industrial revolution. With micros we can bring computing power directly to the user. Moreover, we can tailor microcomputers to meet the needs of individuals.

Parallels in the Management of Industrial and Information Work

The industrial revolution caused not only the centralization of the workplace, but also determined that it be structured to meet the requirements of the power and the machines. A third influence was more subtle. The major production cost was running and maintaining machinery; labor costs were small. Therefore, management maximized the utilization of machines, programming workers to serve them. Programming people to serve machines continued until after World War II when labor costs began over-taking machine costs. Concurrently, productivity began decreasing, despite the best management techniques.

Then came a breakthrough. Progressive managers around the world advanced a new philosophy of management that made the worker the central focus of mechanized work. Suddenly machines were being situated and programmed to meet the needs of the workers. Volvo of Sweden pioneered this approach, as documented by Pehr Gyullenhammar in *People at Work*.

The Japanese have also received much publicity about their management system and high productivity. While their success in these areas cannot be denied, it should be noted that they emphasize group, not individual productivity. Their approach to mechanization is to replace rather than augment workers.

Unlike industrial practices, the management of information work hasn't changed much in this century. We can communicate information faster, and we can store it in a computer, but most of the basic information processes are still handled manually. Consider how we have used computers so far. We still treat them as we did machines at the turn of the century for narrow, specialized purposes—accounting, filing, or text input. We train specialists to fit their work to the function of a machine.

Word processors, for example, are essentially narrow, specialized, and stupid personal computers, though they can significantly increase productivity. Frequently we discover in an office a single word-processor operator who works at the same task all day long. It is not surprising that studies of word-processor use show that productivity gains are not as high as initially expected. Moreover, operators frequently complain about using CRT terminals; their complaints are similar to those of people who work in typing pools. In short, the ill effects are caused by working at boring, repetitive tasks. A better approach to computerizing information functions is to install a general-purpose machine on which workers can perform an expanded range of functions, rather than using a machine to make workers do more of the same.

The microcomputer—the foremost machine of the information age—is really quite cheap. This means more people have the capital to set themselves up as entrepreneurs. The requisite skills can also be acquired at low cost, making the entrance cost for small, information service businesses quite low.

Anybody who doubts this need only look at the booming software industry that has emerged to serve personal computers.

The Computer Is a Left-brain Beast

The theory of bilateral brain specialization suggests that each hemisphere of the brain performs different tasks. The left hemisphere handles objective, quantitative, and analytical tasks, involving numerical and verbal symbols. It breaks problems down into small discrete units and solves them according to well-defined rules. The right hemisphere specializes in subjective and qualitative processes—sensory impressions, gestalts, and concepts. Right brain functions tend to be creative, intuitive, and nonverbal. These different methods of processing information are, for the most part, mutually exclusive.

Computers are left-brain beasts. They cannot think. They can only follow simple instructions, which at the most basic level consist of nothing more than adding and comparing numbers. If an activity can't be broken down into tiny steps, then a computer can't be used to accomplish the task. The activities computers *can* perform are handled very quickly. Computers should be used, therefore, to handle left-brain functions and to support humans' right-brain functions. In short, computers should handle tedious, boring, and simplistic work, freeing people for more interesting and creative tasks.

Computers can check documents for spelling errors, do repetitive calculations for budgets and financial projections, generate standard reports from machine-encoded data, type copies of "personalized" letters, and provide easy access to transaction records. A computer can help you write and edit documents, manage your time, (maintain a calendar) and your information files (names, addresses, telephone numbers, bibliographies, reports), document your activities, identify key words and phrases in documents, evaluate alternative courses of action, and communicate with other people.

A computer cannot make subjective judgments, evaluate and synthesize information, identify patterns when you don't know what you're looking for, or create anything out of whole cloth.

Do You Need a Computer?

Stop for a minute and consider your work patterns. The following questions will assist you.

- How much time do you spend writing and revising written documents?
- How well do your written documents communicate your thoughts?
- How well do you document your activities?
- How much time and dollars do you spend preparing budgets?
- How much time do you spend organizing and maintaining files?
- How well are your files organized? How long does it take to find something in them?
- How well do you spell?
- Do you do much work that uses information stored in computer files?

This isn't a test. You don't get a score. There are no average scores. The main purpose of these questions is to help you be aware of the time you spend on non-interactive information activities (those that do not require face-to-face discussion). You should also be thinking about how effective your work is.

If you spend more than two hours a day working with information then you can probably justify the purchase of a personal computer. Your increased productivity should pay for it in less than one year. As an added bonus, you will find that the quality of your work will increase significantly. Interested? Read on.

Can You Afford Not To Have a Computer?

I assume that you are paid at least $10 an hour. Overhead and support costs in a business environment are generally at least 100 percent of salary, so that makes an hour of your time worth $20.

I also assume (based on personal experience and observation) that a personal computer can double your productivity in information work areas such as writing, financial or numerical analysis, and organizing and using data. For purposes of illustration, let's say that a personal computer will save you one hour a day, once you have learned to use it. Such a saving is equivalent to $20 per day, $400 per month, or $4,800 per year. For that amount, you can easily put together a small, single-user computer system with software.

At this point, it looks like a good investment, particularly if you factor in the tax advantages of buying equipment. Unfortunately, it isn't quite that easy. You have to factor one more cost into the analysis—the time you spend learning to use your computer. This cost will vary, depending on your system, your programs, and the quality of help and training you get. I'll be conservative here and estimate 100 hours, although experience tells me this is 30–50 percent high.

Your total investment is now about $6,800—$4,800 in equipment and programs, the rest in training time. You've recovered $4,800 through increased productivity, plus perhaps another $1,000 in tax writeoffs, but you need to pick up still another $1,000 in benefits. I'm going to write off this last $1,000 against three intangibles—reduced information support costs, improved work quality, and increased computer use. The more you use the computer to support yourself, the less support you require from others. Personal computers improve the quality of your final product by reducing the costs involved in revising and upgrading it. The more you use your computer, the more ways you will find to use it. If you start out using it one hour a day, by the end of the year, you'll probably be using it two hours a day.

In summary, for a capital investment of less than $5,000 and a labor investment of less than $2,000 you should be able to double your productivity in basic information work. Productivity gains, reduced support costs, and tax writeoffs should give you a 100 percent return on investment in one year. Productivity gains in the second and succeeding years are profit, although you should plow some of that profit back into additional hardware and software.

Now $7,000 is not much money. The average capital investment in support of a blue-collar worker is $25,000. Yet, we invest less than $1,000 to support a white-collar worker. It shows.

In case you have any illusions about being a technologically advanced information worker, take a look at your office furnishings. Your desk and chair follow design specifications that haven't changed in centuries. Do you use a typewriter? The first one was patented in 1827; the basic design of subsequent machines was fixed by the turn of the century. The pencil-and-eraser combination was patented in 1858; the ball-point pen in 1888. The telephone dates back to 1876. Dictating machines also date back more than one hundred years. Enough said?

Personal computers are going to increase information-work productivity. Things will get done faster, and—more importantly—they will be done better. The microcomputer will significantly raise the quality and the standards for quality in information work. The value of consistently correct spelling, no more obvious corrections on documents, better sentence construction, clearer reports and financial statements, and better decisions and communications is impossible to compute.

SECTION II

WHY WOULD ANYBODY WANT A PERSONAL COMPUTER?

This section focuses on computer applications at work, in education, and in the home. I'm going to be perfectly direct about what I'm trying to do in these three chapters: I'm trying to get you hooked on personal computers. I've put as much bait into these chapters as I can. I hope you find something you like.

2

Personal Computers and Work

This book is aimed at white-collar workers, whose primary task is to produce and use information. As a member of that rapidly expanding group, I am painfully aware that I spend little time in productive work. I devote too much of my time to support functions—getting organized, communicating with others, and collecting information. The personal computer can improve productivity in these functions, leaving time for more creative work, and it can increase the amount of work accomplished at any given time.

My basic pitch in promoting the personal computer is that if you can use it for two hours a day it will pay for itself in less than a year. Given that assumption, let's look at how you might use a personal computer during those hours, drawing on applications programs that have already been written and require no programming. Keep in mind that they are all available, but some are more efficient than others.

Word Processing

Any list of personal computer applications should start with word processing. As workers in an information economy, we spend much of our time communicating textual information to others. Properly employed, word processing can significantly increase productivity in this area. The benefits of word processing are significantly increased through the use of various support programs: spelling, grammar and syntax check; automatic indexing; table of contents generation; and on-line calculation and thesaurus support.

Spelling programs check your text word-by-word against an internal dictionary. The programs have limitations in that they focus on individual words, not their context, and they can't distinguish wrong words, only words that are misspelled. Nevertheless, they can significantly reduce the time and labor spent on proofreading. Programs vary in speed, but most will check 20 to 50 pages of text in less than a minute. Words not found in their dictionaries are marked for review and, if necessary, correction. Grammar checks frequently find errors the spelling programs miss. They deal with simple syntax problems like repeat words (''the the''), failure to match parentheses or quotes, and simple grammatical errors.

Indexing and table of contents programs create these tables and key them to the page numbers of your document. They require a little extra work—inserting coded index terms or table of contents headings into the text. They significantly reduce, however, the labor required to perform these tedious tasks.

The on-line thesaurus is a recent development. It allows you to call up the thesaurus on the screen while you are writing. This may not seem like much, but it cuts two to three minutes off the time it takes to look up a word in a printed thesaurus. If you are like me, you may use the computer thesaurus more than you would a printed one because it takes less effort.

Financial Analysis

Most of you have probably heard of VisiCalc®—the financial analysis spreadsheet program that is credited with selling thousands of Apple computers. (VisiCalc works only on Apples, so to use it, you have to buy the Apple.) Besides VisiCalc there are a large number of financial analysis packages available. If you base your planning or major decisions on numerical projections, these programs can revolutionize the way you work. They take over the boring repetitive mathematical tasks and give you time to focus on what the numbers mean. Modifications of projections—changing assumptions, extending them another year—require a few strikes on the keyboard.

The net effect of these programs is to improve the quality of decisions based on numerical projections. If you do any "what if" work, you will probably find that the assistance a personal computer can provide in this area alone will justify the cost of acquiring and learning to use it.

Personal Filing Systems

Personal filing systems are currently the rage at computer-software houses. Although the package-software industry is only about four years old, it has already provoked a fad mentality. As soon as a software house releases a new program and it is successful, other houses rush to bring out their version. Personal filing systems followed financial analysis programs, which in turn tailed word processing programs. Your guess is as good as mine as to what will come next.

Personal filing programs organize information so that you can easily search and find your information stored in on-line data base. The file is composed of records, which contain specific pieces of information; perhaps a journal article; a book; or someone's name, address, and telephone number. Each record also stores a set of keywords to describe it. A search routine is used to locate information in the file by searching records for specified combinations of keywords.

If you deal with large bodies of information, then you may find a personal filing system helpful. It requires an investment of time to organize it, but once you have set it up, it is easy to maintain, update, and use.

Personal filing systems are different from data-base management systems. The latter are complex programs used primarily by systems programmers to develop custom-accounting software. Although data-base management systems could function as personal filing programs, these systems are really too complex for the average user.

Numerical Calculations

Most of us use the ubiquitous pocket calculator for simple numerical calculations. (I sometimes wonder if people can still add in their heads.) You can use a personal computer for these tasks and for complex calculations that are beyond the capacity of most pocket calculators. Calculator programs were a popular function of the first personal computers, but interest in them died. One problem is that personal computers can usually handle only one task at a time, and much calculator work is done as an adjunct to other work. Most of the people I know who write on a personal computer keep a pocket calculator next to their terminal to use when they need to do arithmetic.

Recently there has been a rebirth of interest in calculator programs for personal computers, caused, I think, by the popularity of financial analysis programs. I have seen some new programs that include calculator-utility programs, which can be used simultaneously with other programs, for instance, with a word processing program. As personal computers become more popular in the scientific community, I think we'll see more numerical calculation programs.

Project Planning

To help with complex, multitask projects, you might be interested in computer planning programs, which organize, schedule, and manage details using either Program Evaluation & Review Technique (PERT) or Critical Path Method (CPM) techniques. The planning programs I've looked at are fairly simple to use (they generally offer a menu approach), and can handle projects with three hundred steps or tasks.

Appointment Calendar

The desk-calendar appointment pad is a wonderfully simple device, but a properly equipped personal computer, with a clock and calendar board, improves on it. Equipped with small batteries, the board keeps track of the date and time, even when the computer is turned off. The computer can then match appropriate appointments on the calendar program with the date and time.

The calendar program combines the attributes of a desk calendar and a good secretary. You can log in upcoming appointments and also insert tickler messages to alert yourself to upcoming events. In addition to mapping out where you will be going, the calendar program can also tell you where you have been. It can provide an audit trail to document activities related to a specific project.

Interesting options for calendar programs have developed with the advent of local networks, which link independent personal computers so they can communicate with one another and share access to common files and support devices. Stored on personal computers, calendars can be accessed through a local network to speed up the scheduling of intraorganizational meetings. I'm aware of one local-network system organized hierarchically so that the schedules of executives override those of subordinates.

Business Graphics

We are going to be seeing an increase in the business-graphics programs that began appearing in mid-1982. Graphics programs make it possible to summarize numeric data through the display of two-dimensional graphs, bar charts, and pie charts. Some of these programs can be coupled directly to numeric and financial-analysis programs to provide visual comparison of alternative strategies.

The graphics are limited only by your imagination and the sophistication of your output mechanism. The most visually impressive approach is to show them directly on a CRT (terminal) screen or monitor. Plotters and printers can also reproduce graphs on paper. Some new dot matrix printers can print in four colors.

Accounting Support

I generally think of accounting as a specialized function. I wouldn't recommend putting a major accounting package—that includes the "big five" functions—general ledger, accounts payable, accounts receivable, payroll, and inventory—on a personal computer. I think this is a specialized application that requires a computer dedicated to these functions.

On the other hand, personal accounting support seems a valid application for a personal computer. There are a variety of programs available to maintain and document your checkbook, organize expenditures, analyze investments, calculate interest, and help with budgeting.

Income tax preparation is another area where your personal computer can help you. There are many tax preparation programs available, but most tend to be too specialized for my taste. (Besides, the tax laws change every year.) I used one of my financial-analysis programs last year to prepare my taxes. I created supporting schedules to document my income and expenditures and then developed models representing the appropriate IRS forms so I could use the program to do all the tax calculations. I had to type the forms myself, but all the calculations were done using the program.

Electronic Messaging

Through electronic messaging the personal computer becomes part of a person-to-person communications system over dedicated communication channels (local networks) or via telephone lines using an interface device called a modem. There are two primary application areas: electronic mail and computer-assisted teleconferencing.

With electronic mail you type out a message on your personal computer and send it to the recipient over the local network or telephone lines. The instantly delivered message is stored in an electronic mailbox that the recipient checks with his computer. One advantage of electronic mail is that the same message can be sent to any number of recipients with no extra effort.

Computer-assisted teleconferencing uses computers and telecommunications systems to allow a number of people to discuss a problem, unrestrained by considerations of time and distance. Stored in a computer conference file, the dialogue is available to all participants, who use their personal computers to access and read the file and add their contributions. Electronic mail capabilities make it possible for participants to send private messages to one another in addition to the public messages that are stored in the conference file.

Currently electronic mail and computer-assisted teleconferencing systems are found mostly on larger computer systems, but this is rapidly changing. The support components for personal computers are already nationally available through such computer utilities as The Source and Compuserve. There is also a significant body of software available to support computer bulletin boards, which can readily be adapted to electronic mail transmission and computer teleconferencing. As local networks for personal computers evolve, I am certain we will see both these functions become well-supported.

Data Access from Information Utilities

If information is power, as many would argue that it is, then access to information is certainly the key to power. Information utilities offer the fastest, most effective way to access large amounts of up-to-date information stored in online data bases. There are currently more than six hundred online data bases, covering almost any imaginable topic. Two barriers prevent many people from using them. The first is that effective use of these data bases requires a certain amount of skill. The second is the sheer volume of information they contain. You can use your personal computer to help you overcome both barriers.

Planning a search on an information utility is like that conducted on a personal filing system. You must first develop your search strategy by specifying the keywords you want to look for and the relationship between them. Normally this is done in "real time," while you are connected to the utility and paying a connection fee. There are two problems: You have to know the correct keywords for the data base you are searching, and you have to know the search language of the utility you are using.

With your personal computer, you can prepare a strategy in advance. You can then call up the utility and transmit your search request, saving both time and money. I predict that we will see within the next year the advent of programs to help formulate search strategies. They will probably work on a menu basis and will give you a thesaurus (a listing of the keywords for a specific data base) that you can use to identify appropriate keywords. After you have selected the keywords and specified the relationship between them, the program will formulate the search commands for the utility. (I have seen prototypes of these programs. If I don't see one marketed soon, I may get into the software business.)

Another advantage to using a personal computer is that you can store the results of your search for later analysis. Search results have traditionally been printed at the utility and mailed to customers. Why wait? Also, the results are much more useful when they are in machine-readable (electronic storage) form so you can use your personal computer to manipulate them.

Data Analysis and Interpretation

Many of the utility data bases contain numeric information such as stock-market quotes, economic indicators, and census data. Organizations also generate their own accounting, personnel market and production data. This information is extremely important, but usually needs to be reduced and analyzed before it can be used. Personal computers can be of significant help in manipulating numeric data to describe patterns or predict trends.

Statistics and graphics programs are available to summarize and illustrate descriptive data. These are relatively undeveloped program areas for personal computers, and the currently available programs are far from perfect, but I think we will see a lot of action in this area over the next couple of years.

Personal computers can also develop test models to predict events based on currently available data. Some financial analysis packages can construct numeric models, accessing data from other files to run them. There are also some modeling programs available that handle specific data bases, primarily stock market figures. Again, I think this is an area where we will see much software activity in the next few years.

Interactive Learning

I think the personal computer has a major role to play in education, primarily through programmed learning, by which students interact with the computer, and each successive step of instruction depends on their responses. The first of these programs deals primarily with computer literacy. As the demand for personal computers and for continuing education expands, I think we will see a lot more interactive-learning programs.

This is my list of twelve realistic applications of personal computers to white-collar work. It's not exhaustive; you may think of some applications I've missed. But let's move on to how computers can be used in the schools.

3 — goes from pg 24 to 30...

Personal Computers in Education

Despite its apparent conservatism, public education has been subjected to a large number of fads—concepts that seemed good, but never quite realized their promise. The American education community was blitzed with gimmicks in the late 1950s after the Soviets launched Sputnik. When I began studying the diffusion of information and technology in education ten years ago, I was fascinated by how trends hopped from one area of the country to another. I found that the fads that well-meaning local, state, and national administrators imposed from the top down generally fizzled. On the other hand, those that teachers and principals brought in seemed to have a better chance at success.

I mention this because, in most of the cases with which I am familiar, personal-computer programs start when a student or a teacher brings a machine to the school. I think that personal computers are a natural for education and can give us an incredible return on investment in education, *if they are used properly.*

The jury is still out on the question of how to use personal computers effectively in schools. It will probably be several years before the establishment has acceptable data on this issue. I have a few ideas on the subject that I'd like to share with you. As far as I can tell, few educators understand what a personal computer is.

They treat it as an interesting technical device to be used for specialized purposes—programming (perhaps the most popular use of personal computers in schools), stimulation, and repetitive drill.

This is precisely the wrong approach. Support in all these areas has been available for years, primarily through timeshared computers. Computer-aided instruction in schools was one of the big disappointments of the early 1970s, because it had a single narrow focus.

Given that computer-aided instruction has already flopped in education, what can we do better this time around? *We can teach students to become computer literate and to use personal computers as general-purpose information machines to manipulate ideas.* The best method is to provide people with continual access to the computer as an information tool. Some schools have already started. Carnegie Mellon University, Drexel University, and Clarkson College of Technology have announced that they will provide students with computers. Other schools will soon follow suit.

If students are to learn to use computers properly, we will have to restructure the educational system and redesign curricula to be able to most efficiently use these new information tools, teachers' skills, and the schools' physical plants. From discussions I've had with high school and college teachers in Northern California, I've gleaned some ideas of how we could use personal computers in education.

Communication Skills Improvement

Most educators agree that students' communications skills have been deteriorating for a long time. Most high school students are lucky if upon graduation they know how to write a proper paragraph. Think of the advantages of starting students out on word processors at an early age. They would be able to concentrate on expression rather than worrying about penmanship or spelling. Rewriting—the key to good writing—is sadly neglected at all levels of American education. Working with a word processor removes the tedium from rewriting. And, it can also be used competitively.

Consider this scenario: Groups of three or four students are given the same essay on a floppy disk and instructed to rewrite it. Each group can reorganize text with a few keystrokes. The students need not worry about spelling—each computer has a spelling program. Because each computer also has an on-line thesaurus and a grammar program, students can "tune" sentences and phrases for clarity and impact and can check basic syntax. When they've finished, the rewritten essays are combined on one disk, so they can be easily seen by all. Each group then defends its revision against critiques from the other groups.

The students would learn by doing; get immediate feedback on their work; and be forced to defend decisions, confront mistakes, and see alternate solutions to the same problem.

When I present this spiel to teachers, I am often asked if computers will undermine spelling skills. Why learn to spell if a computer can check spelling for you? I tell them that my spelling program forces me to confront my failures every day. It's like taking a daily spelling test. I think my skills have actually improved since I started using a spelling program. After all, the program doesn't do all the work, it just helps you identify misspelled words—exactly what a spelling test does. I'm still coming to terms with my grammar program. Its dictionary of more than 500 trite phrases and weak modifiers seems to contain all my favorite phrases. When I run the program it seldom passes a paragraph without pausing to comment on my linguistic inadequacies. It's not only educational; it's damned humbling.

The personal computer is helping me to improve my spelling and grammar, at the same time that it is supporting me in my work. It's like having Miss Gaines (my high school English teacher) standing behind me, looking over my shoulder, and correcting me every time I make a mistake. Given an environment like this, how can I help but learn? Buckminister Fuller would undoubtedly have called the personal computer a synergistic tool. Properly used, you get more out of it than you put into it. We need to introduce tools like this to students, as quickly as possible.

Tools in Journalism

As a former journalism major, I've always found significant difference between the content of English and journalism courses. English teachers taught me the mechanics of communicating. Journalism teachers taught me how to define and write to an audience.

Journalism is a natural field for personal computers. Nearly every newspaper of consequence in the country now uses computers as a more economical means to capture and edit stories. Why not help students prepare for using computers in this field while significantly reducing the drudgery involved in publishing student-run papers?

Interested in electronic media? In my video-production work I find the computer invaluable in preparing scripts, keeping track of shots, and preparing title and edit lists. We are even working on a computer-based indexing system to track every second of video footage in our archive.

The Meaning of History

History has always struck me as a rote-memory subject. Who did what to whom, when, and where? We tend to segment it into manageable chunks—American history, world history, the Middle Ages, the French Revolution. While this may make teaching easier, I think it provides a very narrow, deceptive view of our past.

Remember ''Connections,'' the PBS series narrated by James Burke? Burke's view of history was dramatically unique in that he focused on the relationships between seemingly disconnected events and episodes. He showed that our past is not composed of discrete events, but rather of a complex intermingling of cause and effect.

Suppose we used the personal computer as an information tool to follow historical connections. If we did, the past would become an information problem. The trick would be to develop a scheme for (*a*) representing historical facts: events, people, organizations, geography, economics, demographics, and other data, and (*b*) for showing connections between these facts. As far as I know, nobody has done this yet, but the person who does will probably go down in history as the person who revolutionized our views of history.

At the Drawing Board

More years ago than I care to remember, I read about Drafting Dan in Robert Heinlein's *The Door into Summer*. Drafting Dan was a computerized machine that created real-time drawings and plans. How I longed for such a machine during my freshman drafting course, which was an exercise in survival. I never really understood what was going on with perspective, scales, and all that. I was too busy trying to letter neatly and keep from erasing too much of the paper surface when revising my drawings.

Drafting Dan exists today. It goes under the generic name CAD (Computer Aided Design), and is revolutionizing drafting. Think what it would be like to focus on technique, to be able to try out hundreds of ideas and variations, to explore the world of shapes and forms without worrying about erasures.

I recently sat down with a high school graphics arts teacher and he described the computer he wanted: "I want a machine that I can use to create color drawings. It should be able to show perspective. It should be able to rotate drawings to show changing views. It should be able to zoom in on or away from drawings. It should be fairly easy to use." What he wants exists; several different machines are on the market at prices ranging from $10,000 to $20,000. I bet he gets one.

Physical Education Enhancement

When I think of computers in sports, I think game theory, statistics, strategy and tactics, and biomechanics. Game theory gives the rules. Statistics describe what happens as a result of given actions. Strategy and tactics link the action and reactions of opposing sides. Biomechanics focuses on the execution of actions by the individual.

I mean to have the previous paragraph sound cold and analytic. Computers in sports can identify and analyze options, but all this work is only an aid to making informed decisions. Computers can help the individual, the player, and the coach understand a sport at an analytic level, which can improve performance. But sports are ultimately a test of human capabilities, and there is a line beyond which computers cannot go. However, you should be aware that the Oakland A's have a staff "Computer Jock" who uses a personal computer to continuously analyze strategies during games.

Mathematical Relationships

Although mathematics are a natural subject for personal computers, many teachers are opposed both to personal computers and pocket calculators. They bemoan the fact that calculators eliminate students' incentive to learn math. These conservative teachers view math as the application of rote memory—knowing that 6 times 9 is 54 or that 155 minus 79 is 76. They view math as an exercise in manipulating abstract symbols.

I spent so much time as a student trying to get the right answers to math and statistics problems that I seldom thought about what I was doing. Who has time to think about relationships when grades depend on right answers? It was only after I had completed a course that I had time to think about what was going on.

If computers in the classroom can bring the demise of rote-memory math, then I say good riddance! I view mathematics as an abstract language that describes reality, and gives us a means of focusing on relationships. Knowing how to perform basic mathematical operations is a survival skill and should not be neglected. But it is also important to understand the relationship between math symbols and the reality they represent.

Educators flirted with mathematical relationships more than a decade ago—the fling was called new math. Unfortunately, new math focused on relationships at the expense of basic survival skills. Had new math come on the scene after the advent of the cheap pocket calculator, it probably would have been a success. Maybe it's time to bring it back.

Support for the Professional

Just before I finished this chapter, I installed a personal computer system at Lowell High School in San Francisco. Teachers and staff donated the computer to the school. They began using it the first week it was delivered to prepare lesson plans and write letters of recommendation for students applying to college. One teacher organized a file of the school's collection of video tapes. Some teachers asked about building files to make exam preparation easier. Most teachers, however, used the machine to become computer literate by exploring ways to increase their personal productivity and to improve the educational program at Lowell. They are also using the machine to write funding proposals for expansion of their computer program.

Your Role

If you are interested in educational applications I suggest you look around for schools in your area pioneering the use of personal computers. If you are a parent, you have a vested interest in bringing personal computers to the schools. Find out what your schools are doing and what you can do to help. If they do not yet have a computer program encourage them to start one. You might check some of the magazines listed in Chapter 16 for ideas. Above all, get involved. It's important to all of us.

4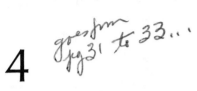

Personal Computers in the Home

Personal computers in the home extend and support their business and education applications. Most of us take work home from the office and school. If you use a personal computer at either of those locations, why not continue to do so at home?

One of the hazards of working with personal computers is that you get spoiled. Once you're hooked, it's hard to go back to old methods. I use a typewriter now only to address envelopes and prepare labels. (Both activities are too much of a bother on a printer.) It's difficult to write longhand or on a typewriter after you've used a word processor, particularly when you know that you will eventually type the piece on the processor anyway. I make outlines and take notes by hand, but little else. I've found that if I don't get my ideas, concepts, or outlines into the computer, I'll never see them.

A personal computer in the home creates a sense of shared learning and exploration of something new. Often it's the child, rather than the parent, who is the guide. It's one of the few areas in the home where parents and children can meet as equals. One problem, though, is that once a personal computer is available

31

and everyone in the family learns how to use it, applications and uses seem to emerge spontaneously. Setting priorities can be difficult.

There is a wide variety of home applications, which include:

- Investing and portfolio management
- Filing of names, addresses, and telephone numbers
- Interactive learning
- Personal financial management
- Household organization and inventory management
- Meal planning
- Games

Except for games, these are extensions of applications I discussed in previous chapters. Suffice it to say that the array of packaged software programs to support these functions increases every day.

Working at Home

The term "the electronic cottage" is becoming as trite as "computer literacy," but it does denote an emerging lifestyle. Much of our society's information work could be done at home, though not everybody wants to or should do so. Many people need a structured work environment; others need the social interaction of a work environment. But I'm one of those people who prefer not only to work at home, but am actually more productive there.

The number of "electronic-cottage workers" is growing. This group once included the self-employed who worked at solitary trades like writing and programming. This is changing. Many employers are encouraging employees to work at home part time. They come to the office to interact with others, but do their solitary work at home. The electronic-cottage entrepreneur is a new phenomenon, beyond which there is still a growing demand for information products that serve the personal computer: software publishing, word-processing services, custom-designed programs and data bases, and mailing services.

Merging Technologies

The sophistication of today's communications technology is increasing the band-width and number of information channels into the home. Many urban homes have cable television service. Almost everyone has a telephone. Computer games abound. Video-cassette machines are becoming increasingly popular. Two-way cable, electronic mail, and videotex are merging computer, telecommunications, and video technology to improve the flow of information into the home. By the end of the decade, all three will be inexorably intertwined, expanding the applications and uses of the personal computer in the home. Eventually we will no longer have telephones, television sets, and personal computers. They will be linked together in one machine that will provide communication, entertainment, and information support. We will live and work in a much more supportive information environment. This sounds suspiciously like what they must have said when commercial television started. I hope we do better this time around.

34

SECTION III

INTRODUCTION TO PERSONAL COMPUTER HARDWARE

A typical personal computer system has four parts. The main component is, obviously, the computer, a general-purpose electronic device designed to process information.

A second component is the terminal, a device used to communicate with the computer. You give the computer instructions by typing them in on the terminal keyboard. The computer sends you messages by displaying them on the terminal screen.

The computer's external memory device saves information and programs and moves them into the computer memory when they are needed. The most common external memory device is the floppy disk drive, which allows you to take information from the computer and store it on the shelf until you want to send it back to the computer. The information is stored on a magnetic disk, the way music is recorded on a cassette tape.

The final component that I will describe in detail is the printer, which records information on paper for storage or transmission to people who do not have facilities to receive electronically stored information.

Manufacturers package these components differently. Some pack them all in one unit, but most keep the printer separate. Others separate the terminal monitor, and combine the other components with the computer. Despite these variations, however, all systems do have these four functional components, so I've organized the hardware section around them.

Before beginning a detailed discussion of the four components, I'm going to take just a minute to describe how computers deal with information.

Most computers, including all personal computers, are digital. They represent information using binary codes. The simplest code is a bit—a binary digit. A bit is essentially a simple switch with two positions—on and off. You can develop complex codes by joining a number of bits together. Each bit doubles the number of codes available. Two bits can represent 2×2, or 2^2, or four different values. Three bits can represent 2^3 or eight different values.

A byte is eight bits and can represent 2^8 or 256 unique values. This provides enough unique codes to represent all the letters of the alphabet (both capital and lower case), all ten digits, and most common punctuation marks.

Bit and byte are physical storage units, but computers are also concerned with logical storage units called words. A word is the unit of information that a computer manipulates. An 8-bit computer can manipulate 8 bits (256 unique codes) at once. A 16-bit computer can manipulate 16 bits at once (65,536 unique codes).

5

goes from pg 37 to 48...

The Computer

The main component of the computer is the central processing unit (CPU), which actually processes the data. Other components include the memory, the I/O unit, and the external-memory controller. The memory is where data and instructions are stored until they are needed by the computer. The I/O unit connects the computer to input and output devices, such as terminals and printers. The external-memory controller moves data and programs into the computer memory from an external storage device such as a disk-drive unit.

These components can be packaged in two different ways. One is to put the components on a single printed circuit board (to make what is called a single-board computer.) The other is to take a modular approach and place each component on its own circuit board. There are advantages and disadvantages to each approach.

The single-board approach is the most cost effective. One board costs less than four (or more). Also, it eliminates worry about connecting the components. Another advantage is that a single board is generally easier to package into the equipment.

The primary advantages of the modular approach are flexibility and ease of service. Modular boards generate less heat than single boards, which prevents hardware failures. Because functions are contained on different boards, it is possible to customize the computer to meet the needs of the user, adding or switching boards according to changing needs. Repair is simplified, because boards can be substituted on site. On the minus side, the cost for individual boards is high and the complexity of the system design is increased. The primary problem is providing communication between the boards. This is handled by a bus system.

What Is a Bus?

A bus is a communications channel that moves electrical impulses between two points. Computer buses provide electrical connections between components.

The computer bus is actually a network of several special-purpose buses. The data bus moves information between the boards. It requires as many lines as there are bits in a word. The address bus identifies a specific memory location so that the computer can either read or write data. The size of the address bus determines how much memory can be addressed. In most 8-bit machines the address bus is 16-bits (lines) wide. This means it can address 2^{16} or 65,526 separate storage locations (or words). The control bus sends control and synchronizing signals to the various boards. The power bus provides electrical power to the boards.

From this basic description, you can see that a bus is an integral part of any computer. Although a bus structure is required on single-board computers, the term is generally associated with modular computers. In modular computers, the bus is represented by a series of connected sockets. Individual modules or boards are plugged into these sockets to connect them.

The CPU Components

The CPU is the "brain" of the computer, and is responsible for the actual manipulation of information in the computer. A CPU has three distinct parts: an Arithmetic Logic Unit (ALU) that performs operations on the data; registers that store the data and the instructions for the ALU; and the control circuitry that coordinates and manages the movement between the ALU, the registers, and other components of the computer.

The ALU is the part of the microprocessor that actually does the computing. It is composed of a number of circuits that are designed to perform a set of functions based on two instructions—adding and comparing values. The ALU actually has a much more complicated set of instructions it can execute, but they are all composed of these two basic operations.

To perform its functions, the ALU follows instructions that are stored on registers. The register is a small block of memory that holds information temporarily so that it can be rapidly accessed by the ALU. Registers store both the locations of instructions and the data. Most microprocessors have several registers. At a minimum, every microprocessor contains four basic registers: the accumulator, a data counter, an instruction register, and a program register.

The accumulator is the workspace for the CPU. It holds data that has either been obtained from external memory and is about to be operated on by the CPU, or data that has just been processed by the CPU and is about to be returned to main memory. The data counter holds the address of a specific piece of data in memory. It keeps track of the memory address for the data being processed by the accumulator.

The instruction register stores the commands for the CPU. The program register or counter holds addresses of CPU instructions, much as the data counter holds addresses for the accumulator. Because program instructions are always stored sequentially, the program register always holds the address of the next command that is to be moved into the instruction register. The program counter automatically moves to the next address location every time a new command moves into the instruction register.

Other registers found in most CPU designs include the stack pointer, which temporarily stores addresses; index registers to keep track of the data; and status registers, which keep track of what's going on. The control unit coordinates the movement of instructions and data between the registers, the ALU, and the main memory of the computer. It must obtain instructions from memory, decode them, and match the codes with the proper registers. At the same time, the control unit must move data between memory and the registers in readiness for ALU processing, according to the instructions in the registers. The CPU's clock, syn-chronizes the operations of the various computer components. As I noted earlier, the basic instructions that the ALU follows are quite simple. The power of the computer comes from the speed with which these instructions are performed.

The Chip Families

The major factor that distinguishes a microcomputer from the larger mini- and mainframe computers is the microprocessor—a CPU on a single chip. In minis and mainframes the CPU is com-posed of many discrete electrical elements.

The 8-Bit Chip

There are currently two major 8-bit microcomputer chip families—the "eights" and the "sixes." The eight family is composed of de-scendants of the INTEL 8008—the first 8-bit microcomputer chip, which was introduced in 1973. Members of the six family are de-scended from the 6800 chip developed by Motorola. There is a third chip family—the "nines"—manufactured by Texas Instru-ments. The nine family, however, has never enjoyed very much popularity, and chips from this family are rarely seen in small-business or personal computers. Differences between these fami-lies can be seen in their number registers, their function and size, the ALUs' instruction sets, the control circuits, and the micropro-cessors' clock speeds.

The eight family currently dominates among microprocessors. Although the family sire is the INTEL 8008, a somewhat later ver-sion, the 8080, was the prototypical design for many of the micros that began to appear in 1976–77. Today the foremost member of this family is the Z80, which is manufactured by Zilog, and has a much larger instruction set than the original 8080. The utility of this expanded instruction set, however, is questionable. Much of the software available for this chip family uses only the 8080 in-struction set to ensure compatibility across a much larger set of micros. Other members of this family include the 8085, an en-hanced version of the 8080, and the 8088, a hybrid 16-bit chip.

TABLE 5–1. The Chip Families

THE EIGHTS

8-Bit Chips

Intel 8008
Intel 8080

ZILOG Z80   INTEL 8080A
ZILOG Z80A   INTEL 8085
ZILOG Z80B
ZILOG Z800

16-Bit Chips
(8-bit word)
ZILOG Z8000   INTEL 8088
                   INTEL 8086

THE SIXES

8-Bit Chips

MOTOROLA 6800
MOTOROLA 6502   MOTOROLA 6805

16-Bit Chips
MOTOROLA 68000

One can think of the eight family as having four generations. The first-generation 8008 is generally not seen today. The second generation 8080 has an ALU, an accumulator, a control unit, seven 8-bit programmable registers, a 16-bit address register, and a set of seventy-eight instructions including binary, decimal, and double-precision arithmetic commands. The 8080A—an enhanced 8080—and the Z80 are third generation chips. The super-chip fourth-generation 8085 and the Z800 have larger address registers and faster clocks than did their predecessors.

The virtues of the 8080 family are low cost, speed, and an instruction set that is well designed for most business applications. Chips in this family function at two, four, or six MegaHertz (MHz). Zilog has announced the development of the Z800 CPU, which will have a larger address capacity and will function at eight to ten MHz.

Another major advantage to the eight family is that it is relatively standardized. For example, it has a standard S-100 bus (although machines are moving toward the single-board design). More important, however, is the family's standard operating system, which allows the development of software that can be used interchangeably by family-member machines.

The six family is represented today by the 6502 chip, a variant of Motorola's 6800. The primary advantage of the family is the simplicity of its architecture. It operates at slower speeds than the 8080 family (one to two-MHz), but has an instruction set that is much more amenable to graphics. Like the 8080, the 6502 can usually address up to 64K bytes of memory. The 6502 is found in the Apple II series and the Apple III, the Atari, and Commodore computers. The 6800 has not enjoyed a great deal of success, however, because of an ineffective bus structure.

The principal problem with the six family has been the lack of hardware and software standardization. Each manufacturer has developed a unique operating system and line of software packages. Apple, Atari, and Commodore software packages can be used only with the machine for which they were written. This restriction can greatly inhibit system expansion and updating.

The 16-Bit Chip

One of the primary measures of computer performance has been the size of the word a machine can process. As we noted earlier, most microcomputers currently use chips that process an 8-bit word. However, there has been considerable research and development done on chips that process 16-bit words, and INTEL has announced an experimental chip that can deal with a 32-bit word. Whereas the 32-bit chips are not yet economically viable for the general personal computer market, the 16-bit chips are coming on fast.

The 16-bit families are extensions of the 8-bit families. The eight family is represented by the INTEL 8088, the INTEL 8086, and the Zilog Z8000. The six family is represented by the Motorola 68000. The 16-bit chips surpass their 8-bit cousins in their ability to manipulate larger words, address more storage, and operate at higher speeds. They also have much more sophisticated instruction sets and are more amenable to performing concurrent multiple tasks.

Most of the personal computers introduced in 1982 and 1983 use 16-bit CPUs, including the highly successful IBM PC, which uses an INTEL 8088 microprocessor. The incredible success of the PC format has established it as a de facto standard that stipulates the CPU (8088), bus (IBM pseudobus), and operating system (PC–DOS or MS–DOS). Many manufacturers have jumped on the PC bandwagon and offer an increasing array of add-on hardware components, software, and complete systems designed to use that format. Actually, the 8088 is a hybrid version of the 8086. It has the instruction set and address bus of the 8086, but it uses an 8-bit rather than a 16-bit data bus.

The increased memory capacity, larger word size, and more sophisticated instruction set of 16-bit computers provide the power to move significantly beyond the performance of 8-bit computers, but this has not yet happened. Most current software is designed to work with only 64K of main memory and with instructions that are common to both 8-bit and 16-bit microprocessors. This will change as the 16-bit market matures, but 8-bit machines will remain in the market for some time, coasting on the greater availability of proven 8-bit software. Fortunately, the emergence of MS–DOS as a standard operating system for 16-bit machines should increase the availability of software for the new machines.

The new Grid Systems COMPASS and Apple Lisa™ mark the beginning of a new trend in personal computers. These high end, sophisticated, user-friendly computers mark a departure from an emphasis on standardization and compatibility. Their unique operating systems, though easier to use, reduce the software available for each machine and make intermachine communication difficult (except between like models). Communication between personal computers will soon be essential in the office and any multicomputer environment. The availability of communication programs for machines, such as the COMPASS and Lisa, should be a necessary condition for purchase.

Given the advantages of the new 16-bit microcomputers, does it make any sense to go with an 8-bit computer? If you are just starting out, probably not. I recommend going with a 16-bit, IBM-compatible computer. You get more performance for the money

and will be able to use a rapidly expanding collection of sophisticated software. If, on the other hand, you must interface with existing 8-bit machines, you might find it more useful to get a compatible computer. An 8-bit machine certainly isn't obsolete; it just
won't be able to take advantage of some of the newest software.

The Bus Structure

The S-100 is the standard bus for 8-bit chips. It dates back to when
the Altair 8008, the first commercially available microcomputer,
was built, and the components could not be placed on a single
card. To provide modularity, the CPU, the I/O port, the memory,
and other components were placed on separate cards by function.
A 100-line bus provided communication between the cards. Originally designed for the operational requirements of the 8008, this
bus has been successfully adapted to meet the requirements of
the entire eight family.

Hundreds of microcomputer boards have been designed to accommodate the S-100 bus, allowing for a wide choice in system
configuration. There are problems, however. Because computer
manufacturers used the bus somewhat differently, consumers
could not assume that all S-100 boards were compatible. Each
manufacturer's bus line might be carrying different signals. To be
certain a system would work, all the components had to be from
the same manufacturer. Consequently it was, and often still is,
nearly impossible to build a mixed-board system.

But this is changing. The Institute of Electrical and Electronic
Engineers (IEEE) has established standards for the S-100 bus.
Many companies are now moving gradually toward employing
the standard S-100 bus.

In six-family computers the SS-50 bus is used with 6800 chips,
and the IEEE 488 bus frequently with the 6502. These are not as
standardized as the S-100 bus. Many of the six-family systems use
either a single-board design or a proprietary pseudobus.

A pseudobus system is a single-board machine with a supplemental bus structure to plug in additional features. The Apple
and the IBM PC have set the standards for pseudobuses. Both
machines are enjoying considerable popularity.

The recently introduced Apple IIe™, with its new keyboard, is
a significant improvement over the Apple II + ™, making it a more

viable business machine. More than 750,000 Apples IIs have been sold, and I am certain the Apple II series design will continue through the 1980s. Although the IBM PC has been well-received, I consider it to be a good but not a "great" personal computer. The keyboard is poorly laid out (see Chapter 6, on terminals), and the basic unit performs only adequately. IBM, however, like Apple, has encouraged other manufacturers to develop add-on hardware for its machine, resulting in the de facto standardization of equipment. It seems that every week a new IBM PC-compatible computer is introduced. This means you can (*a*) use a stock IBM PC, (*b*) modify a stock PC with components from other manufacturers to improve on the basic design, or (*c*) buy a PC-compatible machine from another manufacturer. The IBM XT, with its greater memory and built-in hard disk, provides significant improvements over the original PC design. The PC has already captured a large part of the personal computer arena. The introduction of the XT shows that IBM doesn't plan to rest on its laurels.

The Computer Memory

Computers use two kinds of semiconductor memory, RAM and ROM.

Random Access Memory (RAM)

Random Access Memory (RAM) is used to provide the main memory for computers—that is the semiconductor memory that is directly controlled by the microprocessor. It has two important features: it is reusable—you can write on it, read it, erase it, and write on it again, and it is volatile— it loses its contents when the power is turned off. The term random access actually means that it takes the same amount of time to access any location in memory.

Two kinds of RAMS are used in personal computers. Dynamic RAMS, the most common, use capacitors to store bits. Static RAMS store bits using more complex digital circuits called flip-flop. Dynamic RAMs are simpler to make and cost less, but require complex support circuits to maintain their charges. Static

RAMs cost more, are faster, and are considered more reliable than dynamic RAMs. They are found only in top-of-the-line computers.

Read Only Memory (ROM)

ROMs are special memories that store frequently used information or instructions in the computer. Located on circuit boards, they are nonvolatile memories, meaning that the information they contain is not lost when the computer is turned off. They provide an easy way to store routines that are frequently required by the computer. By storing such routines in semiconductor memory, they can be accessed rapidly, greatly increasing the operating speed and convenience of the computer. Common routines, such as start-up functions and disk-access routines, are typically stored on ROMs, as is the character set used on a terminal. We are beginning to see operating systems and other sophisticated software stored in ROMs.

There are several types of ROMs available. Programmed Read Only Memories (PROMs) are ROMs that are written after manufacture. Erasable Programmed Read Only Memories (EPROMs) are PROMs that can be erased either by exposure to ultraviolet light or electronically (Electronically Alterable Programs Read Only Memories—EAPROMs).

ROMs are used for the mass storage of prepackaged information. Texas Instruments and Hewlett Packard, for example, use ROMs in their software modules that can be plugged into handheld calculators. ROMs are also found in the plug-in game programs in home entertainment systems. We may see increased use of ROMs, particularly in the development of user-friendly features on more advanced systems.

Connections to I/O Devices

To make effective use of your computer you must be able to enter commands into it and retrieve information from it. This is done through input/output devices. Users of the earliest micros communicated through front panel switches, sending coded instructions one byte at a time. Today, we have more sophisticated I/O devices. The two peripheral units you are most likely to use are the computer terminal and the printer, which are discussed in separate chapters. The I/O unit provides the mechanisms to connect these external devices to the computer.

Communication is accomplished in two ways. One is to direct communication with a section of memory DMA (direct memory access). The more common technique is to communicate with a particular memory address through a port.

DMA technology allows peripheral devices to access the memory without the intervention of the CPU. Much favored in earlier computers, this mechanism is less common as systems become more sophisticated. The primary problem with DMA technology is that the connection between the peripheral unit and the computer is unique to each system, greatly reducing the flexibility of system configuration. It also generates problems in dealing with standardized software. Many personal computers, such as the Apple and the Commodore, use DMA, however, it is becoming far less common. It is gaining popularity for operations inside the computer.

The second communication method is through a port, which is essentially a bus that operates between the computer and the peripheral. The CPU transfers information to and from the address that is assigned to each port. This technique is somewhat slower than DMA technology, but allows a greater choice of peripheral devices and software.

The two types of ports—serial and parallel—differ in the way data is moved through them. Data is moved through a serial port one bit at a time. Data is moved across a parallel port one byte at a time—eight bits in parallel. Serial ports are used with both terminals and printers. Parallel ports, on the other hand, are used primarily for printers.

External Memory Devices

Running a computer system without an external memory device, though possible, is not practical. As I mentioned earlier, the internal addressing capability of most 8-bit machines is 64K bytes. Inputting the program and data to fill this space each time you use the computer would become very tedious. An external memory device allows you to store both programs and data and input them into the computer as needed.

External memory devices store information on magnetic media, either tapes or rotating floppy disks. The memory controller oversees the movement of information (data and programs) between the external memory device and the main computer memory.

Apple II Main Board
130 Integrated Circuits
for equivalent function

Illustration 1   A Single-board Computer

The single board of the Davidge 6/4 computer. This board contains a Z80B microprocessor, 64k of memory, and the hardware to support four serial and two parallel ports. The entire board measures approximately six by twelve inches. *(photo courtesy of Davidge)*

Illustration 2 A Pseudobus Computer

The board of the Apple II pseudobus computer. The major elements of the computer are located on a single board. The sockets along the back are used to insert additional boards to augment the basic computer. *(photo courtesy of Apple)*

Illustration 3   A Bus-based System

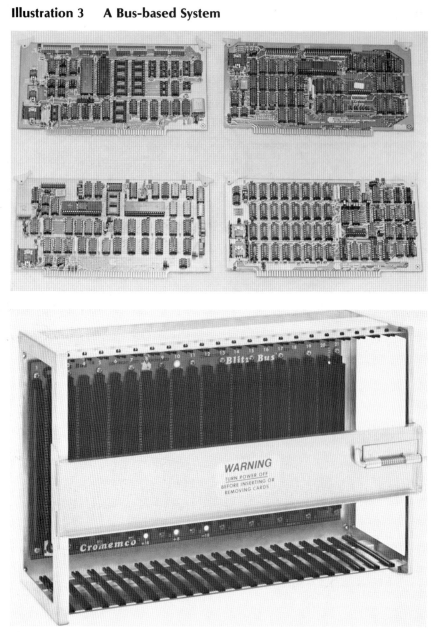

The major components of a bus-based system. Featured are four S-100 bus boards (CPU, memory, disk controller, and peripherals controller) and a card cage and motherboard into which the boards are inserted. Not shown (and needed to complete the system) are the enclosure, power supply, cooling fan, and ribbon cables to connect the boards to external devices such as the terminal, disk drive, and printer. *(board photo by the author, card cage photo courtesy of Cromemco)*

Illustration 4   A Potpourri of Keyboard Designs

Notice variations (in the photos above and on the following pages) in placement of the control (CTRL), escape (ESC), caps lock (CAPS), return (Enter), and back space keys. Check out the variation in cursor control keys (marked with arrows) and the number, placement, and labeling of function keys. If you need a numeric keypad, look very closely. To be effective the keypad should have an enter or return key to the right (where it is on your calculator) and a decimal point and minus sign in close proximity so all these keys are readily accessible to the right hand.

Illustration 4, cont.

Illustration 5   A High Performance Display Screen

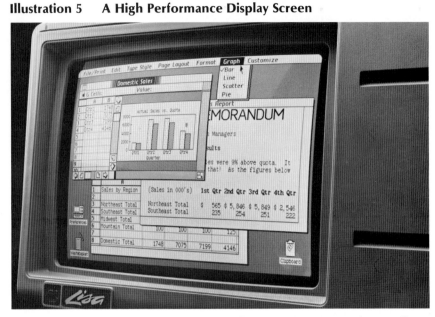

A bit-mapped screen on the new Apple Lisa™. The multitasking software allows you to show four simultaneous applications on the high resolution screen. Notice the different character fonts, graph shadings, and pictographs on the screen. *(photo courtesy of Apple)*

Illustration 6   De Facto Standard Terminal

The Heathkit H-19 is sold in a slightly modified version as the Zenith Z-19 (and also serves as the foundation for the Zenith Z88 and Z89 computers). This terminal is extremely popular. It has a Z 80 microprocessor and there are a number of "add-on" accessories available that enhance its capabilities. The CP/M Users Group (CMUG) is a good source of software specifically designed for the H/Z-19. *(photo by the author)*

6

The Terminal

gros from pgn 49 to 58...

The terminal is your link to your microcomputer system. How comfortable and easy to use your computer is depends on the terminal you select. Choosing the right terminal is an extremely important but difficult task, given the range of products available.

The most popular type of terminal is the video-display terminal (VDT). It is also called a cathode-ray terminal (CRT), because most units have cathode ray tubes for displays. The most common VDT is the alpha-numeric terminal, which displays both numbers and letters, usually in 24 rows of 80 characters each. Graphics terminals are more sophisticated VDTs that can display complex graphic information in addition to numbers and characters. Some printers have their own keyboards and can be used as terminals, but they are extremely slow and are usually unsuitable for use with microcomputers. Because you will most likely be working with an alpha-numeric VDT, I will devote my discussion to this type of terminal.

Terminals usually consist of a display unit (a cathode ray tube similar to the picture screen of a television set), a keyboard, a controller, and a communications interface.

Some personal-computer systems do not have a separate terminal, integrating all the components into a single package. Others have a separate display but combine the keyboard with the computer. Despite these packaging variations, all systems have the following four terminal components.

The Keyboard

The keyboard is the most important part of the terminal, since it is the communication link with the computer. Touch—the tactile sensation you get when pressing the keys—and format—the layout of the keyboard—determine the comfort of a terminal. A bad touch or an unfamiliar or cumbersome keyboard can make the terminal a formidable machine. Good touch and a well-designed format can increase your pleasure and speed in using it.

Some of the more common technologies used to make keyboards include electromechanical switches (keying opens and closes a mechanical switch, sending a signal to the controller), Hall-effect or solid-state switches, capacitance (which generates signals through the contact of two metal plates), and membrane (sealed surfaces acting as semiconductors to generate a signal). You probably won't be able to distinguish between the technologies by appearance or touch. Few modern terminals use electromechanical switches; most use capacitance keyboards. Membrame keyboards are used primarily on low cost home and game computers.

Although all keyboards use the standard typewriter format (called "qwerty," after the top left letter-character line), they include a number of ancillary keys, which may seem confusing at first. Ancillary keys include the punctuation keys and various control keys, such as RETURN, control (CTRL), escape (ESC), and BREAK (ATTN).

The RETURN key is used to signify the end of a line. Hitting the return key on most terminals automatically moves the cursor (the position indicator) to the left margin of the screen and down one line. The control and escape keys, like a typewriter shift key, are used in conjunction with another key to send commands to the computer. The BREAK or ATTN key informs the computer that you wish to terminate work on the current command and return to the previous command state.

Some keyboards also have a numeric pad—a calculator keyboard located to the right of the normal one for handling numerical data. Other ancillary keys you may find issue commands to the terminal to delete or repeat characters on the screen. "Off-line" tells the terminal to disconnect from the computer temporarily; "erase," to clear portions or all of the screen; and "reset," to restore the terminal to a previous state. You may also find a set of keys that move the cursor. They are indicated by arrows pointing right, left, up, and down. The "home" key returns the cursor to the upper left corner of the screen.

Your terminal may also have some special function keys labeled F1-Fn or marked with colored dots. These must be programed to be used. Unless your programs have been custom configured to your system, you will probably find that these keys don't work. Don't worry; it won't affect the usefulness of your terminal or the operation of your programs.

I recommend that you look for a Selectric-type keyboard that has quotation marks and the apostrophe on a single key on the right-hand side of the keyboard. You will find this format the most comfortable. Key placement is crucial to microcomputer operations and slight variations determine whether a keyboard is a joy or a terror to use. Beginners can usually adapt to any terminal format. If you are used to a particular keyboard, however, you should look very closely at the special keys when selecting a terminal. If you work with numbers, for example, you will probably want a numeric keypad in addition to the numbers at the top of the keyboard. You should look closely to make sure that all the functions you need are on the numeric keypad. Minus signs, for example, are often omitted, making it difficult to enter negative numbers. A numeric keypad should also have an ENTER key near the lower right corner of the pad. The ENTER key functions as a return key does, but is placed in a location which is more convenient to those who are used to working with numeric keypads.

You may require special foreign-language character sets that include umlauts and accent marks. These can be found on a few special keyboards. Terminal keyboards are based, however, on a character code called the American Standard Character Information Interface (ASCII). ASCII has 128 character codes, which are used by most computers today. ASCII does not have provisions, however, for umlauts or special accents, so little-used ASCII codes substitute these characters for foreign language applications. Special terminal and printer character sets must be used to write and print foreign language documents.

Touch is a very subjective issue. A large number of terminals don't have a touch that feels good to me. I like a crisp feel, with rapid recovery and rollover to compensate for my tendency to hit keys in rapid succession. A terminal with good rollover "remembers" the order in which keys are struck, even if they are struck almost simultaneously. Try several keyboards to find what feels best for you before you make a decision. Don't assume that keyboards on different models made by the same manufacturer are the same—they generally aren't. You will even find variations between units of the same model.

The Display

The display is an output device that shows you the information that you are typing on the keyboard or that the computer is sending to you. Display types include teletypewriters/printers; cathode ray tubes; and plasma, vacuum-flourescent, and electroluminescent displays. Still in the developmental stage, the latter three technologies all require high cost, integrated driver circuits. The teletypewriter was once the most common display mechanism, but now it is seldom used because of its speed and display limitations. The most popular display mechanism, the CRT, is available in a variety of character sizes and sets. Diversity in character sets will allow you to display nonstandard characters on the screen.

Most CRT displays show 24 or 25 lines of information. Typically, each line contains up to 80 characters, but some sophisticated displays can show 132-character lines. Others display up to 60 lines of 80 characters each. These large displays, however, are rare and expensive.

A character is displayed when a moving electron beam hits phosphors located on the surface of the screen. When the beam hits the phosphors, they glow. The beam is controlled by circuits inside the terminal. The image on the screen is held in an internal memory that is checked by these circuits each time the beam sweeps or refreshes the display screen. One of two approaches are used to control the display.

The simplest uses a character set stored in a ROM chip in the terminal. When the terminal receives the display signal, the controller selects the appropriate character from the ROM and places it in a memory that controls the movement of the electron beam. This technique is the least expensive approach. It permits the display of a predetermined character set, special effects such as reverse video (dark characters on a light background), varying levels of intensity, blinking characters, and underlining.

The second technique, bit mapped display, allows more creative and flexible displays. The screen is divided into small dots called pixels (or picture elements). Display images are created by selectively activating the individual pixels to form patterns, such as characters or lines. The pixels are controlled by a memory bank with storage locations which are "mapped" to each pixel. Changing the value in a memory location alters the brightness level of its associated pixel. The advantage to this approach is that the entire display is managed by software, making it possible to create special character sets and to draw complex lines and figures. The disadvantage is that it requires more complex control circuits and considerable memory to control the display.

A number of other variables influence display quality. One is the surface of the screen. Both regular and textured surfaces are available. A textured surface is the more expensive of the two, but it reduces glare off the surface of the screen. Nylon net and polarizing screens are available to cut the glare on regular display surfaces. This may seem a small point, but glare is one of the major causes of operator fatigue.

Character quality is determined by the number of pixels used to create characters. A character grid is a collection of rows and columns of pixels. The more pixels in the grid, the better the character resolution. Character grids range in size from 7×9 to 13×16.

You should consider the color and type of phosphors used in the display. Although most displays are black and white, green or orange phosphors are gaining in popularity. Proponents argue that these colors reduce fatigue. Other terminals display dark characters on a light background—similar to the printed page. I believe, however, that too much light area on the screen increases fatigue. I suggest sticking with light characters on a dark background.

You can choose any tint available, unless your eyes are abnormally sensitive to some colors. If they are, you should "test drive" various colored displays to find the one that feels best.

I don't really think display color matters as much as does decay speed: the amount of time it takes the phosphor to "turn off" after being hit by the electron beam. A slow decay phosphor leaves a ghost image on the screen. You should not accept a terminal with a slow decay. It will leave ghost images on the screen and make it extremely difficult to change the display rapidly.

Some experts argue that decay and display color are related, on the grounds that your eyes are more sensitive to some colors than to others. If the display is in a color to which the eye is particularly sensitive, the display may temporarily overload the cone cells on the back of the retina and produce a ghost image.

The Controller

The controller is the circuitry that manages the electronic beam and the interface between the terminal and the computer. It is usually located on a single printed circuit board inside the terminal.

Terminals are considered to be "dumb," "smart," or "intelligent," depending on the sophistication of the controller circuits. These are not precise classifications; they are used to group terminals together by the sophistication of their functions and programing capabilities. The advent of the microprocessor revolution has blurred the once-clear distinctions between terminals.

At the most basic level, all terminals are communication devices interacting with a host system in real time. They contain only the basic control circuits to generate displays and buffers to hold lines of text on the screen until they can be transmitted to the computer. Dumb terminals communicate with the computer on a line-by-line basis. Priced in the $500 to $1,500 range, they are the largest selling items on the terminal market.

Smart terminals have large buffers that can hold one or more screens of information. (A screen usually contains 24, 80-character lines.) Smart terminals can usually communicate in blocks—that is, they can send one or more screens of information to the computer at one time, achieving greater speed and efficiency than their dumb cousins. This means they must have larger internal memories (for the buffer) and more sophisticated control circuits. Many smart terminals offer on-screen editing and other special functions, which are either plugged into the machine with PROMs (Programmed Read Only Memories) or are programmed by the user with RAMs (Random Access Memories). A PROM, for example, might provide special editing features; a RAM might store a template to format data entries on the screen.

Smart terminals are designed for timesharing large, multiuser computer systems. In handling text and data editing and error detection, the smart terminal reduces the load on the host computer and improves the response characteristics for the individual user. Smart computers sell in the $1,000 to $3,000 price range.

Intelligent terminals are essentially combination computers and terminals. They can function alone or in connection with a host computer. Often they have both internal main memory and an external disk drive. At the low end they offer data formatting, editing, and compressing; thorough error checking; and other features. The high-end intelligent computer is completely independent, offering a full range of software programmable functions. The low-end machines sell for as little as $2,500. Sophisticated, specialized intelligent terminals can, however, cost as much as $20,000.

The Interface

The interface controls communication between the terminal and the computer. Almost all terminals communicate serially with the computer using an RS232C serial port. Most terminals will communicate at a variety of speeds, which are measured in *baud*. Dividing the baud rate by ten will give you the approximate speed in characters per second.

Higher interface speeds mean faster response to your commands. As a general rule, you want your terminal to communicate as fast as possible with your computer—preferably at least 9600 baud. At this speed it will take about two seconds to completely fill the screen of a typical terminal (1920 characters). Slower speeds are useful only if you plan to connect your terminal to a computer over telephone lines. Communication over telephone lines is generally done at 300 or 1200 baud.

Selecting a Terminal

The first rule in choosing a terminal is: Don't buy one without test driving it. Differences between terminals are often very subtle and not apparent without a direct test. Keyboard feel, for example, cannot be described; it must be experienced. Also, the quality of the character set, the display, and the display color must be experienced. There are some quantitative standards, however, that you can apply to compare terminals.

Keyboard

Many high-end terminals have detached keyboards, which can be moved in relation to the screen for the best combination of comfort and work efficiency. If you wear bifocals, you should definitely consider a detached keyboard. Look for a coiled-cord connection between the detached keyboard and the terminal. It is more flexible than the flat-ribbon cable.

The keyboard should have a comfortable slope—9.5 degrees is considered optimal. The tops of the keys should be slightly dished. The keyboard should have a layout that suits your needs. I recommend a Selectric keyboard if you will be doing much text processing. A numeric keypad will be important if you are going to be doing accounting or financial work. If you plan to use the numeric pad a lot, look for one that has an ''enter'' key and a minus ($-$) sign so you can enter negative numbers without shifting the position of your right hand.

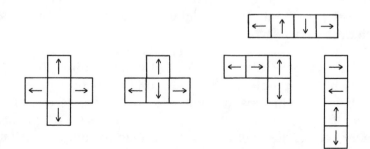

FIGURE 6–1. Cursor-Control Keys. Cursor-control key layout is seldom standardized. Here are some of the variations found in terminals. The two to the left are generally considered to be the easiest to use. *(drawing by Rashida Basrai)*

The Display

The terminal should display at least 24, 80-character lines. The more expensive terminals have a fifteen-degree tilt, which is a nice feature. The display should have a good brightness control. Some terminals automatically adjust the display intensity for changing room brightness.

You should look for a display screen with a no-glare or low-glare finish. If you don't choose a no-glare screen, you might want to buy a glare-reducing screen to fit on the screen. Some terminals have shields to protect the display against glare. Positioning the terminal away from the light and adjusting curtains or blinds can also help.

The character set on the screen should be large and easy to read. Make certain it has both upper- and lower-case characters and that the lower-case characters—*g,y,p,j,q*—have descenders. Make certain that the display does not flicker and that the phosphors decay quickly enough to prevent ghosting. Color, as I mentioned before, is primarily a question of personal preference.

Communications Interface

The terminal should be capable of communicating at rates as slow as 300 baud and as fast as 9,600 baud, though a 19,200 baud rate is nice if you can get it. When you have learned to use your system and to depend on it, you will probably become very sensitive to even minor system delays. It takes only one additional second to refresh the screen at 9,600 baud as compared to 19,200 baud, but the delay can become an intolerable interruption to your chain of thought if you're used to a quicker transmission rate.

Intelligence

Intelligence is mainly useful in a timesharing environment, where you do not have the dedicated attention of the computer. With micros this isn't the case. (Unless, of course, you are one of the unenlightened who is working with a multiuser micro system; more about this later.) Some intelligent features, however, make the terminal much easier to use.

The machine-addressable cursor allows the micro to control the cursor movement. This allows for interactive screen displays, and is essential for many sophisticated programs.

Through reverse video different portions of the screen can be highlighted under computer control. In many sophisticated programs reverse video makes visual distinctions between the program commands available to the user (menus) and the data the program is manipulating.

Variable intensity and blinking are other ways of accentuating material on the terminal screen under computer control. Controlled erase allows portions of the display to be selectively erased under program control.

Other Features

Other features you should look for include the noise level of the terminal and the amount of heat it generates (heat is the number one enemy of electronics). A remote-diagnostic feature will allow you to troubleshoot the terminal at the user end. Many terminals have a speaker that transmits audio signals related to terminal functions.

Graphics capability and pixel addressing can be very useful if you are interested in graphics applications. Remember, they require special software to use. If you aren't going to spring for the software, you probably won't want these features. Color terminal displays look nice and are particularly good for graphics work, but I haven't seen too much software that uses color well. If you have applications that require color, check out the software before you buy the terminal.

Paging, block moves, and scrolling are features related to smart and intelligent terminals. They are functions that allow the user to move information between the screen and the internal memory (buffers) of the terminal. These are useful for time-shared applications, but are not necessary for microcomputers.

Style—the physical design, shape, and appearance of the terminal—is always important. Start with the features you will need, but remember, you are going to have to live with your terminal. An ugly design may not affect terminal performance, but it may affect your performance.

7

The Floppy Disk Drive

The floppy disk drive is the most common external storage device for personal computers. It is called a floppy drive because it stores information on a thin plastic disk coated with a magnetic oxide. The disk is so thin that it easily bends in the hand and flops back and forth during handling.

Floppy drives come in three sizes: maxi, mini, and micro. The maxi uses a disk that is 8 inches in diameter—about the size of a 45 rpm record. The mini uses disks that are 5.25 inches in diameter. The micro format is still in a state of flux with disks ranging in size from 3 to 3.5 inches in diameter.

Floppy Disk Functions

The floppy disk drive serves four important functions for the computer. It is an archive to hold information while the computer is turned off and provides virtual memory support to the computer while it is working. It facilitates the distribution of software and is used to move information between machines.

Archive

The main memory of a computer is volatile—when you turn off the computer, you lose whatever information is stored in it. To archive information—data programs and even some program documentation—you store it on magnetic media. The floppy disk is the dominant magnetic storage medium for personal computers. As a matter of fact, most computers even keep the operating system that "manages" computer operation on floppy disk.

Virtual Memory

Most personal computers have a limited amount of main memory (compared to minicomputers and mainframes). Typically, 8-bit personal computers have 64K of main memory, 16-bit personal computers have 64 to 256K. Virtual memory allows you to work with programs and files larger than main memory. Stored on the floppy disks, portions of both the program and data file are moved from the disk to main memory as they are needed. After the data have been processed, or an instruction carried out, the information is swapped back to the floppy disk, so other information can be moved into main memory.

Virtual memory is extremely important in personal computing, where main memory tends to be small. In word processing, for example, a significant portion—as much as 25 percent—of the main memory may be occupied by the word processing program and the operating system. A single-spaced page of text has about

TABLE 7–1. Comparison of the Storage Capacities of Disk Drives

DISK DIAMETER (IN INCHES)	8	5.25	3[1]
Single side			
Single density	250-300K	100-125K	100K
Double density	575-600K	200-250K	200K
Double side			
Single density	575-600K	200-250K	200K
Double density	1-2M	400-500K	400K

[1] Data on 3-inch drives is an estimate based on Sony literature.

4,000 characters, so a 64K system may only have room for about 12 pages of text in main memory. Spelling programs require as much as 100K for their dictionaries, and my online thesaurus requires more than 200K. Without virtual memory, the performance and utility of these programs would be significantly reduced.

Software Distribution

The floppy disk is also the major method of packaging software. In the "good old days" programs were distributed as printed listings and had to be typed into the computer. Thank God, the good old days are gone. Now, when you buy a program, it comes on a floppy disk, ready to load into your computer and use.

Data Transmission

My double-sided 8-inch floppies hold 1.2 million bytes—that's equal to about 300 single-spaced pages of text. First class postage for one of these floppies is less than a dollar. For less than $10 I can get a floppy delivered overnight via Express Mail. This has got to be one of the biggest bargains going in information transmission. Sending that much information over telephone lines (using a 1200 baud MODEM) would take almost 30 hours and would cost at least $100.

You could send this information in printed form ("hard copy," in computerese), but if the recipient wanted to manipulate it by computer, it would have to be rekeyboarded. Now 1.2 million characters, typing at a steady speed of 5 characters per second (that's about 60 words per minute) would take—anyway, I'm sure you've got the message. Information is most usable when it's in machine-readable form, so it makes sense to transmit it in that form whenever possible. The most effective way to do that is by sending it on a floppy disk.

How the Disk Drive Works

Disk drives store information by selectively magnetizing the disk coating and read by sensing the magnetized patterns. This is done by means of a read/write head, much like the record/play-back head of a tape recorder. The disk rotates under the read/write head, with the head moving across the surface of the disk to record the information in a series of concentric tracks. It can be selectively moved to any track under computer control.

The time required to move to a specific location on the disk is a function of the time it takes to move the read/write head to the proper track and the rotation speed of the disk. Floppy disks rotate at speeds of 300 to 360 rpm.

A technique called sectoring enhances the speed and efficiency of data transfer between the computer and the disk drive. Tracks are divided into segments called sectors, which allow you to store data in small, manageable chunks, several of which can be accessed during a single revolution of the disk. The drive determines sector locations by "reading" a light-emitting diode through an index hole in the disk with a photo sensor. A second

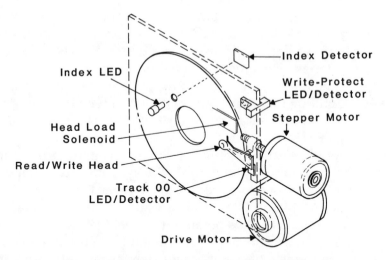

FIGURE 7–1. The Basic Floppy Disk Drive. The floppy disk drive is composed of a number of systems. The drive motor spins the disk. The stepper motor moves the read/write heads to the proper position on the disk. Solenoids load and unload the head. Light-emitting diodes and photocells sense the index hole in the disk and the write-protect notch. There are also mechanical components that load, position, and unload the disk and electronic components that control the operation of the drive and manage the movement of data to and from the drive. (*drawing by Rashida Basrai*)

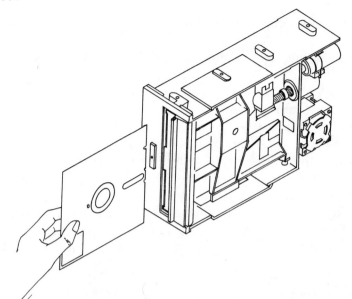

FIGURE 7–2. Loading a Floppy Disk. Floppy disks are loaded into the drive with the label away from the drive, and facing up. For most vertically mounted drives the label should be to the left. Inserting a disk into the drive upside down is embarrassing and should be avoided at all costs. Always hold the disk with your thumb on the label. *(drawing by Rashida Basrai)*

sensor checks a write-protect notch and disables the write mechanism if the disk is write-protected.

Information is stored on the disk in files. A directory on each disk hold the name of each file, together with addresses indicating where the file is stored on the disk. The unit of storage for a file is the block, which is a group of sectors.

To read or write on a disk, the drive controller first consults a directory to find an empty space on the disk (if performing a write operation) or the address of the first block of the file to be read. It then moves the head until it is over the proper track. Called seeking, this operation is done with a precision-stepping motor. The drive next "loads" the head by pressing it against the surface of the disk. When the head is to be moved again, it is first unloaded, then stepped to the new track, and loaded again.

The drive calculates sector locations from the position of the index hole, using a timer. When the proper sector is under the head, it is read and the data are sent to the computer.

Recording Information on Disks

Two formatting techniques are used to locate information on disks. The hard sector format is less flexible, but allows denser data storage. The soft sector format is more flexible, however, and is the most common format in use today.

Hard sectoring uses special disks which have a series of index holes so each sector can be mechanically located with a sensor. Systems using hard-sectored drives have all data recording parameters "hard-wired" into the system. This reduces the work for the user, but also reduces flexibility and makes it difficult to use disks to move information between different machines.

Soft sectoring allows one disk to be used for a variety of different formats. Sector boundaries are set with a computer program

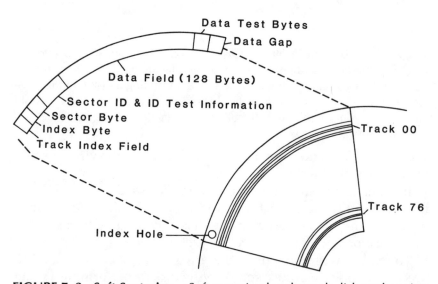

FIGURE 7–3. Soft Sectoring. Soft sectoring breaks each disk track up into sectors under software control. This sector from an IBM standard format 8-inch disk shows the overhead associated with soft sectoring. Notice the space required for the leading and trailing parts of the sector—it totals about 90 bytes. Since the IBM format allows 128 bytes of data per sector, the overhead is very high. You can increase storage efficiency by increasing the size of the sectors—the overhead stays the same. It takes 218 bytes of space to store 128 bytes of data (90 + 128), but you can store 1,024 bytes of data in only 1,114 bytes of space (1024 + 90). In general, larger sector sizes provide more efficient data storage and access (reading and writing). *(drawing by Rashida Basrai)*

called a formatter which writes the sectors onto the disk. Each sector is divided into three sections: a leading section, which indicates the start of the sector and its address; the data section; and a trailing section, which contains test information to check the data sector and an end-of-sector mark.

The size of the first and third sections is fixed by the formatting software and represents the "overhead" required for disk housekeeping with soft sectors. Typically, it is about 90 bytes per sector. Data sections range in size from 128 bytes to 1024 bytes.

Disk storage capacities can be augmented by increasing the density at which information is recorded and by recording information on both sides of the disk. Single density disks store 3408 bits of information per inch; double density disks store twice as much information in the same space. Recording on both sides of the disk doubles the number of tracks and the amount of information stored.

Although you can get greater storage density with hard sectoring because no disk space is needed for sector location, the greater flexibility of soft sectoring has made it the de facto standard for personal computers. The following table shows the formatted capacity of disks recorded at various sector sizes. Note that as the sector size increases, the number of sectors per track decreases, but the amount of available data space increases. This

TABLE 7.2. The Impact of Sector Size on Storage Capacity

Storage capacity of 8-inch, single sided, soft sectored disks (77 tracks) at various sector sizes and densities. Capacities reflect free storage and do not include system or backup tracks.

DENSITY	BYTES PER SECTOR	SECTORS PER TRACK	DISC CAPACITY
Single	128	26	249,600
	256	15	288,000
	512	8	307,200
	1024	4	307,200
Double	128	48	460,800
	256	26	499,200
	512	15	576,000
	1024	8	614,400

is because the amount of overhead space per sector is fixed, so when you increase the amount of data stored in each sector, you change the ratio of overhead to free storage space.

Drive Performance

Drive performance is measured in terms of speed—how fast the drive can access a given sector of data, and how fast that data can be transmitted to the computer. Access time measures how fast the drive can read a given data sector. It is based on the average seek time, settle time (the time it takes the head to settle after it has been moved), load time, and latency, which represents the time it takes the disk to rotate so the proper sector is under the head. Track-to-track seek time is 3 to 6 milliseconds. Typical settle time is about 6–9 milliseconds, and typical loading time is about 35–40 milliseconds. Typical latency or rotation time would be one half revolution, which is about 83 milliseconds and 360 rpm.

The average seek time is calculated by figuring how long it would take to read a track one third in from the edge of the disk, say track 25. Access time for one of my 8-inch drives is the sum of average seek time (25 tracks × 6 milliseconds), settle time (9 milliseconds), load time (35 milliseconds), and latency (83 milliseconds), totalling 277 milliseconds, or about one quarter of a second.

Transfer rate measures how fast data can be transferred from the disk drive to the internal computer memory and is a function of disk rotation speed and data storage density. Eight-inch drives have a greater transfer rate than small drives because they can store more data on each track. Typical transfer rates for 8-inch drives are 250,000 bits per second in single density mode, 500,000 bit per second in double density mode. Typical transfer rates for 5.25-inch drives are about half that rate.

Information is stored on disks in a variety of formats determined by the size of the block, the size of the sector, the number of tracks, the density at which information is recorded on the disk, and whether one or both sides of the disk are used to record information. Larger sectors give greater storage capacity. Larger blocks give faster transfer rates, but reduce storage efficiency because files are saved only in whole blocks. My system uses an 8K block to store either a file containing 8000 characters or a file containing only one character.

The Floppy Disk

Finally, let's take a quick look at the physical characteristics of the different sizes of floppy disks.

Maxifloppies

The maxifloppy looks like a 45 rpm record in a sleeve. When you hold the disk horizontally with the label facing up and closest to you, you will see a center hole, one smaller hole closer to you, an oval cutout, three notches in the opposite end—two small ones beyond the oval cutout and a larger notch to the left of center. The hole closest to you is the index hole. The large hole is used by the drive spindle to rotate the disk. The read/write head moves along the oval cutout to read or write the disk. The two small notches help position the disk in the drive. The large notch is used to write-protect the disk. When the notch is uncovered, the disk is

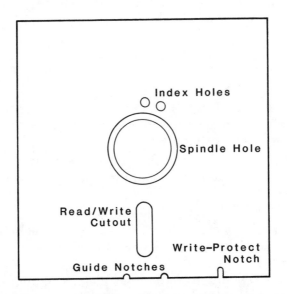

FIGURE 7–4. The 8-Inch Floppy. The 8-inch floppy disk stores up to 1.2 million bytes of information. Note the location of the index hole(s) (disks can have one or two holes) and the write-protect notch. On the 8-inch floppy, the disk is write-protected when the notch is uncovered. You must cover the notch with a piece of tape before you can write on the disk. (*drawing by Rashida Basrai*)

protected and you cannot write on it. To write on the disk, you must cover the write-protect notch with a small piece of metallic tape, which is usually included in the box of disks.

An 8-inch disk has 77 tracks, numbered from the outside in. Most personal computer operating systems reserve the outermost two tracks for the operating system. The disk directory occupies the next track and the remaining ones are used for data storage.

Currently, only 8-inch disks have a standard format—a format that all machines can read. This is the IBM 3470 format, which uses 26 128-byte sectors per track. The total format is shown below:

> Sectoring: soft
> Density: single
> Sides: single
> Sector size: 128 bytes
> Block size: 128 bytes

NOTE: A block is a group of one or more contiguous sectors. Information is moved between the computer and the disk drive in blocks to make the data transfer rate more efficient.

Minidisk

Minidisks are 5.25 inches in diameter, and there are some physical differences in packaging from the maxifloppies: the index hole is to the left of the spindle hole, and the write-protect notch is along the left side of the envelope. The write-protect routine is reversed—you leave the notch open for writing and cover it to protect the disk.

The first minidisks could hold only 35 tracks, but current technology can pack 40, 80, or even 100 tracks on a disk. Some minidrives now have storage capacity and performance equal to that of 8-inch drives.

The lack of a standard format has plagued minidisks until recently, making it extremely difficult to exchange disks between different computers. Now, however, the IBM PC disk format has emerged as a de facto standard.

The minidrive system uses much the same space allocation and formatting routines as the maxidrives. Table 7–3 shows the

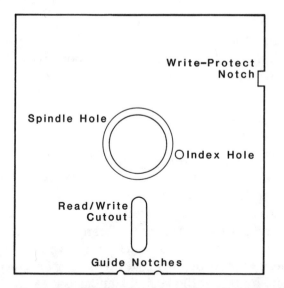

FIGURE 7–5. The 5.25-Inch Floppy. The 5.25-inch floppy disk can store up to 1.2 million bytes of information (in high performance configurations using 96 tracks per inch, both sides of the disk, and double density storage). The index hole and write-protect notch are in different positions than on the 8-inch floppy. The write-protect feature on 5.25-inch disk works opposite from its larger cousin. The notch is left open to write on the disk and is covered with tape to write-protect it. *(drawing by Rashida Basrai)*

TABLE 7–3. Storage Capacity of Minidrives
Formatted storage capacity for single-sided 5.25-inch drives using 35 tracks at various sector sizes and recording densities. (Many manufacturers now use 40–track disks which can store up to 320K. Some high-performance drives can hold a megabyte (Mb) of information.

DENSITY	BYTES PER SECTOR	SECTORS PER TRACK	DISC CAPACITY
Single	128	18	73,728
	256	10	81,920
	512	5	81,920
	512	5	81,920
	1024	2	65,563
Double	128	29	118,784
	256	18	147,456
	512	10	163,840
	1024	5	163,840

capacity of minidrives at various sector sizes and recording densities. Notice that the minidrives behave somewhat differently from maxidrives, and the large sector sizes do not necessarily guarantee maximum storage capacity.

Microdrives

In 1981, Sony introduced a new floppy disk format called the micro drive. The industry has shown considerable interest in the new format, and a number of companies are entering this arena. Typically, the companies have been unable to agree on a common format. At present there are three different sizes for microfloppies—3 inch, 3.25 inch, and 3.5 inch; and a variety of protective envelope designs and recording formats. Performance on these drives is quite high, but the lack of standards creates a significant risk factor. My guess is that this will not change soon, and I recommend waiting until a standard has emerged before buying any microdrive machine.

8

The Printer

The printer is the most independent component of a personal computer system. Most systems come without printers, and you must select one to meet your own specific needs.

Serial printers print one character at a time. They are lowest in both cost and print speed and are most popular for personal computer applications. There are two types of serial printers—those that generate fully-formed characters and those that generate characters from a series of dots (dot matrix printers). Serial printers range in speed from 10 cps (characters per second) to more than 300 cps.

Line printers are faster and more expensive than serial printers. They print an entire line at a time and operate at speeds measured in hundreds of lines per minute. Line printers are found in large computer installations, where their greater speed can be effectively utilized.

Laser printers use a xerographic type process to print full pages at once. They are extremely sophisticated and provide a wide variety of character fonts and good graphics. They are also extremely expensive and are found almost exclusively in large computer installations.

Because serial printers dominate the personal computer arena, the rest of our discussion will focus on them.

Dot Matrix Printers

Dot matrix printers form letters as a series of dots, generally on a 7 by 9 matrix. Dot matrix printers predominate in the personal computer marketplace because they are less expensive, faster, more flexible, and more reliable than fully-formed-character printers. They do not, however, produce extremely high quality type. They are generally smaller than full-character printers and are better suited to graphics applications.

How They Work

Functionally, dot matrix printers are quite similar to cathode ray tube displays. The print head sweeps across the page, just as the electron beam sweeps across the screen. The print head holds a series of pins in a vertical matrix. A control mechanism directs the striking of these pins against a ribbon to produce dots on the paper (just as the electron beam triggers phosphors on a CRT tube). Selective printing of the dots forms characters.

The key variables among impact dot matrix printers are the number and size of the pins and their configuration in the print head. Small dots and closer spacing between them produce better characters. Some print mechanisms stagger the pins so they overlap slightly when printing.

Non-impact dot matrix printers create dots by using either heat or electronic discharge to selectively blacken specially treated paper. Although the non-impact printers were quite popular in the early 1970s, they cannot compete with pin-and-ribbon matrix printers of today in terms of performance, price, or speed. However, their small size and quiet operation make them popular in applications where these factors are important.

Ink jet printers are another type of dot matrix printer. They create dots by squirting small drops of ink onto the page. The placement of the droplets is controlled by an electronic field in response to a character font template. Ink jet print is comparable in

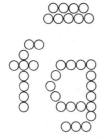

| Interlaced Needles | Interlaced & Overlapped Needles |
| Print Head | One Pass, No Descenders | One Pass, Descenders |

FIGURE 8–1. Dot Matrix Printing. Dot matrix printing has improved dramatically in the last few years through the development of smaller, interlaced needles. This drawing shows how dots are combined to form characters and how interlacing improves character quality. *(drawing by Rashida Basrai)*

quality to that of a good dot matrix printer, and the technology is taking hold for color printing. Early technical problems have been solved, and low cost ink jet printers are now available for the personal computer market.

Dot matrix printing offers great flexibility. Because the character set is created by software (as it is with the CRT), it is possible to create special character sets, including those for foreign languages. Other sets vary the type fonts and sizes. Some enhance type quality by overprinting dots to produce broader, darker characters. Under software control, the more sophisticated dot matrix printers can make multiple passes of each line to produce ultrafine characters that come close to, but do not equal, the quality of fully-formed-character printers. With multiple passes the character quality increases, but output speed drops. Dot matrix printers also produce very fine graphics displays via software programs that control the placement of individual dots on the page.

10 CPI

```
THIS IS NORMAL.
THIS IS NORMAL,ITALICS.
THIS IS NORMAL,DOUBLESTRIKE.
THIS IS NORMAL,DOUBLESTRIKE,ITALICS.
THIS IS NORMAL,EMPHASIZED,DOUBLESTRIKE.
THIS IS NORMAL,EMPHASIZED,DOUBLESTRIKE,ITALICS.
THIS IS SUPERSCRIPT.
THIS IS SUPERSCRIPT,ITALICS.
```

17.16 CPI

```
THIS IS CONDENSED.
THIS IS CONDENSED,ITALICS.
THIS IS CONDENSED,DOUBLESTRIKE.
THIS IS CONDENSED,DOUBLESTRIKE,ITALICS.
THIS IS CONDENSED,SUPERSCRIPT.
THIS IS CONDENSED,SUPERSCRIPT,ITALICS.
```

EPSON
EPSON AMERICA, INC.

Main Office: 3415 Kashiwa Street • Torrance, California 90505 • (213) 539-9140

FIGURE 8–2. Dot Matrix Type Faces. This print sample from an Epson MX-80 demonstrates the variety and quality of type faces that can be generated with a dot matrix printer. The Epson can generate sixty-four different fonts.

Dot matrix printers represent the low end of the serial printer market. Printers that handle 8.5 by 11 inch paper range in price from under $300 to more than $4,000, depending on capabilities and speed. Light weight dot matrix printers cost $300 to $1,000 and offer printing speeds of 60–100 cps, multiple character sets, and some graphics capability. The dot matrix printers that sell in the $1,000 to $2,000 range offer all the features of cheaper printers but are built for heavier duty and have printing speeds of 100–200 cps. Top-of-the-line dot matrix printers, with speeds in excess of 200 cps and multi-pass options which provide character quality approaching that of fully-formed-character printers, sell for more than $2,000.

The dot matrix printer constitutes the most volatile area of the

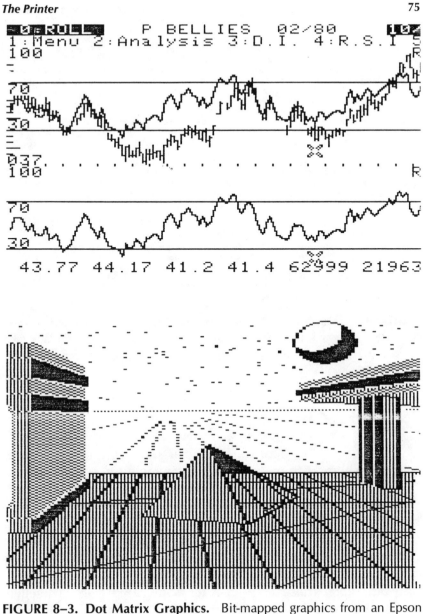

FIGURE 8–3. Dot Matrix Graphics. Bit-mapped graphics from an Epson printer.

printer market. Although unit prices will not go much lower, the price/performance ratio will improve significantly over the next few years.

The advanced 2410 is actually three printers in one: an outstanding correspondence quality printer that prints clean, crisp copy at 85 cps (everything
you're reading here is printed in the 2410 correspondence quality mode), a
data processing printer that goes like the wind at 350 cps; and a draft
quality printer that prints characters with extra dot density at a fast 175
cps for rough drafts and internal paperwork. Add red / black color,
Okigraph(TM) dot addressable graphics for charts, graphs, and pictures, and
an extensive list of features including the Okidata high performance print
head, and you've got yourself a workhorse that runs like a thoroughbred.

Here's a list of some impressive additional 2410 capabilities:

- Short line seeking logic and horizontal/vertical slew to
  increase throughput
- Underlining, super- (R^2) and subscripts (H_2O)
- Double—wide characters
- Proportional character s p a c i n g
- 6 and 8 lines per inch vertical spacing
- 14 channel electronic Vertical Format Unit
- Friction and Tractor Feed paper handling
- Optional Cut Sheet Feeder, accepts up to 200 sheets
- ASCII 96 character set and extension character set
- Downline loadable character set to create original
  characters and symbols
- Optional correspondence quality character set
- Operator status display

FIGURE 8–4. Dot Matrix Printing Effects. Notice the difference between
the first and second paragraphs in this sample printed by an Okidata Pace-
maker 2410. The first paragraph is printed in correspondence quality, the
second in draft quality.

Fully-Formed-Character Printers

There are three types of full character serial printers—selectrics,
daisy wheel, and thimbles. Selectrics were quite popular during
the early 1970s; however, they are now obsolete. Daisy wheel and
thimble printers exemplify the current generation of full character
serial printers. They range in price from about $1,400 to $3,500.

Adapters are available to connect the IBM Selectrics to a microcomputer. One type connects through the electronics of the typewriter; the other activates the selectric keys with solenoids. The
only advantage these adapters offer is low entry price. They generally cost around $500—more than a low-cost dot matrix printer
but considerably less than a daisy wheel or thimble printer. If you
already have a selectric typewriter, must have top quality output,
and want to minimize expenses, you might consider this option.
Generally, however, I think you would be better off with a printer
specifically designed for computer use.

Daisy wheel printers print with a flat spoked wheel that rotates in a vertical plane parallel to the paper. One character is lo-

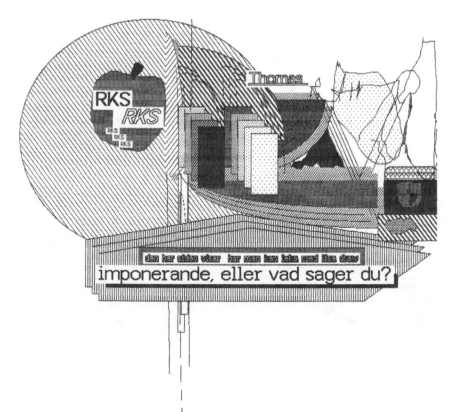

FIGURE 8–5. Dot Matrix Graphics. Graphics generated from a drawing program on the new Apple Lisa™. Notice the shadings. *(drawing generated by Ambjörn Lindskog)*

cated at the end of each spoke of the wheel. The wheel is moved across the page mechanically. At each print position the wheel rotates until the proper character comes under a solenoid-operated hammer. The hammer hits the end of the spoke, pressing the character against a ribbon and transferring a character image onto the paper. They print at speeds of 17 to 65 cps—much slower than dot matrix printers—but they offer much better character quality.

The thimble printer is a variation of the daisy wheel. The ends of the spokes of the print wheel are turned up approximately 80 degrees to form a broad, thimble-like mechanism which rotates in a horizontal plane rather than a vertical one. Spokes can hold two

 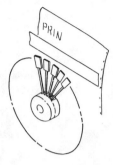

Golf Ball

Daisy Wheel

Thimble

FIGURE 8–6. Fully-Formed-Character Mechanisms. Based on IBM technology, the golf ball can print at speeds of 10 characters per second. It is generally considered too slow for computers, but many people adapt golf-ball typewriters to serve as low-cost printers.

The daisy wheel is faster and easier to manage than the golf ball because the print mechanism moves in only one plane. Most daisy wheels hold one character on each spoke but some special designs can hold more. Daisy wheels print at speeds from 17 to about 80 characters per second.

Thimbles, which hold two characters on each spoke, rotate and move up and down to position character forms. They print at speeds ranging from 35 to more than 50 characters per second.

characters each, and the thimble can be raised or lowered in addition to being rotated, to bring the characters under the hammer. This increases the number of characters that can be stored on the thimble.

Both daisy wheel and thimble printers can print only one type font at a time, but additional fonts can be obtained by changing the print element. Daisy wheel printers have been around longer and have more fonts available. Full-character printers often can control character placement on the paper in a sophisticated fashion. Vertical placement (controlled by the paper feed) is in increments of 1/48th of an inch, and horizontal placement (controlled by the print mechanism) is in increments of 1/120ths of an inch. This allows full-character printers to provide many of the special effects that dot matrix printers offer.

Most daisy wheel and thimble printers offer 10- and 12-pitch type fonts (some also offer 15-pitch). They also allow for line spacings of either six or eight lines per inch. Graphics can be generated using periods and other characters, although the quality is

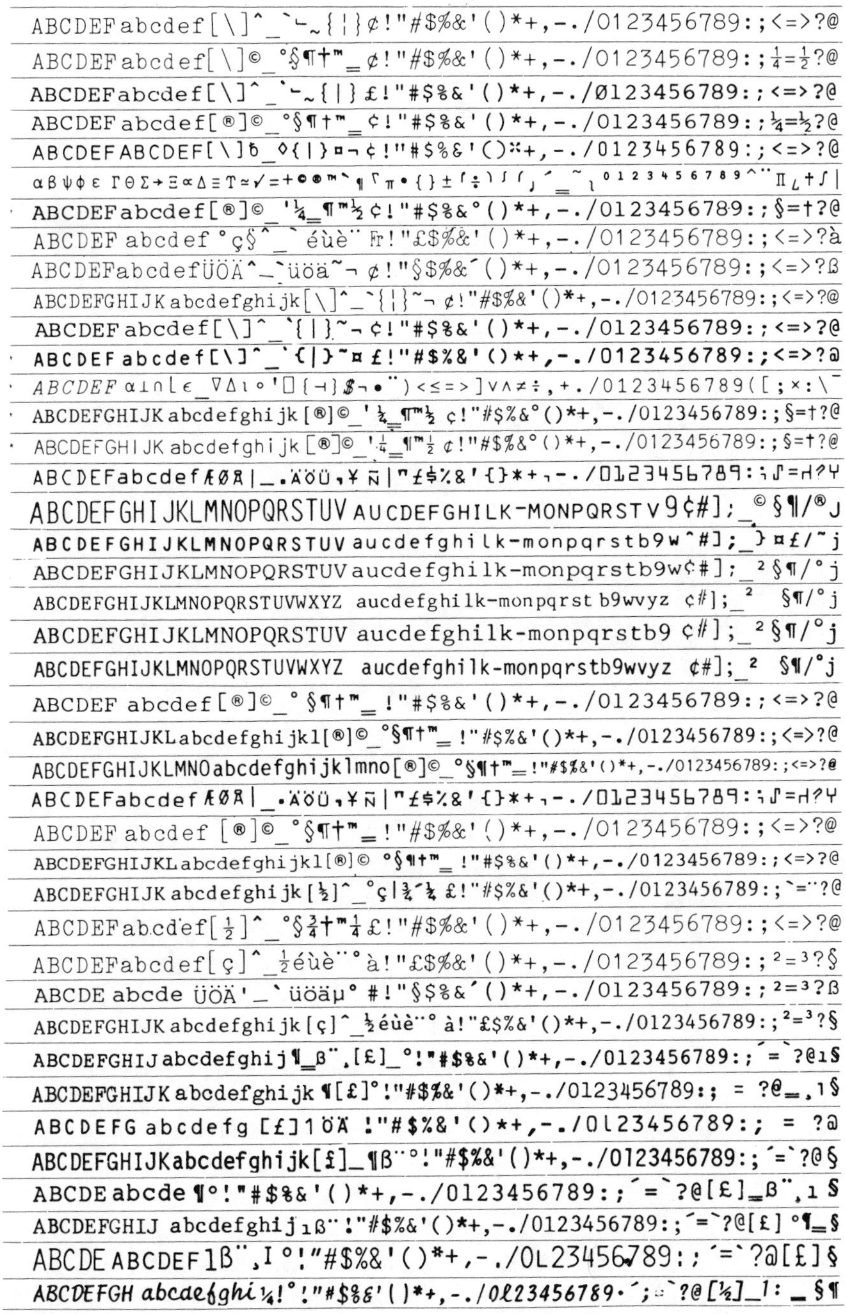

FIGURE 8–7. Fully-Formed Type Faces. Some of the type faces available for fully-formed-character printers. Daisy wheel printers offer the greatest variety of type faces.

```
This is single strike printing.

This is double strike printing.

This is boldface printing.

This is underscore printing.

This is strikeout printing.

This is a super script.

This is a sub script.
```

```
This section of text demonstrates different
justification options. The text was typed in on a 55-
character line. The first paragraph is unjustified--it
has a ragged right margin.  The second paragraph is
justified--whole spaces have been inserted between
words to create an even right margin. Notice the large
gaps between words.  The third paragraph is
microjustified--small spaces, each 1/120th of an inch,
are inserted between words and characters during
printing to smooth out the spacing gaps while
maintaining the even right margin.

This    section   of    text    demonstrates    different
justification  options.  The text was typed in on a 55-
character line.  The first paragraph is unjustified--it
has  a  ragged right margin.   The second  paragraph  is
justified--whole   spaces   have   been   inserted  between
words to create an even right margin.  Notice the large
gaps    between    words.    The    third    paragraph    is
microjustified--small  spaces,   each 1/120th of an inch,
are    inserted   between   words   and   characters   during
printing   to   smooth   out   the   spacing   gaps   while
maintaining the even right margin.

This   section   of   text   demonstrates   different
justification options. The text was typed in on a 55-
character line. The first paragraph is unjustified--it
has a ragged right margin.  The second paragraph is
justified--whole spaces have been inserted between
words to create an even right margin. Notice the large
gaps   between   words.   The   third   paragraph   is
microjustified--small spaces,  each 1/120th of an inch,
are  inserted  between  words  and  characters  during
printing  to  smooth  out  the  spacing  gaps  while
maintaining the even right margin.
```

FIGURE 8–8. Fully-Formed-Character Printing and Spacing Effects. Some of the printing effects you can create using fully-formed-character printers. These printers can also produce graphics by controlled placement of characters.

not as fine as with dot matrix printers. Graphics software packages are available for many fully-formed-character printers, as well as for dot matrix printers, that make it easier to generate graphics.

Many of these printers allows sophisticated printing effects—

This section of text demonstrates horizontal and vertical spacing effects. All
paragraphs are printed with a 12-pitch
wheel (pitch=characters printed per
inch). The first paragraph is printed
with spacing of 10 pitch and 6 lines per
inch. The second is printed at 12 pitch
and 6.8 lines/inch. The third uses 15
pitch and 8 lines/inch. The last uses 8
pitch and 5.3 lines/inch.

This section of text demonstrates horizontal and vertical spacing effects. All
paragraphs are printed with a 12-pitch
wheel (pitch=characters printed per
inch). The first paragraph is printed
with spacing of 10 pitch and 6 lines per
inch. The second is printed at 12 pitch
and 6.8 lines/inch. The third uses 15
pitch and 8 lines/inch. The last uses 8
pitch and 5.3 lines/inch.

This section of text demonstrates horizontal and vertical spacing effects. All
paragraphs are printed with a 12-pitch
wheel (pitch=characters printed per
inch). The first paragraph is printed
with spacing of 10 pitch and 6 lines per
inch. The second is printed at 12 pitch
and 6.8 lines/inch. The third uses 15
pitch and 8 lines/inch. The last uses 8
pitch and 5.3 lines/inch.

This section of text demonstrates hori-

zontal and vertical spacing effects. All

paragraphs are printed with a 12-pitch

wheel (pitch=characters printed per

inch). The first paragraph is printed

with spacing of 10 pitch and 6 lines per

inch. The second is printed at 12 pitch

and 6.8 lines/inch. The third uses 15

pitch and 8 lines/inch. The last uses 8

pitch and 5.3 lines/inch.

FIGURE 8–8, cont.

Subscripts and superscripts, double-struck characters (the hammer strikes each character twice before moving to the next position), and bold-face (the print head produces a broader character
by moving slightly to the right before the character is struck a second time). Some printers offer true proportionate spacing.

Printer Features

Printers come in a bewildering array of models and features. This
discussion should help you through the maze.

Interface

Printers are connected to computers with a serial (RS232) or parallel interface, or a 20 milliamp current loop. Serial and parallel interfaces are the most common. Although parallel interfaces are generally easier to design and cheaper, I feel serial interfaces are worth the extra cost because they offer greater flexibility.

Serial interfaces send information as a series of sequential bits. Although they all use a standard RS232 interface plug, they are not standardized because they do not all use the same lines to move signals between computer and printer. At a minimum, the serial interface requires two lines—one for the data signal and one for a signal ground. A third line, called a handshake, is often used to control the flow of information from the computer to the printer. This allows greater communication flexibility. Sometimes additional lines are used to provide other control signals between printer and computer.

Parallel interfaces send eight bits (a full character) at once, using a set of parallel lines. They require more lines than a serial interface—eight for the signal, one for the signal ground, and one for a handshake. Parallel interfaces are less standardized than serial interfaces. However, they are popular with manufacturers and systems integrators because of their lower cost.

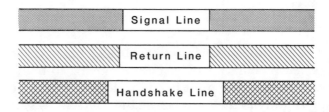

FIGURE 8–9. The Serial Interface. The serial interface is the simplest personal computer communications link. It requires only a data line, a return line (to complete the electrical circuit), and a handshake line (to control the flow of data along the line). Information is transmitted over the line one bit at a time, as a series of synchronized electrical pulses. (*drawing by Rashida Basrai*)

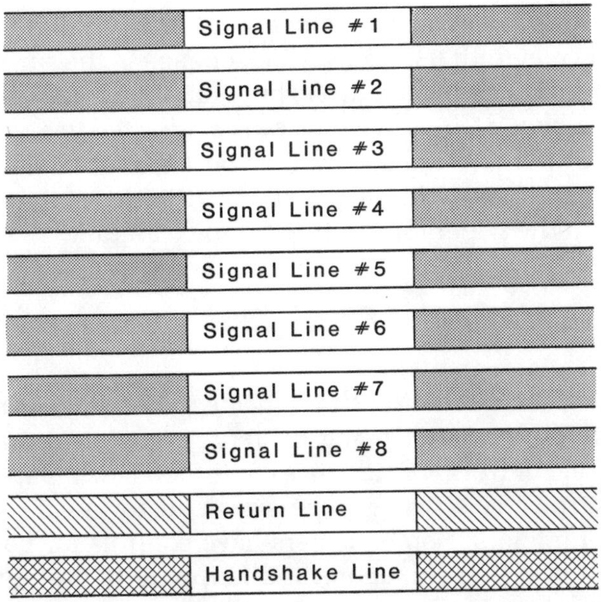

	Signal Line #1	
Signal Line #2	
Signal Line #3	
Signal Line #4	
Signal Line #5	
Signal Line #6	
Signal Line #7	
Signal Line #8	
Return Line	
Handshake Line	

FIGURE 8–10. The Parallel Interface. The parallel interface requires more lines than the serial interface. It transmits one byte at a time—eight bits in parallel—over eight signal lines. It also has a return and a handshake line. (*drawing by Rashida Basrai*)

Paper Feed

One of three basic mechanisms—friction, pin, or tractor—controls the movement of paper through the printer. Friction feed operates just like a typewriter. The paper is inserted behind the platen, which rotates to move it past the print mechanism. Pressure rollers hold the paper against the platen. This method of paper control is very good for correspondence, where you want to use letterheads, but it can be a drag when you have to insert every page of a 200 page report.

Pin feed uses pins on each end of the platen to position and move the paper. The paper has sprocket holes on each side to fit over the pins. The paper comes in rolls—either continuous, or perforated so it can be "burst" into individual sheets. The disadvantage is that only one paper width can be used because the pins are fixed on either side of the platen.

Tractor feed uses a paper moving mechanism that is independent of the platen. It uses pins which engage in the sprocket holes of the paper like a pin feed drive, but, since the tractor is independent of the platen, the drive pins can be adjusted to accommodate a variety of paper widths. The very best tractor feeds, called bidirectional tractors, hold the paper on both sides of the platen and can back up the paper for printing complex graphics.

Controls

Printer controls are located either inside the case or on an exterior control panel, the latter being far more convenient and easy to use. Typical controls will advance continuous form paper one full page; control line spacing, type size, and form size; and reset printer parameters. Some printers have controls for built-in programs to test printer functions and help you figure out why the printer won't work. Some printers will reset internal parameters in response to signals from the computer. This allows you to imbed commands in your text to control printing effects such as font type and size, spacing, and character color.

Buffers

A buffer is an interim memory unit that holds information until it can be processed. Printer buffers moderate the flow of data from the computer and hold multiple lines of text. They allow for bidirectional printing (the printer prints one line left to right, and the next line right to left), which speeds the process by eliminating the time needed to return the print head to the left margin.

Buffers are particularly useful with print spooling—a software feature that allows you to print one file while working on another by switching the computer between the two tasks. Increasing the speed at which data is transmitted to the printer and decreasing the frequency with which the data must be transmitted allows the computer to provide more support to your other task. Increasing the size of the printer buffer helps in both areas. Printer buffers vary in size from one line—80 to 100 bytes—all the way up to 48,000 bytes.

Selection Criteria

If cost and speed are your major concern, dot matrix printers are probably the answer—if you can accept the print quality. If you want the highest possible print quality, you will have to go to a daisy wheel or thimble printer. As with the dot matrix printers, cost is directly related to the output speed. If you are going to be doing a lot of printing, don't try to get by with a light-weight printer. Get a reliable, heavy-duty one.

The following checklist may help you to identify printer features most important to you:

- horizontal tabs
- vertical tabs
- proportional spacing
- bidirectional printing
- multiple type fonts
- graphics
- print speed
- character enhancement
- half-line vertical increments for formulas
- noise
- weight
- warranty
- availability of service contract

I strongly recommend a combination tractor and friction feed mechanism. Bidirectional tractors are more expensive, but are necessary for sophisticated graphics printing. I also recommend wide carriages—they don't cost that much more, and it's often handy to be able to use wide paper—and the more flexible serial interface.

I have no particular recommendation in the dot matrix area, because new products are appearing every month. Among the fully-formed-character printers, my personal preference is thimble printers—in particular, the NEC Spinwriter. It is reputed to be the most reliable of the fully-formed-character printers. It is available in both low cost–low speed and more expensive–high speed models. My personal printer is a modified NEC Spinwriter which has a 16,000 character print buffer and automatic bidirectional printing. It has an honest throughput of about 60 cps.

The feature I can't stress enough is reliability. Printers are the most mechanical computer component and, therefore, are the most prone to failure. When you start using a microcomputer you will begin to depend on it almost immediately. If any part breaks down it is going to hurt. Once you have narrowed down your choice of printers, base the final decision on reliability. Get names of users and call them to determine both the failure rate for the printer and the time it takes for repair.

9

Packaging Computers

The high fidelity/stereo market provides the best analogy for understanding variations in personal-computer packaging. You can get a stereo unit that has everything in one package—turntable or changer, preamplifier, amplifier, and speakers. You can also get a compact system with separate speakers so you can position them for better stereo effect. The next step up is to have a separate turntable, a receiver (a combination tuner, preamplifier, and amplifier), and a set of speakers. The ultimate is to buy each component separately—turntable, tuner, preamplifier, amplifier, and speakers. As components are separated, three things happen: the cost goes up because each component requires its own package, and support system; the performance of each unit improves because each can be designed to do a single function and compromises do not have to be made; and flexibility increases—it is possible to change one component at a time.

Computer packaging is quite similar. It is possible to buy everything crammed into a single package, or you can go the component route and buy everything separately. Of the four basic components in any personal computer system the printer is generally independent. Many different kinds of printers will plug into any system. The remaining components must be carefully integrated so they will work together. They can be combined into a variety of different packages.

Intelligent Terminals

The intelligent terminal packages the computer, terminal, and disk drives into one package. The North Star Advantage, the Televideo 802, the Data Technologies Associate, the NEC APC, the Zenith Z100, the Archives III, and the Data General MPC/100 are examples of this approach.

The advantage to this system is that the components are integrated and ready to go. The system occupies the smallest amount of space, it is usually styled more attractively, and is the least expensive package. The disadvantages are that these designs are the most difficult to keep cool (heat is the number one enemy of microcomputers), are generally more difficult to repair, and are extremely difficult to upgrade, since all the components are packaged together.

```
┌─────────────────────────┐
│                         │
│        Display          │
│                         │
│        Keyboard         │
│                         │
│        Computer         │
│                         │
│      Floppy Disks       │
│                         │
└─────────────────────────┘
```

FIGURE 9–1. Integrated Computers. An integrated system combines all the components in a single package: computer, terminal, and external memory. (*drawing by Rashida Basrai*)

Intelligent Terminals with External Drives

In addition to the intelligent terminal there is one additional box that holds the disk drives. Examples of this package are the Radio Shack TRS-80 Model II and the Zenith Z-89 and Z-90 (both with extra drives), the Xerox 820, and the Hewlett Packard HP125.

This package has many of the same advantages and disadvantages as the intelligent terminal except that it is possible to upgrade the disk drives more easily, though it may cost more because of the additional box and power supply.

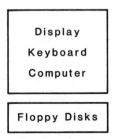

FIGURE 9–2. Integrated System with External Memory. This package is losing popularity as it becomes easier to design smaller disk drives into a single package. *(drawing by Rashida Basrai)*

Integrated Systems with Separate Terminal

This variation will have two components—one houses the computer and the external memory system (probably one or more floppy disk drives and perhaps a hard disk drive) and the other the terminal. Examples of this package are the Cromemco, the North Star Horizon, the RAIR, the ALTOS, and the standard ONYX.

More flexible than the two packages discussed above, this approach allows you to change the terminal. Some of these packages use a single board computer; others use a bus system with independent plug-in computer modules. The latter is more flexible and easier to repair. (See Figure 9–3.)

Modular Systems

A modular system has several components, which are designed by the manufacturer to work together. It has a separate monitor or display, but the keyboard, computer, and external memory may come in one, two, or three packages. Examples of this approach include the Apples (II, III, and Lisa), the DEC Rainbow™,

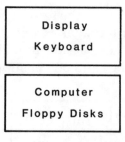

FIGURE 9–3. Computer and External Memory Combined, Separate Terminal. This package combines computer and external memory in one enclosure. A separate terminal is used. *(drawing by Rashida Basrai)*

the Epson HX-10, the Franklin ACE, the IBM PC, the NEC AS-TRA 200, and the Toshiba I-100.

The modular system is currently the most popular package on the market. Most of these computers use a pseudobus design and can be upgraded with plug-in boards. Often other manufacturers offer disk drives, keyboards, and monitors to expand or modify these systems.

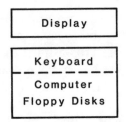

FIGURE 9–4. Modular Systems. Rapidly becoming the most popular packaging format, modular systems use both single-board and pseudobus designs. The more advanced ones (IBM PC, Lisa, Epson QX-10) are designed to interface with specific printers to take advantage of unique software. *(drawing by Rashida Basrai)*

Component Systems

A component system has each function component in a separate box—each probably comes from a different manufacturer. It is difficult to give examples of a component system because they tend to be unique. I have two: one uses a California Computer Systems S-100 bus computer, two 8-inch Tandon disk drives in a Vista box, and a Televideo 950 terminal; the other uses a Davidge 6/4 single board computer, two Mitsubishi 8-inch drives in a Vista box, and a Heathkit H19 terminal.

I prefer this approach for its flexibility. Each component can be upgraded independently of the others. In the last 20 months, I have changed every component in both my systems without having to change any operating procedures. Unfortunately, it is also the most expensive type of system—the components cost more and it takes longer to integrate them for effective performance.

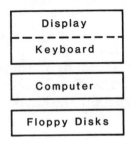

FIGURE 9–5. Component Systems. Popular with computerphiles, component systems provide maximum flexibility and allow quick upgrading and modification of components to maximize performance. (*drawing by Rashida Basrai*)

Portable Systems

Portable systems are designed and packaged so they can be moved from place to place. The package size determines the power, capability, and ease of moving.

Hand-held computers are sophisticated pocket calculators. They are easy to move but are limited in power and utility by their size. Typically they have small (12- to 15-character) displays, limited main memory, and no external memory. They are manufactured by Caiso, Commodore, Hewlett Packard, Radio Shack, and Sharp, among others. They do not compare well with the other computers described in this book.

Briefcase-sized computers weigh under ten pounds and can easily be moved from one location to another. They provide many of the same functions as larger personal computers—word processing, calendar and scheduling, and financial analysis—and are modified to deal with display and memory limitations. They use flat screen displays, which can show 80 to more than 1,000 characters. Internal memories range from 8K to more than 128K. Some use cassettes for external memory, others use bubble memory or small disk drives. Most can operate on either batteries or 110-volt power. Examples include the Epson QX-20, the Gavilan, the Grid COMPASS, and the Radio Shack 100. They range in cost from $800 to $10,000.

Typewriter sized portables offer all the power of full-sized personal computers, but in smaller packages. They have full-size displays, at least 64K of main memory, and built-in disk drives. Most require 110 volt power, but some can be run on batteries. These machines are really transportable rather than portable. They weight more than twenty pounds and are uncomfortable to carry for extended periods of time. Examples include the Compaq, Corona, the Dynalogic Hyperion, the Kaypro II, the Osborne Executive, and the Otrona Attache. These machines cost between $2,000 and $4,000.

FIGURE 9–6. Portable Computers. The portable computer has rivaled the modular system as the most popular packaging approach in 1983. Portable computers come in three sizes: pocket, briefcase, and suitcase. Currently, only the suitcase-sized portables have floppy disk drives and offer performance to equal that of other packaging options. *(drawing by Rashida Basrai)*

10

Other Hardware

In addition to the major hardware components, there are others that you should be aware of and consider adding to your system. None of these components are necessities, but you might find some of them valuable in making your personal computer do more for you.

External Memory Devices

One category of frequent interest is supplemental external memory devices, which increase storage capacity and the rate at which data is moved between the main memory and the external memory.

Hard Disks

Hard or Winchester disk drives provide greater storage capacity and faster transfer rates than floppies. Because the disk on hard disks is stiffer, it can rotate at higher speeds and tracks can be packed more closely together. The read/write heads of hard-disk drives do not actually touch the surface of the disk; they float on a cushion of air a few microns (millionths of an inch) above the surface. Because air-borne particles of dust and smoke can damage the fragile magnetic media, the hard disks and read/write heads are sealed in dust-free chambers. Consequently, the disks cannot be removed from the machine. Storage capacity is expanded by stacking disks on top of each other and adding more read/write heads.

Hard disks measure 3 (more or less), 5.25, 8, or 14 inches. Storage capacities range from 5 megabytes (Mb) (5,000,000 bytes) to more than 160 Mb. Typically, hard disks for personal computers range in capacity from 5 to 40 Mb. Hard disks are primarily used to provide virtual memory. You still need to rely on other devices (primarily floppies) for archive, software distribution, and data transfer.

One limitation of a hard-disk drive machine is that you can't remove the disk from the computer. If you want a duplicate or a back-up copy of your files, you will need to record them on a floppy disk, streaming tape, or hard-cartridge disk. Back-up copies allow you to move programs and data files to another machine if yours breaks down or if you buy a second machine.

Floppies can be used for back-up. After all, you will have to have a floppy-disk drive anyway to load new software and to transfer information between machines. The drawback to floppy back-up, however, is that it takes several disks to do a complete back up of all the files on a hard disk. The best solution is to back-up your hard disk selectively. That is, you back up only those files that have been changed or added to since the last backup.

Streaming Tape Drive

The streaming drive uses a tape cartridge, designed for high-speed data transfer. It has the capacity to record the contents of a hard disk on a single cartridge. This simplifies the back-up procedure. (Typically it takes 10 to 20 minutes to transfer the full contents of the hard disk to the tape.)

While the streaming-tape drive is a good archival device, it cannot provide software distribution and data transfer. I have seen some packages that include only a hard disk and a tape drive. You can't imagine how much trouble it is trying to get new software on one of these machines. Do not get a hard-disk machine that does not also have a floppy drive.

Cartridge Drive

A cartridge drive uses a removable hard disk. This is how hard disks were built in the old days, when computers were mainframes and only programmers played with them. Recently several manufacturers have started offering cartridge drives for the personal computer market—either alone, or in conjunction with a true Winchester drive. Although cartridge drives provide both archive and virtual memory support, they do not replace the software and data-transfer functions of a floppy.

Telecommunications Features

Telecommunications refers to the electronic movement of information. The principal telecommunications concern for personal computers is moving information over telephone lines. Typical applications are to communicate with other personal computer users or to access information utilities.

Communication over telephone lines requires a MODEM (a modulator-demodulator) and a telecommunications software package. A MODEM is an electronic device that translates digital computer signals into analog signals that can be sent over telephone lines. They are serial devices—that means they send the information one bit at a time. MODEMS come as stand-alone devices which connect with your computer via an RS-232 serial port or as boards which plug into the bus of your computer.

Two issues govern selection of MODEMS—speed and compatibility. Speed is measured in baud, which indicates the number of bits being sent per second. Personal computers generally use either 300 baud or 1200 baud MODEMS. Compatibility means that your MODEM must use the same communications protocols as the MODEM connected to the computer you are calling. Most personal computers use Bell standards—103 for 300 baud, 212A for 1200 baud. Some manufacturers offer MODEMS which will handle both standards.

Some MODEMS automatically answer incoming calls and dial outgoing calls. When coupled with a clock/calendar device and auto dial–auto answer MODEM, your computer can be programmed to communicate at specific times. This allows you to communicate with other computer users at late hours, when telephone rates are lowest, without the bother of staying up.

A dual speed MODEM (103 and 212A compatible) with auto dial and auto answer will give you maximum flexibility for telecommunications.

There are a number of telecommunications software protocols on the market. Some are generic, others are designed to work with specific MODEMS. This is one place where I recommend you get specific software as it will make using your MODEM much easier.

Power Conditioners

Computers require stable power. While I was writing this book, a friend of mine once tried running his computer during a thunderstorm. The power fluctuations played such havoc with his system that he had to replace many of his disk programs. The storm had caused voltage fluctuations in the power lines that adversely affected his computer. Data stored in main memory was damaged but was still swapped on to the floppy disk replacing good data with bad. Power fluctuations can damage the delicate electronic innards of your machine. Power interruptions can cause your computer to crash without warning, resulting in lost data. If you live in an area with marginal power, you might want to consider purchasing a power conditioner.

A surge and spike protector acts as a buffer against power fluctuations. It is a relatively inexpensive—$50 to $100—form of insurance. I strongly recommend one.

Emergency power supplies provide battery back-up to keep your computer going in a power outage. Plugged into the wall socket and your computer, they switch on automatically when the power fails. They don't last long—about ten minutes—but they give you enough time to perform an orderly shut down of your computer.

The automatic shut down is valuable for floppy disk machines (you can save your working files and avoid lost data) and essential for hard disk systems, which can be easily damaged by power failures. These devices cost $400 to $1,000, depending on the amount of power supplied. If I had a hard disk, I'd buy one of these devices.

Output Devices

Although the printer will probably be your primary output device, you might not want to restrict your system to just one. For example, I often recommend that clients get two printers—a dot matrix for fast printing and proofs and a fully-formed-character printer for correspondence quality printing. Here are two other output options you might want to consider.

Printer Buffer/Controller

A buffer/controller mediates the flow of information between your computer and printer. It takes information to be printed from your computer, stores it, and feeds it to the printer, allowing you to use the computer for other tasks. If your printer does not have a large internal buffer, I'd recommend getting one of these gadgets. Some can hold more than 48K—that's almost 16 pages of single-spaced text.

Plotter

One of the curses of computers is that we can generate much more information than we have ways to digest. I once ran off sixteen different cash-flow estimates for a new business venture. Each estimate was based on a variation in the basic assumptions about the performance of the new business. When I showed them to a potential investor, he went into shock. There was too much information for him to grasp what was going on.

At the last computer show I attended, I saw several graphic programs that generate graphs based on spreadsheet results. This capability is a significant breakthrough in graphics output. These programs can be used with both printers and plotters, but a plotter gives much better graphics output than either a fully-formed-character printer or a dot matrix printer. Lines are straight and clean. Some even give you a range of colors. If you plan to use your personal computer to work with financial information, you are going to need a plotter. Start looking.

Interactive Graphics Support Tools

Graphics support tools provide entrance into an exciting new medium; one in which you can dynamically create and alter any visual image—text, a drawing, a line diagram, even a picture. Not only can you generate these images, you can string them together to form a continuously changing picture. I've just started working with interactive graphics and I find it to be one of the most exciting communication innovations of the past decade. I've started exploring video production so I can fully employ these new tools.

Graphics-processor Board

Graphics-processor boards—add-ons for bus-based computer systems—give you the capacity to store and manipulate visual images. They have lots of on-board memory, processors, and ROM to hold command sets. These boards vary in the degree of resolution and color control they offer. The more pixels (or picture elements) a board has, the better its graphics resolution and definition. Inferior graphics have resolutions on the order of 50 x 50 or 2,500 pixels. Quality graphics systems have resolutions of five hundred to one thousand pixels. As a standard of comparison consider that your home television set has about 250 x 300 pixels of resolution. Color control determines how much you can vary the color of a pixel. The lowest level of control would be one bit, which gives two color grades—generally either black or white. Eight bits give 256 color codes; twenty-four bits, more than sixteen million codes. Now you see why the memory is required. A quality image might require 512 x 512 units of resolution and 24 bits of color control. That would require 512 x 512 x 24 (6,291,456) bits or about 800,000 bytes of storage.

You can get low-resolution graphics systems with computers like the Apple and Atari. Medium- and high-resolution graphics systems are usually built around the S-100 bus or add-on devices.

A medium-resolution graphics board (512 x 512 x 8 bits) costs about $5,000 to $10,000. A top level (512 x 512 x 24 bits) costs $15,000 to $20,000. This may seem high, but costs will drop as that of memory does and as the demand for color graphics increases. Color graphics capability is already offered as an option on some 16-bit packaged systems. All you need is a color monitor.

Color Monitor

To work in color you are going to need a good color monitor. The two key variables in monitors are resolution and type of input.

Resolution is measured in lines—the number of rows of pixels that it will resolve. Your television set is a low resolution device— it will display about 225–250 lines. A medium resolution monitor can display 350–400 lines. High resolution monitors display more than 500 lines. The amount of resolution you will need is determined by the resolution of your computer. An IBM PC standard video board will generate 200 lines. The Corona (an IBM look-alike computer) generates 325 lines. Better graphics boards can generate close to 500 lines.

Color monitors use either RGB or composite inputs. The RGB input provides separate signals for each primary color—red, green, and blue. The RGB interface generally uses a multi-pin plug. The composite input is the NTSC standard signal used in television broadcast. It generally uses a coaxial cable and a BNC or an "F" plug.

Monitor prices are primarily a function of resolution and size. Low resolution color monitors currently sell for $250–$400. Medium resolution monitors sell for $500–$1,000. High resolution monitors start at $1,000 and go up and up.

Graphics Tablet, Digitizer, Light Pen, and Mouse

All these devices send information to the computer. They can all send coordinate information (as in drawing an image), control the movement of the cursor on the screen, and respond to questions on the screen.

The graphics tablet is an electronic drawing board with a broad, flat surface (on which to draw) and a stylus (with which to draw). Sensors under the board report the position of the stylus to the computer, which shows it on the monitor. The monitor is also used to display a menu of commands for use with the graphics tablet.

A digitizer is like a graphics tablet system, but it does not require a tablet. It is placed over a flat surface and sensors on the bottom report movement to the computer. Digitizers are very good for "reading" a drawing into the computer.

A light pen is a stylus that works with a display screen. It's like a graphics pad, except that you use the display screen itself as the tablet.

The mouse is a less precise version of the digitizer, used to control cursor movement and send commands to the computer. Like the digitizer, sensors on the bottom of the mouse discern movement and send signals to the computer (which, in turn, moves the cursor). Buttons on the mouse also are used to send signals to the computer. A mouse and a screen menu are used to control the operation of the Apple Lisa.

The graphics pad, digitizer, and light pen are all useful tools for graphics work. Which one to use depends on your specific application, personal style, and graphics software. Quite frankly, I must confess that I have never been impressed with the mouse system. It isn't accurate enough for graphics work, so it tends to be used mostly to send commands to the computer. I find it much easier to use a keyboard to enter commands; any device which requires that I take my hands from the keyboard slows my work.

SECTION IV

INTRODUCTION TO PERSONAL COMPUTER SOFTWARE

Software is a generic term for sets of instructions given to a computer to have it accomplish a specific task. You will be using four types of software with your computer. *Operating systems* provide overall communication and control between the various hardware components and between your hardware and other software products. Your software programs, therefore, must be compatible with both your computer hardware and your operating system. *Utilities* are primarily simple programs for conducting housekeeping operations such as transferring, cataloging and formatting disk files, maintaining hardware, and providing telecommunications links.

Computer *languages* provide the vocabularies and syntactic structures for writing program instructions. They come in a bewildering array of levels and variations, ranging from easy-to-understand, higher-level languages with English-like vocabularies and structures, to simple, but difficult-to-understand, binary codes. *Applications programs* are packaged sets of instructions that tell the computer to perform specific tasks such as word processing or financial analysis. They make it possible for you to use your computer to do useful work with a minimum of preparation or previous experience.

The software industry is in a constant state of flux, but de facto standards point to the best packages.

11

(handwritten: pre fm pg 103 to 112 old with photo illustration (fm I to VIII paper))

Operating Systems

A disk operating system (DOS) is a software program that performs the overall communication, control, and housekeeping functions for the computer. It controls the disk drive by creating, opening, and closing files and keeping track of the storage and retrieval of programs and data. In addition, it provides the interface between the various system components (computer, external memory, terminal, printer) and all other software run on the computer.

An operating system also includes a basic set of utility programs which are used for specific functions. An editor utility creates programs; a debugging utility is used to correct them. File copy programs move stored information under operator control between the various system components. System statistics programs provide information on the status of different components.

The disk operating system is the interface between the hardware and software and determines which languages and applications programs can be used on a computer. Disk operating systems can be system specific or generic.

System-specific DOSes are developed by hardware manufacturers and are custom tailored to their computer system. They offer the greatest sophistication and are generally the most user friendly, but at a cost. The cost is that they do not provide a standard software interface so it is often difficult, if not impossible, to move programs and languages designed for a system-specific operating system to another computer. Apple, Atari, Commodore, Radio Shack, and Zenith computers all come with system-specific operating systems.

Generic DOSes are created by independent software houses to run on a variety of machines. These operating systems come in two parts. The main part is common to all machines and provides a standard interface. Programs designed to work with that interface can run on any computer running the generic DOS. The second part "wires" the DOS to a specific machine. Generic DOSes give you a much broader choice of software, but they are less sophisticated than machine-specific DOSes because they cannot use the full power of a specific computer design.

There are two de facto standard generic DOSes. CP/M80 (Control Program for Microcomputers) is the standard for 8-bit computers using the Z80, 8080 and 8085 microprocessors. Many 8-bit personal computers with system-specific DOSes, such as Apple, TRS-80, and Heath, can be adapted to run CP/M80. There are also a number of system-specific DOSes which are compatible with CP/M80, such as CDOS and TURBODOS. Distributed by Digital Research™, one of the major microcomputer software houses, CP/M is a very powerful DOS, but is considered somewhat difficult to learn.

The de facto standard 16-bit DOS currently appears to be MS-DOS from Microsoft®, a software house previously best known for their powerful, user-friendly BASIC language. It is designed to work with the Intel 8088 and 8086 microprocessors. The incredible market success of the IBM PC is the major factor in the emergence of MS-DOS as the 16-bit de facto standard DOS. PC-DOS, the IBM personal computer operating system, is a proprietary version of MS-DOS, but most programs designed for the PC will also operate under MS-DOS. MS-DOS is considered easier to use and more user-friendly than CP/M, but is somewhat less powerful.

Digital Research remains a major competitor in the 16-bit DOS arena. It offers versions of CP/M for the 8088 and 8086 (CP/M86) and 68000 (CP/M68) microprocessors, as well as a multi-tasking DOS called Concurrent CP/M86. Although Digital Research has not ceded the 16-bit DOS arena to Microsoft, it has recently taken steps to ensure that its products are compatible with MS-DOS.

Sharing and Maximizing Computer Resources

Both CP/M and MS-DOS support a single user performing a single task on a "stand-alone" computer. This can be a problem where workers must have access to the same data, where they must be able to communicate, where circumstances require several users to share a computer, or where the user must perform several tasks simultaneously. There are four approaches to these problems, all requiring special configurations of both DOSes and hardware.

The Multiuser Approach

A multiuser approach, in which several operators draw on the power of a single CPU chip, is a form of timesharing brought down to the microcomputer level. The attention of the computer is divided among the users, each of whom has access to the full power of the machine for a short segment of time. In theory, the computer operates so rapidly that each user appears to have full use of it.

Multiuser operating systems use a special DOS and require considerable computational power and memory to successfully juggle the competing needs of their users. As with mainframe timesharing, the operation is often less than ideal. Eight-bit microcomputers are not suited for multiuser operations. Their memory sizes and data-transfer rates limit their capacity to a maximum of four users. Any more users and the CPU begins to degrade. The service provided to each user is considerably less than that available on a comparable single-user system. Each user gets 48K of main memory for an individual work space and all the users share a common 16K of memory, which holds the operating system. This is not enough memory for some of the more sophisticated software programs available today. As with any form of timesharing, the system is only as strong as its weakest link. Any one user can crash the entire system.

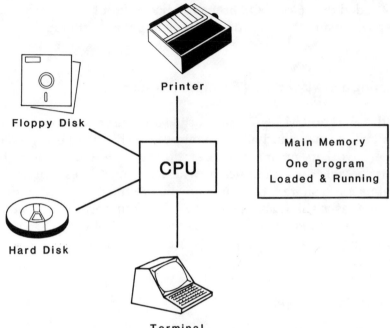

Floppy Disk

Printer

CPU

Main Memory

One Program
Loaded & Running

Hard Disk

Terminal

FIGURE 11–1. Single User Architecture. The most common configuration for a personal computer is one person using a dedicated computer to perform one task at a time. *(drawing by Rashida Basrai)*

Sixteen-bit microcomputers are more amenable to multiuser systems, since they can achieve greater speeds (up to ten MHz, compared to the four to six MHz on 8-bit machines) and have much more memory. If you must have a multiuser system, you should have a 16-bit machine. Remember, however, that greater speed and memory are no protection against user errors; a "down" system idles several people, not just one.

MP/M-II (Multiprogramming Control Program for Microprocessors) is the most common generic multiuser system, but there are also a number of proprietary ones developed by hardware manufacturers (e.g., ALTOS and Cromemco). Multiuser systems have their place—primarily where you have several people who are doing exactly the same thing and must have access to common information. I feel, however, that the future belongs to distributed, general-purpose computers, rather than centralized, specialized ones.

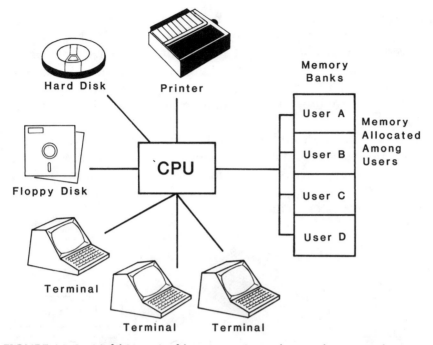

FIGURE 11–2. Multi-User Architecture. Several users share a single computer (CPU, main memory, external memory device). This is similar to timesharing on mainframes and minicomputers. Computer cycles (operations) are divided among the users so that each user has a portion of the machine's attention. As a rule, the current 8-bit computers are not particularly well suited to multi-user systems. *(drawing by Rashida Basrai)*

Multiprocessor Systems

Users engaged in multiprocessing each have their own CPU and memory, but share external memory and peripherals. A common CPU and memory manage the system and move information between users, the external memory, and the peripherals. Multiprocessor systems require two different operating systems. A single user DOS resides on each processor board and a multiuser DOS is used on the common CPU to control interactions between the users and the shared support functions.

Theoretically performance does not degrade as users are added. But this is true only when they are not doing I/O-dependent work. Herein lies the catch. Most applications programs, particularly those designed for 8-bit computers, require frequent information transfers between main and external memory, especially during word processing. Spreadsheet programs are usually stored in main memory, but require I/O functions for prompts and processing. Therefore, multiprocessing is not the most efficient approach to these tasks. The shared external memory also makes it more difficult to maintain individual archives on floppy disks.

If you are interested in a multiprocessor system, I would definitely not recommend using this approach on a system with 5.25-inch drives. The drives are too slow and have too little capacity for shared use. I strongly suggest you get a machine with an 8-inch hard-disk for external memory.

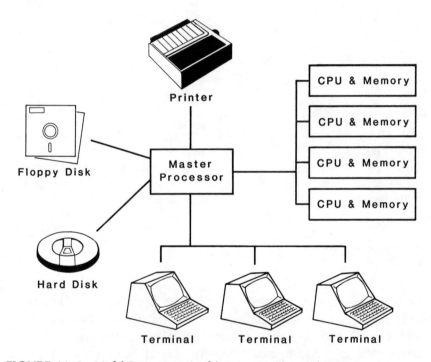

FIGURE 11–3. Multi-Processor Architecture. The multi-processor system is an attempt to overcome the weaknesses of the multi-user approach. Each user has a dedicated CPU and main memory, and all share the external memory device and peripherals. A master processor controls the flow of data between the external memory device and the individual users. This provides each user with full processing power, but applications that require an extensive transfer of data between the external memory and individual users may have problems. *(drawing by Rashida Basrai)*

Multitasking Systems

In a multitasking system, two or more programs run simultaneously in a computer, drawing on a single CPU and memory. The system supports one user. I'd like to see more innovation in multitasking, which is in a very primitive stage. In my work I'm constantly juggling several things at once—writing, doing calculations, talking to people on the telephone, referring to files, setting up appointments.

My simple 8-bit system is super reliable, but it can support only one application at a time. When I write, I use my word-processing program. If I want to check my personal filing system, I have to close out work on the word processor and load the personal filing program and appropriate data base. This transition takes a couple of minutes and involves saving the text file, exiting from word-processing program, removing the program and data disk from drive, finding the filing and data program disks, inserting both disks in the drive, and loading the filing program in the computer. A good multitasking system would allow me to work with two or more programs simultaneously. I could then work more like my normal, schizoid self.

For some reason there really hasn't been much development on multitasking. That's really what the MP/M was designed for, but it was diverted to multiuser service. Part of the problem has been the limits in hardware. The current generation of 8-bit CPUs doesn't really have the power for multitasking. But this is changing with the new generation of hardware.

Three approaches to multitasking have recently been introduced in programs, machines, and operating systems. Multitask programs are essentially single programs that can perform multiple functions. They require a significant amount of memory and, so far, are limited to 16-bit machines (primarily the IBM PC). The programs I've seen—MBA Contex and Lotus 123—have data-base management programs with spreadsheet and text-editing capabilities.

Lisa, the personal work station developed by Apple, is a good example of a true multitask machine. You can work on several different functions at once, and it is user friendly. The concept isn't new—it has been tried by a number of groups including the Augmented Human Intellect Group at SRI International, Citibank, and Xerox (the Star system). Lisa seems to be the best packaging of this concept that I've seen. Unfortunately all this power doesn't come easy. Lisa is an expensive machine at an entry price of $7,000, and its unique operating system limits software applications. Time will tell if Lisa will succeed, but the concepts embodied in the design—user friendliness and multitasking—are making a significant impact on the industry.

Concurrent CP/M86 is a generic, multitasking DOS designed for use with the 16-bit 8088 and 8086 microprocessors. Introduced in 1983, Concurrent CP/M has yet to prove itself in the marketplace. However, Digital Research has announced that new versions will have an emulator which will enable Concurrent CP/M to run most MS-DOS software. This may make it more attractive in the 16-bit arena, where MS-DOS has become the de facto standard.

One simple example of a multitasking device is a printer spool. Spooling programs allow you to print one document while

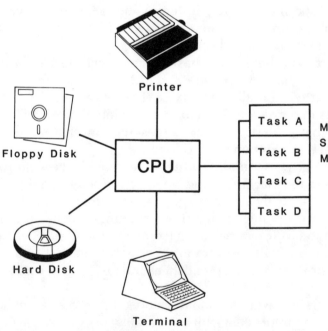

FIGURE 11–4. Multi-Tasking Architecture. Multi-tasking is an adaptation of multi-user architecture. Instead of several users sharing a single computer to do several tasks simultaneously, one person uses the machine to perform several tasks simultaneously. *(drawing by Rashida Basrai)*

doing some other task on the computer by having the CPU check the printer and, if it is idle, send a burst of text from the print file before returning to the work file. I use a printer spooling through my word processor program, WordStar®. I have noticed that spooling degrades performance of my editor, particularly in I/O-intensive commands. However, my machine has been rated as extremely fast, and my printer has an abnormally large buffer. Both factors should reduce degradation.

As we move toward faster and more sophisticated CPUs, I think we will see more multitasking. I think it would be a huge boost to productivity to be able to pause in the middle of a page to check a fact from another file or run a quick calculation.

Local Networks

A local network is a system of stand-alone personal computers that are connected by high-speed data lines to allow intermachine communication and the sharing of printers, hard-disk drives, and common data files.

Individual computers in a local network use single user operating systems. The network itself uses a unique system to control the movement of information through the network. There are a number of networking systems available. As with DOSes, there are both generic and system-specific approaches to networking. The generic approach uses a standardized communications protocol such as CP/Net, EtherNet, or HiNet, which will run on hardware supplied by a number of manufacturers. The system-specific approach, offered by firms such as Corvus and Nestar, bundles the communications protocol with specially-designed support hardware. Local networks are very new and no de facto standards have yet emerged. If you can't wait for market concensus, get a good consultant to help.

I foresee a strong future for local networks. They overcome the disadvantages of multiuser and multiprocessor systems, and achieve the goals of intrasystem communication and the sharing of peripherals. In addition, local networks can serve as interfaces between personal computers and larger computers. The major advantage to this approach is the efficient allocation of processing power and resources.

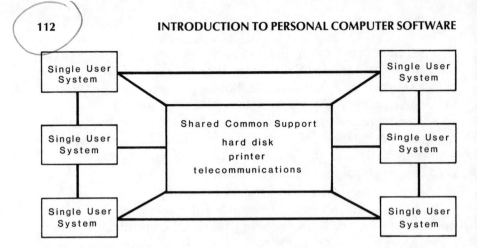

FIGURE 11–5. Local Network Architecture. A local network connects a number of independent single-user systems so they can communicate with one another and share common files and access to expensive peripherals. Most organizations will eventually use local networks. *(drawing by Rashida Basrai)*

Illustration 7   A De Facto Standard Terminal

Originally designed as a terminal for timesharing, the TeleVideo 950 has been adopted by many personal computer users who require a detached keyboard. The 950 has a finely detailed character set. Add-ons are available that convert the 950 to a graphics terminal. Customization programs are available that can adapt popular applications programs (such as WordStar) to take advantage of its special function keys. *(photo courtesy of TeleVideo)*

Illustrations 8-9   The New Look in Terminals

The new, erometric terminals are highly stylized and structurally flexible. The keyboards tend to be low, and the screens can be swiveled and tilted.

Illustration 8 (left)

The TeleVideo 970. All the electronics for the terminal are located in the vertical tower for better cooling. This same package is used for the TeleVideo 803 integrated computer. *(photo courtesy of TeleVideo)*

Illustration 9 (right)

The Qume 102. Long a major figure in the printer and disk drive arenas, Qume has just entered the terminal market. *(photo courtesy of Qume)*

Illustration 10   Big Screen Terminal

Although most terminals offer the standard 24 (or 25)-line by 80-character column display, it is possible to find larger displays. This MicroTerm Ergo 4000 is designed for word processing and has 66 lines of 80 characters each—enough for a full page with room to spare for menus. Other terminals have displays with longer lines—up to 132 characters—to accommodate those who think in terms of 14-inch computer printout rather than manuscript pages. *(photo courtesy of MicroTerm)*

Illustration 11   Variations in Floppy-Disk Drives (center)

Shown from left to right are 8-inch full-size, 8-inch half-height, 5.25-inch full-size, and 5.25-inch reduced-height floppy-disk drives. *(photo courtesy of Shugart)*

Illustration 12 The Microfloppy Drive

Microfloppies range in size from 3 to 3.5 inches (standardization is being debated as we go to press). Here we see a Shugart 3.5-inch drive (on the right) compared with a full-size minifloppy. The single-sided SA300 microfloppy has a storage capacity of 500,000 characters. *(photo courtesy of Shugart)*

Illustrations 13-15   Integrated Computers

All of the components of a computer system—computer, terminal, and external memory—are combined into a single package.

Illustration 13

The TeleVideo 802 is based on the TeleVideo 950 terminal. It has a Z80 microprocessor and two 5.25-inch disk drives. *(photo by the author)*

Illustration 14

The North Star Advantage has a 5.25-inch hard disk, a 5.25-inch floppy, and a Z80 microprocessor. It can be upgraded with a 16-bit INTEL 8088 microprocessor via a plug-in board. *(photo by the author)*

Illustration 15

This ergonomically designed Tele-Video computer is available in both 8-bit and 16-bit configurations. This model has two 5.25-inch floppy-disk drives in the tower (to the right of the screen). The design is based on that of the TeleVideo 970 terminal. *(photo courtesy of TeleVideo)*

Illustrations 16-17

Illustration 16

The Cromemco System One uses an S-100 bus and has both a hard disk and a 5.25-inch floppy-disk drive. Note that it has a keyed power switch for security. *(photo courtesy of Cromemco)*

Illustration 17

Focus Data, a systems house computer, combines an Exo single-board computer (with an 8-inch hard disk and an 8-inch floppy) with a TeleVideo 925 terminal. This system can be expanded to serve four users or as the hub of a local network. *(photo courtesy of Focus Data)*

Illustrations 18-20   Modular Systems

Both the Apple *IIe* and the IBM PC use pseudobus designs—the main computer components are on a single board, and add-ons are plugged into bus sockets on the main board.

Illustration 18

The Apple *IIe* uses a 6502 microprocessor and the AppleDOS 3.3 operating system. A plug-in Z 80 CPU module allows it to run CP/M. The Apple *IIe* is a redesign of the Apple II+. It has a redesigned keyboard, 64k of RAM, and upper and lower case characters. *(photo courtesy of Apple)*

Illustration 19

The IBM PC uses an 8088 microprocessor and both the PC-DOS and MS-DOS as operating systems. It can also run a version of CP/M86. A plug-in Z 80 card allows it to run CP/M80. The 8088 allows the PC to control considerably more memory than most 8-bit personal computers. IBM machines with 256k of RAM are not uncommon. *(photo courtesy of IBM)*

Illustration 20   The Fortune 32/16

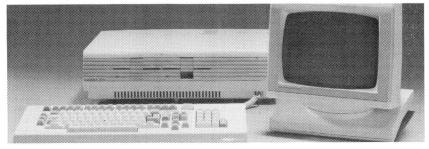

The Fortune 32/16 is a business-oriented modular computer system. Based on the Motorola 68000 16-bit microprocessor, the Fortune 32/16 can control up to one megabyte of main memory. It uses a modification of the UNIX operating system. *(photo courtesy of Fortune Systems)*

Illustrations 21-22   User-Friendly Systems

As personal computers become more popular and designers more sophisticated, increased emphasis is being placed on engineering computers that are easy to use.

Illustration 21

Lisa™, the new Apple personal computer, is a high-end personal computer that uses a Motorola 68000 microprocessor, currently the most sophisticated of the 16-bit chips. It offers multitasking, a very sophisticated, high resolution display screen, and a mouse (located to the front right), which is an analog input device used to control cursor position and to send commands to the computer. This machine is also equipped with two Apple-designed 5.25-inch floppy-disk drives and a hard-disk drive. *(photo courtesy of Apple)*

Illustration 22

The Epson QX-10 has a HASCII keyboard, which has hard-wired keys to perform basic operations (such as print, save, stop), call up bundled applications programs (word processing, filing, spreadsheet, calendar, drawing), and control type fonts and sizes. Like the Lisa, the QX-10 has a very high resolution screen, which displays text in the size and font that will be printed. *(photo courtesy of Epson)*

Illustrations 23-24 Low-Cost Modular Systems

Following the trail blazed by the Osborne 1, several manufacturers now offer bundled systems—hardware plus a software package that includes an operating system, a language (generally a version of BASIC), and word processing, spelling, and spreadhseet programs. Some of these packages are modular (most are portables).

Illustration 23

The Cromemco C-10 is the first general market product from one of the original microcomputer companies. Prior to the C-10, Cromemco had focused on the scientific and engineering market. *(photo courtesy of Cromemco)*

Illustration 24

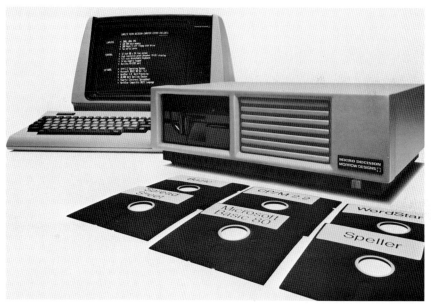

The Morrow Designs MicroDecision can be purchased with or without the terminal and with one or two disk drives. Like Cromemco, Morrow is another pioneer in the microcomputer business. *(photo courtesy of Morrow)*

Illustrations 25-26   Component Systems

These two component systems were used by the author in the preparation of this book.

Illustration 25

A system composed of a Focus Data single-board computer, a pair of Qume half-high 8-inch drives, a Heathkit H-19 terminal, and a Sellum 1 printer. *(photo by the author)*

Illustration 26

An S-100 bus system using a California Computer Systems 2200 computer (top removed to show boards), Qume half-high 8-inch drives, and a TeleVideo 950 terminal. *(photo by the author)*

12

gre fm pg 113 to 119...

Utilities

Utilities—the least glamorous form of software—provide specific system support functions: cataloging disks, moving files from one disk to another, moving files from one machine to another. Utilities are small programs that help you manage your computer. This may not seem like much, but experienced personal computer users will do almost anything to get a good utility program.

Some utility programs are included in your operating system; others you will have to buy individually. Many utilities start out in the public domain and are passed about freely or at a low price through clubs and user groups. Usually, some entrepreneur takes a public-domain software program, cleans it up, improves the documentation, and puts it out on the market. Market versions are often easier to use, but if you are on a budget, look for public-domain programs.

A format utility formats soft-sectored disks. It lays out space for the operating system and the directory, and splits the rest of the disk into sectors. If you are using soft-sectored disks, you must have a formatter. AppleDOS uses a program called "init" for formatting. CP/M uses programs written by the computer manufacturers, generally named either "init" or "format." The IBM PC and MS-DOS use a program called "format."

A system-generation program writes the basic operating system on the disk (assuming your system is not kept in ROM). A CP/M operating system is usually stored on the first two or three tracks of the disk. The operating system cannot be copied by the usual file move programs. The only way to get system tracks on a disk are with a system-generation program or a disk-to-disk copy program. AppleDOS copies the operating system to the disk as part of the "init" program. CP/M requires a separate utility to load the operating system called "sysgen." The IBM PC and MS-DOS will copy the operating system onto a new disk as part of the "format" routine, or you can use a separate utility called "sys."

A file-control program moves file information around in the system. It can copy a file from one disk to another, rename a file, send a file to a peripheral, and perform various other functions. CP/M includes a file-control program called PIP (Peripheral Interchange Program). AppleDOS uses a file utility program called "FID" (file development). The IBM PC and MS-DOS use "copy."

A disk-to-disk copy program makes literal track-for-track copies of entire disks. This is a very efficient way to copy a disk, since it combines formatting, copying the operating system, and copying all the files into a single step. It is also much faster than making file-by-file copies. The AppleDOS disk-to-disk copy program is called "copya." CP/M does not offer a generic disk-to-disk copy program, but one should come with your computer. It will probably be called "copy." "Diskcopy" is the disk-to-disk copy program for the IBM PC and MS-DOS.

Directory routines can be built into the DOS or they can be separate programs. "Catalog" is used to display the directory of a disk in AppleDOS, "DIR" is used in CP/M and MS-DOS and for the IBM PC.

A statistics program (STAT) reports the status of various parts of the system. It can tell you how much space is left on a disk, the names of files stored on it, how much space each file occupies, and how a disk is formatted. CP/M uses STAT. AppleDOS, MS-DOS, and the IBM PC show file size as part of their directory displays. The IBM and MS-DOS use a second program (chkdsk) to get disk statistics. The CP/M program "stat" provides a variety of disk statistics and other system support functions.

A communications utility transfers data from files between computers. If you plan to use your computer to access information from a utility service (such as The Source or Compuserve) or electronic bulletin boards or to communicate with another computer user, you will definitely need some type of communications utility program.

A hardware-test utility performs diagnostic routines that check hardware components—CPU, memory, disk drive, printer, and terminal—for preventive maintenance and identification of major problems.

A floppy-disk maintenance utility is particularly important. The floppy disk is the most fragile part of the microcomputer and disk-maintenance utilities can often be a godsend. One type scans a disk, identifies bad sectors, and adds them to a dummy data base so you can continue to use the disk, even though some sectors are damaged. Disk-patch programs can rescue you from disasters by resurrecting erased files and recovering data from damaged files. Disk editors, the most sophisticated maintenance utility, access and manipulate any data stored on the disk. Disk editors require some knowledge of how an operating system works.

A catalog utility develops and maintains a master-file directory of all your disks. These programs are handy for keeping close tabs on files.

A good source of public-domain utilities is the CP/M Users Group (CPMUG), which offers more than 90 volumes of software. Costing $15, each volume consists of documentation and an IBM-formatted 8-inch disk of programs contributed by CPMUG members. A catalog of volumes costs $6; *Lifelines* lists the contents of new volumes as they become available. Some of these programs are a little rough, but you would be surprised how many of them end up as commercial products with price tags of fifty to one hundred dollars. For more information contact:

CPMUG
1651 Third Ave.
New York, NY 10028

If you don't want to wade through all the CPMUG directories to find the "good stuff," entrepreneurs have already done it for you. Workmen & Associates, which sells a series of disks at a reasonable price, have gone through the CPMUG files, selected the good stuff, cleaned up the documentation, and packaged a number of programs by applications areas. They currently have two disks of general utilities, one each of disassemblers and backup/dump programs. For more information contact:

Workmen & Associates
112 Marion Ave.
Pasadena, CA 91106

```
    DIR B:
  B: PIP      COM : XD       COM : SECTION1     : SECTION2
  B: SECTION4     : SECTION3     : SECTION6     : SECTION5
  B: SECTION7     : GLOSSARY     : TOC          : ILLUSCAL
  B: ILLUS    BAK : ILLUS        : ILLUSCAL BAK
  A>
```

FIGURE 12–1. Directory Utility. The directory of the working-file disk for this book as given by the standard CP/M directory command (DIR). The files are listed in the order they are stored on the disk. There is no indication of file size. (*example created by author*)

```
    STAT B:*.*

    Recs  Bytes  Ext Acc
    810   104k     1 R/W B:GLOSSARY
     39     8k     1 R/W B:ILLUS
     39     8k     1 R/W B:ILLUS.BAK
      8     8k     1 R/W B:ILLUSCAL
      6     8k     1 R/W B:ILLUSCAL.BAK
     58     8k     1 R/W B:PIP.COM
    355    48k     1 R/W B:SECTION1
    325    48k     1 R/W B:SECTION2
   1016   128k     1 R/W B:SECTION3
    818   104k     1 R/W B:SECTION4
    514    72k     1 R/W B:SECTION5
    951   120k     1 R/W B:SECTION6
     77    16k     1 R/W B:SECTION7
     18     8k     1 R/W B:TOC
     18     8k     1 R/W B:XD.COM
   Bytes Remaining On B: 496k

    A>
```

FIGURE 12–2. Directory Utility. The CP/M utility STAT used to display the files stored on the disk. STAT lists the files alphabetically and shows the number of 128 byte records in each file, the storage space occupied by each file (in increments of 8K because I store in 8K blocks), the number of directory entries for the file (each entry holds 16 blocks), file access permitted (these are read/write files), the drive on which the disk is located, and the name of the file. At the bottom it shows how much storage space is left on the disk. (*example created by author*)

```
    F B:
**XDIR v3.5 - April 9, 1981**

GLOSSARY.       104k
ILLUS    .        8k
ILLUS    .BAK     8k
ILLUSCAL.         8k
ILLUSCAL.BAK      8k
PIP      .COM     8k
SECTION1.        48k
SECTION2.        48k
SECTION3.       128k
SECTION4.       104k
SECTION5.        72k
SECTION6.       120k
SECTION7.        16k
TOC      .        8k
XD       .COM     8k

Disk B:  8K blocks, Size= 1200K, 15 Files, Used=  704K, Space=  496K
A>
```

FIGURE 12–3. Simplified Directory Utility. The utility (SD) lists the files alphabetically, and the space occupied by each file. It gives some disk-use statistics at the bottom (block size, storage capacity, number of files, storage used, free space). This utility is from the CP/M users group. *(example created by author)*

```
    XD B:
Extended Directory (C)'82 PEi V2.06 K
GLOSSARY.       102K | SECTION5.        65
ILLUS    .        5K | SECTION6.      119K
ILLUS    .BAK     5K | SECTION7.       10K
ILLUSCAL.         1K | TOC      .       3K
ILLUSCAL.BAK      1K | XD       .COM    3K
PIP      .COM     8K
SECTION1.        45K
SECTION2.        41K
SECTION3.       127K
SECTION4.       103K
    496K unused of 1192K, Drive B:  User  0        113 files remaining
A>
```

FIGURE 12–4. Extended Directory Utility. The XD program from Proteus Engineering lists the files alphabetically, but also shows the size of each file, rather than the space it occupies. It also shows how much space is left, the drive, the user number, and the number of file names (directory entries) left on the disk. The discrepancy between the size of a file (in bytes) and the space it occupies is caused by disk control software. Files are saved in space units called blocks. In this example, the block size is 8K bytes. This means disk space is consumed in units of 8K bytes. A file with one character (i.e., file size = 1 byte) still occupies 8K bytes (one block) of space. *(example created by author)*

INTRODUCTION TO PERSONAL COMPUTER SOFTWARE

```
B 0
                DRIVE B:  TRACK 2  SECTOR 0
0000   00 50 49 50 20 20 20 20   20 43 4F 4D 00 00 00 3A   .PIP      COM...:
0010   01 00 00 00 00 00 00 00   00 00 00 00 00 00 00 00   ........ ........
0020   00 58 44 20 20 20 20 20   20 43 4F 4D 00 00 00 12   .XD       COM....
0030   02 00 00 00 00 00 00 00   00 00 00 00 00 00 00 00   ........ ........
0040   00 53 45 43 54 49 4F 4E   31 20 20 20 02 00 00 63   .SECTION 1    ...c
0050   03 04 05 06 07 08 00 00   00 00 00 00 00 00 00 00   ........ ........
0060   00 53 45 43 54 49 4F 4E   32 20 20 20 02 00 00 45   .SECTION 2    ...E
0070   09 0A 0B 0C 0D 0E 00 00   00 00 00 00 00 00 00 00   ........ ........

                DRIVE B:  TRACK 2  SECTOR 1
0080   00 53 45 43 54 49 4F 4E   34 20 20 20 06 00 00 32   .SECTION 4    ...2
0090   0F 10 11 12 13 14 15 16   17 18 19 1A 1B 00 00 00   ........ ........
00A0   00 53 45 43 54 49 4F 4E   33 20 20 20 07 00 00 78   .SECTION 3    ...x
00B0   1C 1D 1E 1F 20 21 22 23   24 25 26 27 28 29 2A 2B   .... !"# $%&'()*+
00C0   00 53 45 43 54 49 4F 4E   36 20 20 20 07 00 00 37   .SECTION 6    ...7
00D0   2C 2D 2E 2F 30 31 32 33   34 35 36 37 38 39 3A 00   ,-./0123 456789:.
00E0   00 53 45 43 54 49 4F 4E   35 20 20 20 04 00 00 02   .SECTION 5    ....
00F0   3B 3C 3D 3E 3F 40 41 42   43 00 00 00 00 00 00 00   ;<=>?@AB C.......

                DRIVE B:  TRACK 2  SECTOR 2
0100   00 53 45 43 54 49 4F 4E   37 20 20 20 00 00 00 4D   .SECTION 7    ...M
0110   44 45 00 00 00 00 00 00   00 00 00 00 00 00 00 00   DE...... ........
0120   00 47 4C 4F 53 53 41 52   59 20 20 20 06 00 00 2A   .GLOSSAR Y    ...*
0130   46 47 48 49 4A 4B 4C 4D   4E 4F 50 51 52 00 00 00   FGHIJKLM NOPQR...
0140   00 54 4F 43 20 20 20 20   20 20 20 20 00 00 00 12   .TOC          ....
0150   53 00 00 00 00 00 00 00   00 00 00 00 00 00 00 00   S....... ........
0160   00 49 4C 4C 55 53 43 41   4C 20 20 20 00 00 00 08   .ILLUSCA L    ....
0170   54 00 00 00 00 00 00 00   00 00 00 00 00 00 00 00   T....... ........

                DRIVE B:  TRACK 2  SECTOR 3
0180   00 49 4C 4C 55 53 20 20   20 42 41 4B 00 00 00 27   .ILLUS    BAK...'
0190   55 00 00 00 00 00 00 00   00 00 00 00 00 00 00 00   U....... ........
01A0   00 49 4C 4C 55 53 20 20   20 20 20 20 00 00 00 27   .ILLUS        ...'
01B0   56 00 00 00 00 00 00 00   00 00 00 00 00 00 00 00   V....... ........
01C0   E5 49 4C 4C 55 53 43 41   4C 42 41 4B 00 00 00 04   eILLUSCA LBAK....
01D0   57 00 00 00 00 00 00 00   00 00 00 00 00 00 00 00   W....... ........
01E0   00 49 4C 4C 55 53 43 41   4C 42 41 4B 00 00 00 06   .ILLUSCA LBAK....
01F0   58 00 00 00 00 00 00 00   00 00 00 00 00 00 00 00   X....... ........

                DRIVE B:  TRACK 2  SECTOR 4
0200   E5 E5 E5 E5 E5 E5 E5 E5   E5 E5 E5 E5 E5 E5 E5 E5   eeeeeeee eeeeeeee
0210   E5 E5 E5 E5 E5 E5 E5 E5   E5 E5 E5 E5 E5 E5 E5 E5   eeeeeeee eeeeeeee
0220   E5 E5 E5 E5 E5 E5 E5 E5   E5 E5 E5 E5 E5 E5 E5 E5   eeeeeeee eeeeeeee
0230   E5 E5 E5 E5 E5 E5 E5 E5   E5 E5 E5 E5 E5 E5 E5 E5   eeeeeeee eeeeeeee
0240   E5 E5 E5 E5 E5 E5 E5 E5   E5 E5 E5 E5 E5 E5 E5 E5   eeeeeeee eeeeeeee
0250   E5 E5 E5 E5 E5 E5 E5 E5   E5 E5 E5 E5 E5 E5 E5 E5   eeeeeeee eeeeeeee
0260   E5 E5 E5 E5 E5 E5 E5 E5   E5 E5 E5 E5 E5 E5 E5 E5   eeeeeeee eeeeeeee
0270   E5 E5 E5 E5 E5 E5 E5 E5   E5 E5 E5 E5 E5 E5 E5 E5   eeeeeeee eeeeeeee

                DRIVE B:  TRACK 2  SECTOR 5
0280   E5 E5 E5 E5 E5 E5 E5 E5   E5 E5 E5 E5 E5 E5 E5 E5   eeeeeeee eeeeeeee
0290   E5 E5 E5 E5 E5 E5 E5 E5   E5 E5 E5 E5 E5 E5 E5 E5   eeeeeeee eeeeeeee
02A0   E5 E5 E5 E5 E5 E5 E5 E5   E5 E5 E5 E5 E5 E5 E5 E5   eeeeeeee eeeeeeee
02B0   E5 E5 E5 E5 E5 E5 E5 E5   E5 E5 E5 E5 E5 E5 E5 E5   eeeeeeee eeeeeeee
02C0   E5 E5 E5 E5 E
```

FIGURE 12–5. A Directory Block Listing from a Disk Editor Utility. Here I had the utility print out the directory entries for the disk. These are the first block (block 0), of the disk. Each line shows 16 bytes. On the left is the data in hexidecimal format, to the right is the same data in ASCII format. The first line (16 bytes) of the directory contains the file name. The second line contains the addresses of the blocks where the file is stored. Notice that almost all file names start with a 00 byte. This indicates that the directory entry is "active." On Track 2, Sector 3, the next to the last file has been erased by placing an E5 as the first byte of the entry. With the editor, you could recover this file by changing the lead byte from E5 to 00. *(example created by author)*

```
MAP

    BLOCK ALLOCATION MAP DRIVE B:

    11111111 11111111 11111111 11111111
    11111111 11111111 11111111 11111111
    11111111 11111111 11111110 10000000
    00000000 00000000 00000000 00000000
    00000000 00000000 000000

    62 BLOCKS REMAINING ON DISK OUT OF 150

*
```

FIGURE 12–6. A Space Allocation Map from a Disk Editor Utility. This map shows 150, 8K blocks—a total of 1,200,000 bytes of storage. The 1's indicate blocks that are used. The 0's indicate blocks that are not being used. Notice that there are 62 empty blocks—this gives 62 × 8 or 496K of unused storage. *(example created by author)*

13

Programming Languages

Computer languages provide the vocabulary and structure for writing instructions. Initially, program instructions were written in cryptic "machine code," which could be directly executed but was very difficult to write and understand. As computers became more sophisticated, computer languages did too, and today some computer languages are almost as easy to read and write as English. I think most microcomputer users can get by without ever having to write their own programs. One reason I waited so long to buy a personal computer was that I wanted to be certain there would be a good set of applications programs available. Today's booming microcomputer software industry is turning out programs as fast as it can, obviating the necessity of users writing their own.

Given the abundance of software programs available, why buy programming languages? One reason is that after you have worked with your computer for a while, you may want to try your hand at programming just out of curiosity. I recommend learning to program in one or two languages, not necessarily because you will ever use the skill, but to better understand how your applications programs are put together. Another reason is that as you expand your computer literacy, you may eventually become less tolerant of packaged applications software. You may find it easier at this point to write your own program than to live with one that almost, but not quite, does the job. A third reason for buying languages is that many applications programs require a host language to run on your computer. Finally, and perhaps most important, learning to program can introduce you to a new method of thinking about and solving problems.

Languages have their tradeoffs. Some are relatively simple to use, but lack sophistication and power. The more sophisticated languages are difficult to learn and use well. In selecting a language you should consider its exportability. Can the language be used on a variety of machines? This question considers the varied dialects of some languages. There are numerous versions of BASIC, for example, many of them machine-specific. Programs written in one BASIC dialect will have to be rewritten before they can be used on a computer that uses another version of the language.

Another selection criteria is language structure. The more a language resembles English syntax, the better off you are. Working on an English-like language makes it easier to write programs and understand those written by others. It is most frustrating to go through a program that somebody else has written to try and figure out how it works. Few writers bother to document their programs well, so you must usually work with the program commands. English-like structure makes this much easier.

Interpreters and Compilers

Today, most computer programs are written in higher level languages which must be translated into machine code for execution. Interpreters and compilers accomplish this task.

Interpreters translate the source code of a language into machine code on a line-by-line basis. As each line of the program is translated, the computer executes it. If the computer finds an error in a line of code, it stops and returns an error message. The interpreter works simultaneously with the program being run. Interpreters make it easy to detect and fix errors (debug the program). Interpreters, however, are quite large and consume a significant amount of main memory. Program execution with an interpreter is quite slow, since they work on a line-by-line basis.

Compilers translate the program source code from a higher-level language to machine code in one step. The resulting machine code version (the object code) is saved and directly executed by the computer in a separate step. Compiled code executes very quickly, and since the compiler is not needed when the program is executed, more main memory is available for the program. Error correction, however, is cumbersome. Errors must be corrected in the source code, and the program recompiled before it can be run.

Some compilers take a different approach. They produce an intermediate-program file rather than a machine-level code. At run time a second compiler program translates the intermediate-level code to machine level code. (CBASIC-2 uses this approach.)

Modular vs. Structured Programming

Modular and structured programming are two extremes in approaches and styles. Modular programming ties a number of independent elements together by a supervisor program. For example, one element might be a routine which calculates the mean and standard deviation of a set of numbers. You call up the element and give it the numbers. It sends back the mean and standard deviation. The advantage to this approach is that each element can be tested independently, before being plugged into the program. Also, a single element can be repeated at different points in the program, thereby reducing the number of lines of code. The disadvantage is that the supervisor program must make extensive use of conditional commands to direct the use of the modules. This means that the flow of control in modular programs is extremely confusing. BASIC and FORTRAN are modular-programming languages.

Structured programming organizes a program so the code appears in the order in which it is executed. Hierarchical levels of program execution are often shown visually through indentation of program statements. The advantage to structured programming is that because the flow of control is immediately apparent, it is easy to follow the programming logic. The disadvantages are that the languages and programming style tend to be complex and the programs tend to be longer. Pascal and C are examples of structured programming languages.

Table 13–1 shows the continuum of computer languages. The vertical scale indicates level of sophistication, with higher languages being more English-like in vocabulary and structure. The horizontal scale indicates the programming approach. The less sophisticated languages to the left of the table require you to tell the computer *how* to accomplish a task by breaking it down into a set of individual steps and controlling the execution of those steps. More sophisticated languages (to the right side of the table) let you focus on *what* you want to do and take care of the ''how'' for you.

TABLE 13–1. The Language Continuum

Natural Human Language
CAI Languages (LOGO)
AI Languages (LISP)
APL
Ada
C
Pascal
ALGOL
COBOL
FORTRAN
BASIC
Forth
Assembler
Monitors
Machine Language
Microcode
Hardware

HOW TO DO IT <————————————————————> WHAT TO DO

A Potpourri of Languages

Ada

Ada has been designated the standard programming language for the U.S. Department of Defense. It has been named after Lady Ada Augusta Burton, the daughter of Lord Byron and the first computer programmer, who worked with Charles Babbage on his prototype computer in the late 19th century. The language has been designed to manage the complex computing activities of multiple processors with almost unlimited memory.

Ada is currently in the development stage. Compilers have been written for several mainframe computers and others are being prepared for some of the larger, more sophisticated microprocessors (such as the Motorola 68000). Ada requires too much main memory to fit on the current generation of microcomputers. Its importance comes from the fact that it will be mandatory for the Defense Department and all its contractors by 1985.

Assembly Language

Assembly languages are commonly used to adapt operating systems and programs to hardware and software requirements. They are a sophisticated form of machine language that use mnemonic (memory aid) symbols to stand for instructions. Programs are written by combining these symbols with memory addresses and data (generally represented in octal or hexidecimal notation), using syntactical rules.

Assembly-language programs are written in source code and translated into machine-level object code. The object code is then read by a loader program and run on the computer.

Assembly-language programs are tied to specific operating systems (and microprocessor chips) and may include independent editor, assembler, loader, macroassembler, and debugger programs. Some of these programs may be included with your operating system; others may have to be purchased separately. Assembly languages produce very efficient codes, but they have a rigid format. The mnemonic instructions are difficult to follow.

BASIC

BASIC is probably the most popular language available for microcomputer applications. Invented at Dartmouth University as a teaching language, it is extremely simple and user friendly. Because it is English-like in structure, its programs are usually easy to follow. It is not very sophisticated, however, and it tends to be slow and inefficient in execution.

BASIC is designed as an interactive language. The computer checks each statement of the code as it is being written and flags syntax errors immediately. This makes BASIC very easy to learn, since the most common mistakes can be corrected as you make them. The semantics of the program are checked when the program is run; again, each error is flagged.

There are a variety of BASIC languages, each offering unique features. Some versions are designed to run on specific machines such as Apples, TRS-80, or North Stars. Others are compatable with a generic DOS such as CP/M. Programs written in one version of BASIC must be modified to run under another version. There are three generic versions of BASIC.

BASIC-80 is a general-purpose language from Microsoft, which offers both an interpreter and compiler versions of it. This allows you to have the advantages of both an interpreter and a compiler. Programs can be written and debugged in interpreter BASIC-80 and then compiled for more efficient execution.

CBASIC-2 is a compiler-based, business-oriented version of BASIC developed by Compiler Systems and now distributed by Digital Research. Since it is compiler-based, it runs very quickly. It is not, however interactive. CBASIC-2 has a number of features that make it suitable for business applications, including sophisticated disk-access functions, output functions that can be formatted under operator control, longer variable names, and mathematical functions offering fourteen digits of accuracy. Many financial and business programs are written in CBASIC-2 and you may find you will have to buy it just to support these programs.

SBASIC is a special version of BASIC developed by TOPAZ Programming. It is a compiler version of BASIC that accommodates the writing of structured programs. It is more flexible than either BASIC-80 or CBASIC-2, but is more complex and difficult to learn. In many ways it is more similar to Pascal than to BASIC.

C

C is a computer language designed at Bell Telephone Labs that is closely tied to the Unix operating system. A structured, compiler language, it is function-oriented and extremely flexible. Unlike Pascal, it has not proliferated into a number of incompatible versions, but has remained in a single version. C is not particularly pervasive, although it is being used for some applications programs. Acceptance of C will probably be linked to the success of Unix, although there are versions of C that can run under CP/M.

COBOL

COBOL (COmmon Business Oriented Language) is a very popular business language, used primarily on mainframe and minicomputers. It is a statement-oriented, compiler language. Rigid in format, it is designed to match the flow of data in business applications. It emphasizes extensive internal documentation. Although COBOL is available for micros, it has not achieved the level of popularity that it enjoys on larger machines.

Forth

Originally developed by Charles H. More to control the telescope at Kitts Peak Observatory, Forth is a threaded language: It is built on modules of increasing complexity. Its basic operators (called words) are combined to form new, more complex words. This provides an exceedingly powerful tool, since the vocabulary continues to expand as more applications are developed. It is an interpreter language, which can be later compiled into machine-readable code.

Forth evolves as you use it. Each time you define a new word your version of Forth becomes more powerful, but it also becomes more unique, because your new words may be different from those defined by other programmers. This makes it very difficult for the novice to understand, since all "created" words must be defined in terms of the basic words before they can be understood.

The advantages of Forth are that it is very powerful and that it requires little memory. Initially, Forth requires less than 8K of storage. Power increases dramatically as new words are added, but each new word requires very little additional memory. Forth is readily available for most machines and there are a lot of programs in the public domain. Its disadvantages are structural uniqueness and the lack of commercial Forth programs.

FORTRAN

FORTRAN (FORmula TRANslator) is a general-purpose scientific language long used on mainframes. A compiler language, it is highly efficient and powerful, but not particularly English-like. More rigid than BASIC, its statements require a specific format and they are executed in order. Programming in FORTRAN is much more tedious than in BASIC. Housekeeping details that BASIC and some other languages handle automatically must be coded by the programmer.

Because of its rigidity, FORTRAN tends to be used modularly. Some versions of the language provide a library of program modules (called subroutines) that can be called and linked together by the main program. FORTRAN requires a fairly large amount of memory. Since early microcomputers were limited in memory, FORTRAN was adapted to them much later than to BASIC, and has never achieved BASIC's popularity in micro circles.

LISP

LISP (LISt Processing language) is a nonnumerical language designed for artificial intelligence applications. It is based on the work of John McCarthy, a leading AI researcher. LISP is composed of two units: basic words called atoms and combinations of words called lists. LISP has functions, variables, and operators just like any other language, but it looks strange because all mathematical operations are in Reverse Polish Notation and parentheses are used to separate lists. LISP is extremely powerful, but is difficult to learn. It is not particularly popular in the micro community.

Logo

Logo is a variation of LISP, designed for computer assisted instruction (CAI) by Seymour Papert of MIT. It is an interactive, procedural language that is both easy to learn and very responsive. It has very flexible processing rules and powerful graphics commands.

Logo is really a language for learning, rather than a language for programming. It is primarily a tool for computer-facilitated intellectual exploration. It is not well suited for applications programs, but is useful for learning about programming.

Until recently, Logo was only available for the Apple and Texas Instruments computers, where the size of its interpreter (almost 64K) and its implementation favored educational applications. Digital Research now offers a more generic version of Logo which should make it more available to the personal computer community.

Machine Language

Each computer has a unique set of instructions that define the basic set of operations it can perform. Instruction sets vary in size and complexity, depending on the CPU. All programs must be reduced to machine language before they can be executed by the computer. Normally, however, programs are written in a high-level (for easier programming), which is translated into machine language by a compiler or an interpreter.

It is possible to program directly in machine language by providing the computer with a set of instructions (in machine code), memory locations, and a data sequence appropriate to the task you wish to accomplish. Instructions, memory locations, and data are all given in binary code. The syntax of the program (form and sequence) allows the computer to distinguish between instructions, addresses, and data. Machine-language programming generates an efficient code, but it is extremely tedious and time consuming. Memory space or efficiency considerations may lead to machine-language programming.

Pascal

Pascal was developed by Nicholas Wirth as a general-purpose, structured programming language, based on an earlier teaching language called ALGOL. Pascal is very powerful and complex. It is frequently used as a teaching language, and is quite popular in the computer community.

There are a number of versions of Pascal available, perhaps as many as there are of BASIC. Most are intermediate code languages. The source code is compiled into an intermediate pseudo-code (p-code) that is saved on a disk file. At run time the p-code is interpreted into machine code. This approach allows considerable sophistication, while still providing machine independence. To move Pascal to a different computer or operating system, all you need is a new interpreter to translate the p-code into machine code. There are also some true compiler versions of Pascal that move directly from source code to machine code. These are generally hardware-specific.

Pascal is quite popular as an applications language. Application software is delivered in p-code, together with a run-time package. But Pascal does have a primary drawback. It requires a great deal of memory, leaving little space for the program.

14

Applications Programs

With the advent of the microcomputer has come one of the major advances in computing—the package applications software industry. Applications programs accomplish specific tasks like word processing and financial analysis. Most applications programs for mainframe and minicomputers are custom-written for each installation. Microcomputers, however, have created a purchasing base for creating and marketing off-the-shelf programs. The software business is extremely new and going through growing pains. Software houses are not yet certain exactly what it is they ought to be selling.

The typical software package consists of the programs usually some stored on a floppy disk, documentation, and ideally some kind of support service. All three are bundled in the purchase price, although you may have to pay extra for updates and new versions. This may not be the best way to charge for software, given that all users do not exhibit the same degree of reliance on work application progams. What happens frequently is that users pass through three phases as they become more familiar with their software programs.

130

The trial phase is the exploration and testing of programs to "see what they can do." This is where most informal software piracy occurs as people "borrow" and duplicate programs to try them out.

The second phase is learning how to use the program effectively. The major concern is obtaining a copy of the program documentation which, ironically, is more expensive to borrow and copy than software itself. Because documentation is printed, it must be photocopied, which can cost five cents or more per page.

Dependence on the software, the third phase, means using the software consistently to support your work. Software support is the prime factor—getting help with problems and upgrading the program as new revisions become available.

Each phase emphasizes a different part of the software package and has different economic ramifications. Ideally, software packages should be "unbundled" and each part sold separately to accommodate these phases, but as yet this is not the case. This is unfortunate, for software houses have much more to gain from establishing long-term relationships with their customers through the continuing provision of support than they do from the current system.

Word Processors

For my money, word processing is probably the most important application of personal computers in the office, where much time and money is spent on generating and using information. Using a personal computer for information work requires an investment in a good software package to support the writing, editing, and printing of documents. Most word processor programs are fairly complex, requiring an initial learning period of three to ten hours, depending on the sophistication of the program.

There is an incredible array of word processor programs on the market today (see Table 14-1), all of which entail four different functions. The first is inputting: creating the document and typing it into the machine. The second is editing: correcting and revising the document. Making those inevitable major changes in your document is very easy on a word processor, since editing does not entail retyping to document. The third function is formatting: organizing a text the way you want it to appear on the page. This includes setting the margins and page boundaries, and creating titles. The final function is outputting: printing the document.

Some word processor programs actually have two different programs: one for inputting and editing, the other for formatting and outputting. The advantages to this approach are that the software can be more specialized and efficient, and it reduces the number of commands you must learn. The disadvantage to this approach is that you can't see how the printed document will look on the screen.

The more modern approach is to combine all four functions into one program. The trade-off is that although you can see exactly how the document will appear on the screen, you will have to learn a complex set of commands. I recommend this approach, however, because I think it is extremely valuable to see what your document will look like while you are creating it.

I strongly recommend that you research different kinds of word processors before selecting one. Start by checking magazine software reviews and talking to people about their microcomputer word processing programs. Visit local dealers and places that rent time on micros. Some public libraries offer this service. Try to test drive as many word processing programs as you can to get a feel for how they work. Remember that this will only give you a general feel for how the program works.

For your test drive I suggest you standardize procedures. Try to spend an hour with the program. Remember, you are looking at the program, not the computer, terminal, or printer. Observe the following routine and make notes of your impressions.

1. Type in three or four paragraphs of text. Note the way the text is displayed on the screen.
2. Go back and change part of one paragraph. Delete the paragraph.
3. Insert and delete text within a paragraph.
4. Try a block command—copy the first paragraph to the bottom of the page.
5. Change several words to bold face.
6. Insert a page break between paragraphs.
7. Print out the text.

When evaluating the program, you should consider the following features. Ask about those you don't see. Be certain to examine the software documentation.

TABLE 14–1. Word Processor Programs (machines or operating systems on which the program runs)

Apple Writer (Apple)
Atari (for Atari 800)
Autoscribe (North Star)
Bank Street Writer (Apple)
Benchmark® (CP/M)
Copywriter + (CP/M)
Datacopy Scribe (Apple)
EasyWriter™ (Apple, IBM PC)
Electric Blackboard (CP/M)
Electric Pencil (TRS-80 Model II and CP/M)
The Final Word (CP/M)
Lazy Writer (TRS-80 Model II)
Lettergo (North Star)
Letter Perfect (Apple)
Magic Typewriter (CP/M)
Magic Wand (CP/M)
Magic Window (Apple)
MBA (Apple III and IBM, integrated with a
    data base management system and
    financial analysis)
Memorite (Vector Graphic)
Multimate (PC-DOS, MS-DOS)
Paper-Mate (Commodore)
Pense Write 2 (TRS-80 I and III)
Perfect Writer™ (CP/M)
PIE/Format (Apple)
Pro-Type (CP/M)
Scripsit (TRS-80 I, II and III)
Select (CP/M and IBM)
Spellbinder (CP/M)
SuperWriter™
Superscribe II (Apple)
Super Scripsit (TRS-80 I and III)
Super Text (Apple)
Volkswriter (IBM–PC)
VTS/80 (Apple [with Z 80 card], CP/M)
Wordcraft 80 (Commodre CBM 8032)
Wordmagic II (TRS-80 Model II)
WordPro 4 Plus (Commodore CBM 8032)
Word Processing (TRS-80 Model II)
WordStar™ (Apple [with Z 80 board], CP/M,
    and IBM PC)
WpDaisy (CP/M)
Write-On I (Apple)

Features You Should Look For

Your first concern in choosing a word processor program should be how does it present the text on the screen. Here are some display features you should consider:

- Is text displayed on the screen as it will be printed?
- Does the program show upper and lower case characters?
- How many lines of text are displayed on the screen?
- How long is a line of text on the screen?
- Is there horizontal scrolling for lines that extend beyond the width of the screen?
- Are words wrapped to a new line as the previous one is filled?
- Is there a status line to show what is happening?
- Are page boundaries displayed?
- Is reverse or half-intensity video used to accentuate screen data?
- Are help messages displayed on screen?
- Are tabs displayed on screen?

Command complexity is the second most important feature you should consider. It correlates directly to the overall power and sophistication of the word processor software and to the transportability of the program. Programs designed for a specific system often take advantage of special function keys to reduce command complexity. Programs designed for a variety of computers generally use commands built of character sequences combined with the control and escape keys. Some programs use a two-key command combination (control or escape plus one letter); others use a three-key combination (control plus one letter, followed by a second letter).

Related to the issue of command complexity is on-screen assistance. Many programs display command menus on the screen so you don't have to memorize all the commands. Some allow you to reduce the menu display as you become more proficient, leaving more space to display text. In addition to menu displays, many programs offer on-line help—usually abbreviated explanations of how the various commands work.

Cursor control commands are particularly important in word processing. The cursor controls the placement of text and indicates the positions where program commands are to be performed. Some cursor control commands you should look for in a word-processing program include:

- up/down/right/left
- tab
- scroll up/down
- jump to a marker
- beginning/end of text
- forward/back a word
- forward/back a sentence
- forward/back a screen
- forward/back a page
- scroll horizontally

Delete and insert commands remove or add characters, words, lines, and blocks of text. The insert commands should work dynamically—that is, the text adjusts automatically as you type. A replace command gives you the ability to remove existing text from the screen by typing new text over the top of it.

Block operations delineate and move large amounts of text. You should be able to mark the start and end of a block; copy, move, or delete it; write a block to a new file; and delete block markers.

Search commands tell the computer to find a specific sequence (string) of words or characters in a document. Commands include:

- search for the first occurrence only
- search for a specific number of occurences
- search for all occurrences
- match on whole words only (accept "bed," not "embedded"
- search forwards or backwards from the cursor position
- ignore case (accept "This" when looking for "this")
- continue searching after making a match

Replace operations are extensions of searches. In addition to finding words, the program replaces them with new ones. Commands include:

- replace first occurrence only
- replace a specific number of occurrences
- replace all occurrences

- query before replacing
- continue after replacement

Disk operations support your work on a document by providing utilities such as saving, copying, reading, erasing, and renaming files.

Most word processing programs are designed to work with 64K of main memory, and up to half of that may be needed to hold the operating system and word processing program. This doesn't leave much space for your document. A single spaced page of text requires about 4,000 bytes of storage, so there may only be room in main memory for eight to ten pages. To provide space for larger documents, most word processing programs use disk buffering. A temporary work file is created on the disk to hold the document so parts of it can be moved back and forth between the disk and main memory as you work on them.

The work file holds a document only while you are working with it. When you are done, if you wish to keep the document, you must *save* it on the disk in a permanent file. If you do not, the document will be lost if you turn off the computer or if you clear the working file to start another document. Saving creates a permanent file on the disk that contains a copy of your document. It is a good idea to periodically save your document while you are working on it to protect yourself against accidental loss of the work file.

Another word processing feature is file revision and back-up. After you have created a document, you can save it on the disk. You may wish to modify it at a later date. With the revision and back-up feature you can automatically convert the initial file to a back-up file so you can save the revised file under the same name. This back-up feature is very important because an idle flick of a finger can quickly erase a large chunk of text. Back-up files provide insurance.

Other disk operations you should look for include the ability to copy files to another disk, rename or delete files, read a file into a working document, and display all the files on the disk.

The major purpose of a word processor is to provide printed documents. Many programs offer a variety of print features that dress up the final document. These features generally require inserting special control characters into the text before printing. Some of the printing effects include underlining, boldfacing, double striking, kerning (varying the space between letters), over striking, and proportionate spacing. Others give flexibility in ribbon color and allow for superscript, subscript, and special character printing.

Formatting determines the physical layout of text on the printed page. Here are some features and capabilities you should look for:

- automatic pagination (setting page boundaries)
- automatic page numbering
- inserting header and footer lines
- automatic footnote insertion and numbering
- right margin justification
- setting right, left, top, and bottom margins
- double and triple spacing
- line centering
- two column printing
- indent variation
- page number prefixes
- alternating layout for even and odd pages

Various print utilities control the movement of text to the printer. Some useful ones include:

- write to disk (to save formatted print file)
- spooling (print one file while editing another)
- print partial document (i.e., specific pages)
- single-sheet printing (automatic pause after each page)
- pause during printing
- print multiple copies
- merge data files (combines letter and address files)
- merge text files (combines small files into one document)

Word Processing Support Programs

In the past year a number of programs to support word processing have been introduced. Here are some you might wish to consider. Whether you need any of these programs is a matter of personal opinion.

Spelling programs are a godsend. Finding typos is one of the most tedious parts of document production. All spelling programs work in roughly the same way: They scan text, sort the words alphabetically, and compare them against a dictionary. Words not found are flagged. Some programs will automatically correct common spelling errors; others mark the word for author correction. There are a number of spelling programs available that come in a range of costs and conveniences. Here are some tips for making comparisons:

- Check the size of the dictionary.
- Find out how the program handles hyphens.
- How easy is it to upgrade or revise the dictionary?
- How easy is the program to use?
- How fast does the program operate?
- What extra features are offered (e.g., special dictionaries, prompting of possible correct spellings)?

Grammar checkers are quite new. They go one step beyond spellers by checking syntax and repeat words—one of the most common typos. They also check for trite phrases and weak modifiers.

Footnote programs automatically number and insert footnotes. They even adjust page boundaries to make room for the footnotes. This program is a must if your work requires extensive text documentation.

Indexing programs are program-specific. They allow you to insert keys that automatically generate an index or a table of contents. When you have completed the document, you run the program and it ties the chapter headings or index entries to specific pages in the document.

Format checkers are also program-specific. They check for formatting errors. For example, this page was written with WordStar, which requires that special characters be embedded in the text to command such special features as superscripts and **boldface**. Here is how they look in the text: ^Tsuperscript^T, ^Bboldface^B. Notice that the control characters are used in pairs—one to initiate the effect; the other to discontinue it. Sometimes I forget to type in the second control character or I insert the wrong one. **This <u>causes</u> <u>all</u> <s>sorts</s> of** interesting **effects.** A format checker goes through and checks that the control characters appear in pairs.

Merge programs allow you to combine automatically portions of two files. They are used to generate form letters by combining information stored in a text file (for the body of the letter) and an address file (for the names and addresses of all those to receive the letter).

Financial Analysis Packages

A financial analysis program is a software tool which allows you to create models to make various types of financial decisions. They evolved from the spreadsheet—a set of rows and columns on paper used to organize numeric and financial information.

A budget is a kind of spreadsheet. Some rows and columns are used to hold starting data, the information you use to start your model (for example, the amount of money available). Other rows and columns are used to hold calculated data, information that is calculated from the starting data using formulas you provide. (For example, you might decide to allocate 20 percent of your available money to transportation.) The spreadsheet allows you to explore different assumptions and strategies by changing either the starting data or formulas.

Paper spreadsheets are very cumbersome because all the calculations must be done by hand. Computerized financial analysis programs are very easy to use because the computer does all the calculations for you. Once you type in the labels, starting data, and formulas, the computer calculates all the remaining values in the spreadsheet for you. Changes in starting data or formulas take a few keystrokes and revised spreadsheets are created with the flick of a key.

Working with a financial analysis program entails five steps. First, you plan what you want to do. Determine what information you need from the analysis. Define the variables and determine the relationships between them. Work out the formulas required to calculate data. Next, you setup your spreadsheet, defining and labeling rows and columns and typing in the formulas to calculate values. Then you input the starting data into the spreadsheet. In the calculate step you instruct the computer to calculate the rest of the spreadsheet and show you the results. Then you can go back and revise or tune your model by changing either the starting values of the formulas that use them. When you are satisfied with the results, you can have them output to a disk file or to the printer.

Financial analysis packages have become one of the most visible microcomputer software products of the 1980s. The trend started with the introduction of VisiCalc, which was developed by Dan Bricklin for the Apple computer. Rumor has it that Visi-Calc has been responsible for the sale of X-thousand (fill in the number you heard) Apples. Other software houses, quick to spot a sure thing, have rushed into the market.

The result is that we are now being confronted with an incredible array of financial analysis packages. Reading the ads (read, but never believe) might lead you to assume that each of these programs is essential and can do everything except take out of the garbage. If you are interested in a financial analysis package, you should prepare yourself for a lot of research. New programs (and new versions of existing programs) are appearing every week. To make a selection, follow the general guidelines of the word processor screening procedure described earlier in the chapter. Then, you should engage in a more rigorous analysis of each package's features.

Features You Should Look For

Does the program use a spreadsheet approach or a modeling language? The final output in both approaches is a matrix, but they use different methods to create one. In the spreadsheet approach, all work is done by directly manipulating the matrix on the terminal. All labels and formulas are instantly visible. In the modeling-language approach, you write a high-level language program, which controls the creation of the matrix. The spreadsheet approach is more visual and easier to learn, but has limited capability for printing reports. The modeling language approach appears to be more flexible and powerful and allows more creativity in printing reports, but it is less convenient to use and more difficult to learn.

Financial analysis programs vary significantly in the size (number of cells) of problem they can handle. Most use main memory for all cells to maximize computing speed. This means that the number of cells is limited by the size of main memory and the amount of main memory required for your operating system and the program. Other programs use disk buffering techniques like those used in word processing. They can deal with larger problems but take longer to do calculations because cells must be swapped between the disk and main memory.

How does the program round off numbers? Many financial analysis programs store numbers in scientific format (a decimal fraction times some power of ten). Calculation results are rounded off to meet the cell display requirements. Rounding off can cause problems in that rows and columns don't total properly. I found this out when using one of these programs. It took almost an entire day to clean up rounding-error problems of ten spreadsheets. The moral is: Find out how the rounding works and make certain the package provides the accuracy you desire before you buy the program.

Does the program transfer data between spreadsheets? If you are making multiyear projections, it is very handy to be able to read the totals from the previous year's spreadsheet into the starting columns of the present year's spreadsheet. Some programs allow you to do this; others do not.

Does the program interface with other programs? Several of the newer financial analysis programs (generally those from publishers with potentially complementary products) allow you to share data and spreadsheets with other programs. This can be a very handy feature.

How easy is it to move from cell to cell? Can you move horizontally and vertically with minimum keystrokes? How difficult is it to jump to a distant cell? How similar is the cursor control to that of other programs you regularly use (obvious differences generate frustration).

How easy is it to change assumptions? The advantage of financial analysis programs is that it is very easy to change assumptions—either data projections or the way in which different values are calculated. If you plan to be doing a lot of "what if" work with your program, changing data and calculation formulas can be very important.

How easy is it to print out results? Printer interface and the production of a finished report from your financial analysis are very important if you will be presenting the results of your work to others. Spreadsheet programs generally are limited to printing what you see on the screen, although you can restrict printing to portions of the matrix. Modeling programs allow you to create custom reports to reorganize the results of your analysis. Be certain you see printed output from the programs. Find out how you can tidy up print output to make it more readable.

How sophisticated are the calculation features? All financial analysis programs offer the standard math functions; some offer more sophisticated ones such as linear regression. Still, it's easy to run up against the limits of many of these programs. Two problem areas I have experienced are the inability to create dummy variables to store intermediate results and to control the sequence in which calculations are made.

How sophisticated is the visual presentation on the terminal? Does it use reverse video? Does it provide horizontal and vertical scrolling of the spreadsheet? Table 14–2 lists some currently available spreadsheet programs.

Filing Systems, Data Base Management Systems, and Program Generators

These programs all organize information for storage and reuse. Although they serve similar functions, their use and applications are quite different.

Filing systems are relatively simple programs designed to organize similar but unrelated information for storage and retrieval. Information is stored in records, organized by index terms called key words. Using simple commands, records can be identified and retrieved by telling the program to look for specified combinations of key words. These programs can be used for a variety of applications. They can organize letters (typed on a word processor, of course) in a correspondence file, indexed by date, project, topic, addressee, and writer. They can also be used to arrange collections of magazine articles and papers so they can be searched by topic, source and author.

Filing programs are quite easy to use, but somewhat narrow in range and scope. They might best be described as electronic filing systems.

A Data Base Management System (DBMS) is a more sophisticated filing system providing an integrated approach to data management with greater power and flexibility. It can organize information into a number of related files and move information

TABLE 14–2. Financial Analysis Programs
Here is a list of most of the currently available financial analysis programs. Creativity is clearly not a major issue in naming these programs. Expect to see a lot more with similar sounding names. Where possible, I have indicated most machines or operating systems and the type of program.

Business Plan (Apple)
CalcStar™ (CP/M, a spreadsheet program)
DigiCalc
ExecuPlan (Vector Graphics Computers)
Financial Planning Language FPL (CP/M)
Forecaster (CP/M, a modeling language
 program)
LogiCalc
MagiCalc (CP/M)
MBA (Apple II and IBM, integrated with
 word processor and DBMS programs)
Micro-DSS/Finance (Apple)
MicroFinesse (Apple)
MicroPlan (CP/M, a modeling language
 program)
Model I
MultiPlan™ (CP/M and IBM) 1-2-3™ (IBM)
PerfectCalc™ (CP/M, IBM)
PlannerCalc (CP/M)
Plan80 (CP/M)
PlanStar™ (CP/M, IBM)
Report Manager (NEC computers)
ScratchPad (CP/M)
SuperCalc™ (CP/M, a spreadsheet program)
Target (CP/M, a modeling language program)
T-Maker (CP/M, a modeling language
 program)
UltraCalc
VictorCalc
VisiCalc® (Apple, a spreadsheet program)

between them. It can also create reports by drawing related data from different files. Custom accounting systems are a primary application for DBMS programs. A DBMS is essentially a high-level, English-like, special purpose langauge. It is used to create the application by defining files and the relationships between them, specifying procedures for submitting data to the files and updating them, and describing how file data is to be used to generate reports.

DBMS programs are described by the way they organize data. Hierarchical systems link data elements into vertical hierarchies. Individual elements are stored dynamically by the program based on their relationship to other elements in the file. To locate a specific element, you must know how it is related to other elements in the file. Relational systems organize data elements in matrix format according to an externally specified system. The location of each element in the file is specified in advance, making it easier to find. Hierarchical systems require less storage, since storage locations are used dynamically as data are received. However, they are more complex to work with than relational systems.

DBMS programs are very complex and require more time to master than simpler applications programs such as word processing and financial analysis. Although designed for experienced programmers, they can be used for simple applications if you are willing to spend the time. You can find software tools, such as predefined applications and interfaces to other applications programs, to make using the more popular DBMS programs easier.

A program generator is a high level program which helps you to write a custom program for your own application. It is used for applications similar to those for which you would normally use a DBMS. The difference is that it produces compiled programs which execute more quickly than comparable programs running in a DBMS.

The program generator writes the custom program based on specifications defined in an interactive dialogue between you and the computer. You describe what you want to do in response to questions from the program. Using internal algorithms, the program generator then "writes" a custom applications program for you in a high-level language such as MBASIC or CBASIC.

Table 14-3 lists some of the software packages that are available in each of the three categories. These lists are not exhaustive, but they provide a starting point.

Accounting Packages

Accounting packages are the raison d'etre for many business computers. Supporting the financial management of a small-to-medium-sized business is well within the capability of micros. The change, however, from a manual or a time-shared accounting

TABLE 14–3. Data Base Programs (Host machines and operating systems shown in parentheses.)

PERSONAL FILING

CardFile (CP/M)
Conquest (Apple)
Data Factory (Apple)
Data Manager (Apple)
Data Master (Apple)
Datex (Apple)
DB Master (Apple)
Information Master (Apple)
IRS (CP/M)
Parfact Filer™
SuperFile (CP/M)
Whatsit (CP/M)

DATA BASE MANAGEMENT SYSTEM PROGRAMS

Access/80 (CP/M)
Compumax (CP/M)
Condor (CP/M)
Datadex (Apple)
DataStar (CP/M)
d BASE II™
FMA-80 (CP/M)
GBS (CP/M)
InfoStar™ (CP/M)
Lotus 123 (IBM, MS–DOS)
MBA (Apple III, IBM, MS–DOS)
MDBS (CP/M)
Microbase (CP/M)
PFS (Apple)
Profile (TRS-80)

PROGRAM GENERATORS

The Formula (CP/M)
The Last One (CP/M)
Pearl (CP/M)
Vanloves (Apple II and III and CP/M)

---

service to one implemented on a microcomputer can be an extremely time-consuming and often difficult operation.

There are four basic ways to develop a microcomputer-based accounting system: Use a full software package, use function-specific software modules, build a program from a high-level DBMS or a program generator, or write the program from scratch. The amount of time, the level of difficulty, and the degree of customization varies with each approach.

Buying a pre-packaged software program is the easiest and fastest approach. You install the package in your system, learn how to use it, and you're ready to go. The drawback is that you are getting a system designed by somebody else. It probably won't be exactly what you want and it will probably require some procedural changes.

Functional modules provide a little more flexibility: You buy only the modules you need and you add others later. There are five basic accounting modules: general ledger, accounts payable, accounts receivable, payroll, and inventory. When you buy a complete system, you generally get all five, but many software houses offer the modules individually. With most, the modules can be linked together so that all of them can be updated to reflect changes in one.

Building your own system using a DBMS or a program generator is the most flexible approach. You can design your own input and reporting formats. The basic program provides housekeeping functions—file definition and data movement—and an English-like language defines the various input and reporting functions. In this approach you develop the specifications for your accounting system and then write them or have them written in the high-level language. If you have no programming experience, you will have to find an applications programmer who is familiar with both accounting systems and your DBMS or program generator. The advantage to this approach is that you can customize the program to meet your requirements. The disadvantage is that it takes time and money. If you plan to go this route, you should work with your accountant in developing the program specifications.

The ultimate in custom approaches is to write your own program in a standard language such as BASIC or Pascal. Given the abundance of packaged software, DBMSes, and program generators, I can't see why anyone would take this approach unless they wanted to develop a program that could be sold commercially.

Here are some issues you should consider in thinking about accounting programs.

1. What functions do you require? Can you get by with one or two modules, or do you need a complete package?

2. Are you starting a new business or converting an intact accounting system? How flexible can you be?
3. What is your transaction volume? How many accounts do you have? How much do you expect your business to grow over the next two or three years?
4. What kinds of reports do you need? What kinds of reports would you like to have, over and above the essential ones? Will you have to break out reports by division or groups? Will you have to consolidate division or group reports?
5. What kind of hardware do you plan to use? Do you already have it or will you be purchasing new hardware? Do you plan to do other things with this hardware in addition to supporting the accounting package?
6. Who will be responsible for operating the program and what is their level of expertise? How much training and handholding will be required?

The next step is to go out and explore the available programs. Consider the following questions in researching complete and modular accounting packages.

1. How easy is it to modify the program? Is the program available in source code? Many software companies provide only object code, making it impossible for you to modify the program. It makes you totally dependent on the company for maintenance.
2. Determine the basic principles behind programs. If a program does not require or automatically make double entries, it is possible to "unbalance" the system by making entries on one side, but not the other. See if the program checks all entries against a chart of accounts to prevent the use of erroneous account numbers. How much flexibility will you have in setting up the chart of accounts? How good an audit trail does the program provide? What kind of protection measures are employed to maintain the integrity of the data files?
3. What kind of support does the software house and the dealer provide? Is there a hotline you can call for help? What is their policy on service and updates?
4. What is the capacity of the system? How many digits can be entered in an account code? How many account codes

can it handle? How many transactions can the system handle in an accounting period? How much room is there for descriptive data? What is the dollar capacity in digits?

5. How good is the human interface? How is information displayed on the CRT screen? How easy is it to keyboard data onto the program? How easy is it to generate reports? How easy is it to design new reports?

6. What kinds of reports does the program provide? Can you modify the layout and headings of reports?

7. How good is the documentation? Does the manual include a flow chart? Are blank coding or entry forms available to help you organize input data? Are sample reports provided?

8. What hardware does the program run on? Which operating system is required? What language is it written in? How much memory is required to run the program? Will the program run on multiuser or multitasking operating systems?

9. What kind of security features are there?

10. What guarantees are offered that the program will perform as described? Can you return the system if it does not perform as promised?

This list is not exhaustive. Use it to help guide your search. Have your accountant review the program for acceptability. Make certain you see the program in operation on another system so you can get some hands-on experience before you make a decision. Talk to people who are already using the program.

Specific Business Support Packages

Some software houses offer packages tailored to meet the needs of specific businesses. Examples of these businesses include medical, dental, law, insurance, and real estate offices; restaurants, farms, and construction companies; and auto parts, liquor, and book stores. These packages are sold either as software packages that can be mounted on existing hardware or as bundled systems that include both the hardware and software.

The software package allows you to use hardware you already own or be flexible in your hardware choices. You can also use the same software on a number of different machines, which is a real advantage if you decide to upgrade or expand your system. On the other hand, you may have to install the software yourself or pay your hardware dealer to do it for you. This, however, is not usually too difficult.

The bundled package is likely to be more sophisticated, since the software is designed for a specific hardware system. However, you lose flexibility. If you change or upgrade your hardware, you may have to replace the software.

The advantage of purchasing such "vertical market" packages is that the needs of a specific business are met at a relatively low cost. The alternative is to develop custom software, using a DBMS or program generator package.

The key to success is careful evaluation. Start with an analysis of your business: Develop a flow chart of your procedures, figure out your transaction volume, and decide that kinds of reports you need and want. Then start scanning the software directories and computer magazines to identify potential candidates. Find and talk to people with a similar business who already have a microcomputer system. Take your time and don't be rushed.

Mailing and Letter-generating Programs

Mailing programs can be extremely useful to small businesses that need to contact prospective clients. Of the variety of programs on the market, some are integrated with word processing programs (Mail Merge™, for example, with WordStar) and others stand alone.

A mailing program supports the production and sorting of mailing labels. You should be able to change its format for label input. It should be capable of sorting the addresses by zip code and by your own set of indexing terms. You should be able to edit your address list easily. The program should allow you to type labels on individual and continuous-form envelopes.

More sophisticated programs also support the production and printing of letters using the address files. The program should allow some flexibility in formatting the letter. For example, you should be able to vary the placement of the address and the margins, and whether a first or last name is used in the salutation. (Some programs will allow you to store a letter salutation along with the address on the file.) Letter programs may not have an editor as sophisticated as that of your word processor, but they should make it fairly easy to enter and correct text. The program should give you the option of having either justified or ragged-right margins on your letters. It should allow you to print letters on continuous forms and on single sheets.

Some very sophisticated letter programs allow for varying the fields inside the body of the letter so that form letters can be individualized. You must type in the individual phrases and somehow associate them with specific addresses. This requires more work, of course, than does a program without this feature. Programs with text inserts should automatically adjust the body of the letter for inserts of varying lengths.

Special Business Programs

Calendar programs maintain appointment schedules. Many offer a tickler system that reminds the user of deadlines and events several days in advance. The program is tied to a calendar/clock board to correlate appointments with the time and data. Powered by batteries, the boards continue to operate when the computer is turned off. To use this program effectively, you must establish a standard routine for checking your calendar program on a regular basis.

Graphics programs display tables and charts of numerical findings and trends. When looking at these programs, remember that output quality will be determined by both the program and your printer. Try the program on your printer before making a decision.

Statistical programs summarize and interpret numeric data. The popularity of these programs began with VisiCalc, although the first microcomputer packages predated it. We'll probably see an increase in these packages as more people start applying micros to numerical data.

Planning programs allow you to plan and document the performance of multitask projects on your micro. They frequently use the critical path method, which organizes tasks to minimize completion time. These programs can be very useful for planning and managing complex projects.

Games

Games are an important part of any software library. While they may seem to be most important for the home, they are also useful as "ice breakers" for business and professional systems. It's a lot easier to seduce a staff into using a machine to play some games than to learn how to use an applications program.

Computer games use sophisticated screen display techniques that give players immediate feedback on their actions. Visual display is a key element of these games. The most sophisticated games rely on "memory mapped" displays. The screen is linked to and displays a portion of the computer memory. Therefore, the display can be changed very rapidly—just by changing the contents of a memory location, and portions of the screen can be changed selectively in response to user actions, while the remainder of the screen stays static. Memory-mapped machines (such as Apple, Atari, and TRS-80) offer games stressing hand-to-eye coordination, as do popular electronic arcade games.

Machines that use terminals, rather than memory-mapped monitors, can also be used for games, but the visual portions of these games are less sophisticated. The faster the communications link between the computer and the terminal, the better the visuals.

Games fall into three different categories. Hand-eye coordination games like Asteroids and PacMan stress fancy visuals. They are very easy to learn. Action is very rapid. Little reflection or thought is needed. Fantasy games or role-playing games like Dungeons and Dragons have elaborate rules and require extensive user activity and thought. These games can be very complex. Branching algorithms determine the computer's response to a player's action. The third category is composed of traditional games that have been computerized. The machine takes the place of a human opponent. The visual display provides a record of the game. Chess, Othello, and various gambling games are examples of this category.

Most of these games are available for home and personal computers. Those keyed to memory-mapped displays tend to be the most visually sophisticated. They are available in most computer stores at reasonable prices. The market is highly competitive.

Fewer games are available for business machines. What games I've seen tend to be visually unsophisticated, and often require a lot of player effort and thought. These games are difficult to find. One of the best sources for games is the CP/M users groups, which distributes public domain software.

TABLE 14–4.   Hints for Buying Applications Software

1. When in doubt, go with the de facto standard. There are more users and dealers (making it easier to get help locally) and more add-on products available.

2. Larger, well-known, successful companies generally have more money for supporting and upgrading products.

3. The best documentation for applications programs usually comes from secondary sources, not from the program publishers.

4. Try it before you buy it.

5. Don't expect support from a local dealer unless you buy the software there.

SECTION V

BUYING A PERSONAL COMPUTER

This section is devoted to strategies for buying and maintaining personal computer hardware and software. It includes a list of information sources, and some random bits of information I think will be helpful during the purchase process.

A friend who was in the process of buying a house once commented to me: "Normally I consider it fun to spend money. Why is it that now, when I'm getting ready to spend more money than I ever have before in my life, I'm not having any fun?" Buying computers can be like that. It starts out being fun, but when you are ready to buy, you need accurate information and some way of comparing options. At this stage, visiting computer stores can become an exercise in total frustration. But it doesn't have to be like that. If you have a strategy and do your homework, it can be a fairly enjoyable and highly rewarding experience. I hope these five chapters will be of help.

15

A Buying Strategy

General Guidelines

A popular fiction says that you don't have to know anything about how a computer works to be able to use it; all you need to know is how to make it perform for you. While this theory is technically correct, it handicaps you. You won't be able to fix anything, work out problems for yourself, or, worst of all, grow. Your computer is a general purpose tool and it can help you do a great many tasks. Each time you learn to do something new on your computer you will grow—your perception of that task, of yourself, and your relationship with the computer will change.

Computer illiteracy is an extension of the way we have been dealing with technology for decades. Few people know how televisions, automobiles, or pocket calculators work. Now, I'm not going to be preaching that we should all become computer programmers or electrical engineers (although there are shortages in both areas at present). Rather, I will be describing a pragmatic approach to computer literacy and my basic philosophy on selecting and purchasing both hardware and software.

A second popular myth is that you should first decide what kind of software you want and then choose your hardware accordingly. Following this advice can lead you into trouble because it ignores the learning curve. If you use your personal computer with any regularity, you will undergo an incredible learning experience during the first few months you have the system and the demands you make on your machine will change significantly. Believe me, it will happen; I know both from personal experience and from direct observation. Watching these changes in clients over the past two years has been one of the most rewarding experiences of my life. Six months after you get a computer system your perspective will be completely different from what it was when you started. It is difficult to predict how you will eventually be using your computer, but you will be doing things with it that you never imagined.

I strongly recommend that you buy a system you can grow into. The best way to do this is to make system flexibility a major goal. Try to get a system that can expand to meet your changing needs. Stick with standards. Avoid fancy gimmicks and features that may tie you into a specific piece of hardware. Avoid getting locked into a single manufacturer for hardware, unless the accompanying software is transportable to another system without major cost in either programming or relearning. When you change or upgrade your hardware, you won't want to lose your software investment.

Over the long run, your major investment in a personal computer is the time you spend learning how to use it. Hardware is changing rapidly; you can expect to replace it within three years or less as new systems are developed that perform jobs faster and more reliably. In choosing a sytem be as conservative as possible and opt for flexibility over performance. Peak performance is achieved only through specialization and often precludes hardware independence. On my word processing program, for example, I give commands by pushing a combination of two or three keys. It is possible for me to customize the special function keys on my terminal. If I did so, I could send a command by pressing one special function key instead of three regular keys. On the surface this seems like a good idea. The problem is that once I learned to work with the customized keys, it would be very difficult for me to change terminals. I would have to relearn the commands—a step, I think, that should be avoided.

Avoid programs that are hardwired to specific hardware. Maximum independence is achieved, of course, through a component system, but such a system is expensive, takes up space, and is relatively inconvenient to use.

The Vanilla Computer

The key to success in selecting a system is to look for and follow standards. Although manufacturers do their best to avoid standards—they want to lock you into their equipment for life—the microcomputer industry is moving toward de facto standards that are generated by the marketplace, rather than by formal agreement. The odds favor them as long-term successes.

What I suggest is that you build your system around these standards. This should maximize your flexibility and minimize your vulnerability to technological obsolesence. This approach has some cost; your system will be a middle-of-the-road vanilla computer. It will be a pickup truck rather than a high performance sports car such as a Ferrari. It's hard to spot de facto standards. You can ask sales representatives, but often they won't know what you are talking about. Instead, look for common features across systems; multiple manufacturers making the same or compatible components and second-level support programs.

I have included some examples of standardized hardware components and software programs on the market. There is only one standard format for recording information on floppy disks. This is the IBM format for 8-inch floppies, which store information in single density on one side of the disk in 128-byte sectors. Any microcomputer with an 8-inch drive can read and write data in this format. This means that data on disks can be transferred between any two machines that have 8-inch drives. The IBM PC single side, single density format is becoming the 5.25-inch standard.

CP/M (Control Program/Microcomputer) is a de facto standard operating system for 8-bit microcomputers. Hundreds of manufacturers make these kinds of microcomputers, and hundreds of software houses publish programs to run on them. If you select these specifications, you will achieve almost complete hardware independence. The IBM PC is making the 8088 CPU, MS-DOS, and the IBM bus de facto standards in the 16-bit arena.

WordStar™, a word processing program from MicroPro, is rapidly becoming the de facto standard for word processing software as evidenced by the number of manufacturers who have adopted it for their systems, the program's popularity and the availability of many add-on programs that extend and augment the power of WordStar.

A Six-Step Purchase Strategy

Here is a step-by-step approach to help you make a purchase decision. It may not be foolproof, but I guarantee it will reduce the chances of buying an unsuitable computer system.

Needs Assessment

Determine why you want a computer and what you plan to use it for. Do you want a personal computer to support you in your work? As a way to enter a new field or life style or to simply learn about computers? For entertainment and games? To benefit from educational programs? For home management or recreational activities?

Who will be using the computer? You alone? Other business colleagues? Other family members? If other people are going to be using the computer, I recommend that they be involved in the selection process.

Other questions to consider include: Will your computer be dedicated to a few support functions (such as accounting or word processing) or to a variety of tasks? Are there any environmental constraints you should consider? How much space do you have? How much noise can you tolerate? How long do you plan to live with this system? How long will you have to or want to wait before you can upgrade it? How much time can you invest in learning how to use your computer? Will you be working exclusively with one computer or will you have to move information from one machine to another? If so, what will be required in transferring information? And, finally, what is your budget?

System Specifications

Your needs assessment will help you decide the basic specifications of our system. For example, if you know that your system must support more than one user, then depending on what they will be doing, you will have to determine whether a local network, multiuser, or multiprocessor system best suits your needs.

First, determine the kind of software you will be running. Do you want a single manufacturer system, or would you prefer to maintain hardware and software independence? If you want the latter, then you should get a generic operating system, which is available on many machines and for which a great deal of software is available (a de facto standard). At this time CP/M-80 is the de facto standard for 8-bit machines; MS-DOS appears to be the 16-bit standard.

Now, work out the general specs for your hardware system. The first issue is to decide between 8-bit and 16-bit CPUs. Sixteen-bit machines have a more sophisticated instruction set to allow for more complex operations, greater numerical precision, slightly greater speed, and the ability to control a large amount of memory (as many as one million locations). In addition, 16-bit machines are better for multiuser and multitasking systems.

Eight-bit systems are less expensive, they utilize a mature technology, there is a de facto operating standard, and there is a lot of good software available. But 8-bit machines address only a limited amount of memory (about sixty-four thousand locations) and are less amenable to multiuser situations unless multiple CPUs and memories are added, and they are not as effective in dealing with complex operations.

Given the incredible success of the IBM PC and its various clones, and the increasing array of sophisticated second and third generation software that uses the extended addressing capability of the 16-bit microprocessors, today I strongly recommend 16-bit machines that run MS-DOS. You will need at least 128K of main memory; get 256K if you can.

For external memory I recommend 8-inch drives for 8-bit systems, but with 16-bit systems 5.25-inch drives are generally standard. You can get around the slower transfer rate of the smaller drives by installing a RAM disk. My 16-bit system (a Corona) will hold 512K of main memory on the mother board and comes with a program that allows me to configure a portion of it as a RAM disk. (Remember, RAM disks are volatile and you must copy files onto floppy disk for archive and backup.)

In choosing a terminal you should carefully evaluate the keyboard and the display. If you will be doing a lot of numeric calculations, your keyboard should have a numeric pad with minus-sign, period, comma, and enter keys. Many top-of-the-line terminals also have function keys. Generally they are useful only with customized software. If you wear bifocals, you should get a terminal with a separate keyboard. I have no recommendations on display color. I've worked with white-on-black, green-on-black, and amber-on-black. I don't really see any significant differences between them. The key to adjusting to a display is to tune the brightness to your working situation. A larger character grid will allow better character resolution.

In choosing a printer, you should first decide whether you want dot matrix or fully-formed characters. I strongly recommend getting a printer with a form tractor and a wide carriage. Bidirectional form tractors are necessary for graphics. Unless you will be doing a lot of printing, you should probably not buy a top-of-the-line printer. They provide features and speed that are usually unnecessary. I think that best printer package contains two low- to medium-level units: a dot matrix printer for high-speed drafts and graphics and a lower cost fully-formed-character printer for correspondence and documents. This two-printer package usually costs less than one top-of-the-line printer. Moreover, you will have more flexibility with two printers—if one printer goes down, you still have the other one as a back-up.

Choosing a system package may rest on issues of space and appearance. If space is at a premium and the look of your computer is important, you should probably go for an intelligent terminal with the computer, terminal, and disk drive combined in a single unit. If you can afford the space, I recommend you get either a component or a modular system. For maximum flexibility and serviceability, get a system that uses a socketed bus or pseudobus and plug in cards. This will allow you to upgrade your computer and will make it somewhat easier to repair. This is particularly important if you will buying several systems. You can then swap cards between units to identify problems.

Last, but not least, set your budget. A reasonably equipped hardware package (computer, terminal, two disk drives, and printer) should cost between $5,000 and $10,000. If you are buying more than one unit, you can probably share a printer, so add-on units should cost from $3,000 to $5,000. (These prices do not include software.) Work out a time budget, also. Figure that it will take 20–40 hours to become familiar with the system and roughly the same amount of time to become comfortable with each new software package.

Identify Candidate Components and Systems

Once you've got your system specifications worked out, start looking for candidates. Read computer magazines. Visit as many dealers, and computer shows, as possible. Computer users are an excellent source of information. These ubiquitous buffs are generally willing to talk computers the second you show the slightest interest. I have been in some stores where the best source of information was a customer. One good way to find users is through computer clubs. You can probably pick up more from discussion before and after a club meeting than you can in a day of reading computer magazines.

When you visit dealers, give them a fair shake. Remember that they frequently expend a great deal of effort and as much as five to ten hours in customer education before they make a sale. If you have a lot of questions or want to test drive equipment, visit when the dealers aren't busy. Avoid weekends and late afternoons. Weekday mornings are usually slow. Tell the sales representative where you are in the decision-making process and the conclusions you have reached. This will help them suggest the equipment that best meets your needs.

Collect Evaluative Data

The next step is to collect data for evaluating candidate components and systems. Look at performance and comparative statistics. Check operating systems—are they generic or specific? Consider how easy would it be to upgrade a particular computer system? Do you have to replace the entire system or can you replace individual components?

Collect as much subjective information about the candidates as you can. There are two sources: your impressions from looking at and trying the equipment—and the impressions of others who have used the system. Focus on reliability, flexibility, and ease of use and service.

Compare Systems

Rank the systems, using both the objective and subjective data you have gathered. The first step is to separate the systems into groups and eliminate those in the lower half of the ranking. You should end up with a list of several comparable systems at the top of your list. Now you can consider the last-ditch factors like availability, the best deal, and personal preference.

Make Selection

Your final choice should be subjective and will probably be based on a gut feeling as much as anything else. How do the system components look? How does it feel to operate a system? How good a package does it seem to be? If you've opted for de facto standards and if you've selected a system at the top of your ranking, chances are you won't go wrong.

16

gross from pg 163 to 17

Where To Look for Information

Finding out about software is a difficult task. New kinds of programs appear every week; others disappear. Perhaps the best way to distinguish between programs is to scan the microcomputer publications for comparative evaluations of applications software. *Interface Age* has been particularly good at this.

Software Directories

One way to get a capital-intensive rather than labor-intensive picture of available software is to buy a software directory. Because I haven't reviewed them, I can't make any recommendations. Given the rapid changes in the software market, however, I'd think twice before spending more than twenty-five dollars on one.

> *The Apple Software Directory*
> WIDL Video
> 5245 W. Diversey Ave.
> Chicago, IL 60639
> $19.95: Thousands of Apple software programs categorized by application.

Commodore Software Encyclopedia
Commodore Dealers or Commodore Business Machines
Computer Systems Division
300 Valley Forge Sq.
681 More Rd.
King of Prussia, PA 19046
$4.95: Listing of all currently available software for all Commodore machines.

Dataguide
Sentry Database publishing
5 Kane Industrial Dr.
Hudson, MA 01749
$50: Catalog and directory of hardware and software products. Published semiannually.

Directory of Microcomputer Software
DataPro
1805 Underwood Blvd.
Delran, NJ 08075
$340: More than two thousand programs indexed alphabetically, geographically, by application, and by product name. Monthly updates and newsletter.

The International Microcomputer Software Directory
Imprint
420 S. Howes
Fort Collins, CO 80521
$34.95: More than five thousand programs cross-referenced by application, machine, operating system, and vendor. Quarterly updates.

Software Directory
Digital Research
P.O. Box 579
Pacific Grove, CA 93950
$14.95: 150 programs written in CBASIC.

Software Vendor Directory
Micro-Serve
P.O. Box 482
Nyack, NY 10960
$100 ($200 on floppy disk): More than nine thousand pro-

grams of systems and applications software. Semiannual updates.

TRS-80 Applications Software Sourcebook
All Radio Shack stores
$2.95: More than two thousand programs for the TRS-80 Models I, II, and III; indexed by application.

Microcomputer Magazines

Here is a listing of personal computer journals and magazines. I'd like to say the list is exhaustive, but it isn't. Publications catering to the personal computer market are in boom times. It seems like a new one hits the stands every week. This list was current as of June, 1983. It's difficult to single out which magazines to recommend, but here are some comments that might help you. *Personal Computing* emphasizes the human and work function side of computing, rather than hardware and software. Articles deal with people using microcomputers in a variety of situations. *Popular Computing* and *Desktop Computer* are aimed at the white-collar novice who wants to use a micro to support information work. *Byte* and *Microcomputing* are aimed at the hobbyist and dealer. They tend to be fairly technical in nature, although they occasionally have some easy-to-understand reviews. *Interface Age* is intended for the business market and has some fairly good comparative reviews of hardware and software. The point of view is objective (based on technical specifications) rather than subjective (based on user impressions).

Infoworld is a weekly tabloid with subjective software reviews of individual products. The manufacturer of the product is offered space for comment and rebuttal (both review and comments run together). *Infoworld* is uneven, but it is probably one of the best sources of news on what's happening in the personal computer field.

The User's Guide provides good, in-depth reviews and tutorials on CP/M software—perhaps the best ones I've seen. This is a new publication. It started life as *DataCast*. I recommend it highly.

Lifelines is a technical publication aimed at the sophisticated CP/M user. It provides good update information on problems with packaged applications programs. It also lists the programs offered by the CP/M Users Group, an incredible source of public-domain software for people who aren't afraid to modify programs. Many of the commercially offered CP/M utility programs are based on programs that were initially listed in Lifelines.

Mini-Micro News is aimed at professionals, but their hardware technology reviews are excellent. Most of the weekly papers— *Computerworld, MIS News, Computer Business News*—are aimed at professional markets. They provide more news than technical information.

I have coded the listing of publications to show the topics covered and the intended audiences.

Topic Codes
   A–all products
   H–hardware and peripherals
   S–software
   MS–machine specific
   U–use and application

Audience Codes
   B–business
   C–consumer
   E–education
   M–mixed
   P–professional (engineers and programmers)
   T–trade

Micro Computer Index offers a quick way to scan computer publications for information on specific topics. Published quarterly, it offers a subject index and abstracts of articles that are published by most of the major personal computer magazines. This information is also available for online searching via DIALOG Information Services Inc. For more information contact:

   Microcomputer Information Services
   2462 El Camino Real, Suite 247
   Santa Clara, CA 95051

Some Computer Publications

Antic
297 Missouri St.
San Francisco, CA 94107
(MS, Atari)

Apple Orchard
908 George St.
Santa Clara, CA 95050
(MS, Apple/M)

Business Computer Systems
221 Columbus Ave.
Boston, MA 02116
(A/B)

Byte
P.O. Box 590
Martinsville, NJ 08836
(A/M)

Classroom Computer News
P.O. Box 266
Cambridge, MA 02138
(A/E)

Color Computer News
REMarkable Software
P.O. Box 1192
Muskegon, MI 49443
(A/C)

Compute
Small Systems
P.O. Box 5406 Ave.
Greensboro, NC 27403
(A/E)

Computer Business News
375 Cochituate Rd. Route 30
Framingham, MA 01701
(A/B—primarily OEM market)

Computer Dealer
P.O. Box 1952
Dover, NJ 07801
(A/T)

Computer Decisions
Hayden Publishing Co.
50 Essex St.
Rochelle Park, NJ 07662
(A/P)

Computer Gaming News
Golden Empire Publishers
1337 N. Merona St.
Anaheim, CA 92805
(S/C)

Computer Systems News
333 East Shore Rd.
Manhasset, NY 11030
(H/P)

Computer Teacher
Computer Center
Eastern Oregon State College
La Grange, OR 97950
(A/E)

Computerworld
375 Cochituate Road, Route 30
Framingham, MA 01701
(A/P)

Computing Newsletter
2611 Northridge Dr.
Box 7345
Colorado Springs, CO 80933
(A/M)

Computronics
50 North Pascack Rd.
Spring Valley, NY 10977
(H/P)

CP/M Review
2711 76th Avenue, Southeast
Mercer Island, WA 98040
(H,S-CP/M)

Creative Computing
39 West Hanover Ave.
Morris Plains, NJ 07950
(A/M)

Some Computer Publications, cont.

Curriculum Product Review
530 University Ave.
Palo Alto, CA 94301
(A/E)

Data Management
505 Busse Highway
Park Ridge, IL 60068
(A/P,B)

Datamation
Technical Publishing Co.
666 Fifth Ave.
New York, NY 10103
(A/P)

Desktop Computing
Elm St.
Peterborough, NH 03458
(A/M,B)

Dr. Dobbs Journal
People's Computer Company
1263 El Camino Real
Box E
Menlo Park, CA 94025
(S/M)

EDP Weekly
7620 Little River Turnpike
Annandale, VA 22003
(H/P)

Educational Computer
10439 North Spelling Rd.
Cupertino, CA 95015
(A/E)

Educational Technology
140 Sylvan Ave.
Englewood Cliffs, NJ 07632
(A/E)

80 Microcomputing
80 Pine St.
Peterborough, NH 03458
(MS,TRS-80/M)

80US
80-Northwest Publishing, Inc.
3838 S. Warner St.
Tacoma, WA 98409
(MS,TRS-80/M)

Harvard Newsletter on Computer
Graphics
730 Boston Post Rd.
P.O. Box 89
Sudbury, MA 01776
(A/M)

High Technology
38 Commercial Wharf
Boston, MA 02110
(H/M)

Hobby Computer Handbook
380 Lexington Ave.
New York, NY 10017
(A/C)

Home and Education Computing
P.O. Box 5406
Greensboro, NC 27403
(A/C,E)

In Cider
1001001 Inc.
80 Pine St.
Peterborough, NH 03458
(MS/C)

Information System News
333 East Shore Rd.
Manhasset, NY 11030
(H/P)

Infosystems
Hitchcock Building
Wheaton, IL 60187
(H/P)

Infoworld
530 Lytton Ave.
Palo Alto, CA 94301
(A/P,B,C)

Interface Age
P.O. Box 1234
Cerritos, CA 90701
(A/M)

*Journal of Community
   Communication*
Village Design
P.O. Box 996
Berkeley, CA 94701
(A/M)

*Journal of Computers in Science
   Teaching*
P.O. Box 4825
Austin, TX 78765
(A/E)

Lifelines
1651 Third Ave.
New York, NY 10028
(S/M)

LIST
3381 Ocean Drive
Vero Beach, FL 32963
(S,B)

Micro
34 Chelmsford St.
P.O. Box 6502
Chelmsford, MA 01824

Microcomputing
Elm St.
Peterborough, NH 03458
(A/M)

Micro Cornucopia
11740 NW West Rd.
Portland, OR 97229
(A/M,C)

Micro Moonlighter
2115 Bernard Ave.
Nashville, TN 37212
(S/M)

Mini-Micro Systems
Cahners Publishing Co.
5 South Wabash Ave.
Chicago, IL 60603
(H/P,B)

Nibble
Box 325
Lincoln, MA 01773
(MS/S,Apple/M)

99er
Emerald Valley Publishing
P.O. Box 5537
Eugene, OR
(MS, Texas Instruments/M)

Northwest Computer News
P.O. Box 4193
Seattle, WA 98104
(A/M,E)

PC
1528 Irving St.
San Francisco, CA 94122
(MS,IBM/M)

Some Computer Publications, cont.

PC World
555 DeHaro St.
San Francisco, CA 94107
(MS,IBM/M)

Personal Computer Age
10057 Commerce Ave.
Tujunga, CA 91042
(MS,IBM/M)

Personal Computing
Hayden Publishing Company
50 Essex St.
Rochelle Park, NJ 07662
(A/M,B)

Perspectives in Computing
IBM Corporation
Old Orchard Rd.
Armonk, NY 10504
(MS/M,B)

*Physician's Desktop Computer
    Letter*
Information Research
10367 Paw Paw Lake Dr.
Mattawan, MI 49701
(A/P)

Popular Computing
P.O. Box 307
Martinsville, NJ 08836
(A/C)

Rainbow
Falsoft, Inc.
5803 Timber Ridge Dr.
P.O. Box 209
Prospect, KY 40059

Recreational Computing
1263 El Camino Real
P.O. Box E
Menlo Park, CA 94025
(A/C)

6502/6809 Journal
34 Chelmsford St.
Chelmsford, MA 01824
(H/M)

68 Micro Journal
P.O. Box 849
Hixson, TN 37343
(MS,6800/M)

Softside
6 South St.
Milford, NH 03005
(S/M)

Softalk
11160 McCormick St.
North Hollywood, CA 91601
(S/M)

Software News
520 Riverside Ave.
Westport, CT 06880
(S/M)

S—100 Microsystems
93 Washington St.
Morristown, NJ 07960
(S/M)

SYNC
Ahl Computing Inc.
39 E. Hanover Ave.
Morris Plains, NJ 07950
(MS, Sinclair, Timex)

T.H.E. Journal
P.O. Box 992
Acton, MA 01720
(A/E)

TRS-80 Software Review
92 Washington Ave.
Cedarhurst, NY 11516
(MS/M)

17

goes from pg. 171 to 175...

Buying Hardware

There are three approaches to buying hardware. The first is to do everything yourself, the second is to work with a dealer or retailer, and the third is to work with a consultant. Each has its pros and cons.

Buying Hardware on Your Own

The do-it-yourself approach puts the entire burden of hardware selection, purchase, and integration on you. You research the field and decide what you want. Next, you identify sources for the equipment you have selected and buy it. Then, you must put the system—hardware and software—together.

If you know what you are doing or are willing to invest the time to learn and if you like doing things for yourself, this might be the way to go. You will probably get a computer at the lowest possible cost. With luck, you should be able to purchase hardware components at 25 to 30 percent below list. On the other hand, this is a risky path to take and one that will require a lot of your time. Service contracts and warrantees are minimal on discounted components. The time required for selecting and integrating a system is directly related to the number of individual components you purchase. When you start out in computing you must learn to operate your system and work with the software—a formidable task in itself. If you also have to get the hardware running this will significantly increase the difficulty and frustration of implementing a computer system.

The safest do-it-yourself approach is to buy an integrated computer, terminal and drive system from one manufacturer, packaged either as a single component (intelligent terminal) or as a modular system. This ensures that the integrated components are matched to work together. An integrated system usually comes with the operating system already in place. All you have to do is plug in the computer, load the software, and start to work. At some point you may have to connect a printer to the system, but this is usually easy to do.

Buying from a Dealer

The second approach to buying hardware is through a local dealer whom you can call on for help in choosing the system and for after-sale training and service. The dealer has equipment on the floor that you can look at and try out before you buy. With a dealer, in contrast to the other approaches, you have the greatest opportunity for recourse should post-sale problems occur.

Dealers, however, can handle only a small subset of the available hardware and software. They are not inclined to be objective about their recommendations. Their jobs are to push the hardware they carry. Be aware that dealers differ in their integrity and their knowledge of microcomputers. Service is even more uneven. Prices at a dealership are, of course, higher than those at discount and mail-order houses.

You should take great care in selecting a dealer. Do not assume that all dealers are willing or able to support (service and training) what they sell. Your dealer should have a good balance of hardware and software experience, and be able to understand what business applications will meet your needs.

To select a dealer, you should start by surveying the yellow pages and the business section of your local paper. Collect descriptive data on each dealer. Visit various dealers and determine whether they are knowledgeable. The smartest dealers have sales representatives who have specialized in specific applications. You may have to talk with several reps and not just one to get the information you need.

Determine how much and what kind of hardware the dealership carries. You want a dealer who has a good range of options, but not more than can be supported. Avoid dealers who carry more than five or six basic systems, or specialize in lower-level equipment. If more than half the equipment in a store is devoted to games, you probably should leave.

Determine the dealer's specialty areas. Some stores specialize in particular types of equipment or applications. In my area I can find general dealerships, those that specialize in home and game machines, and others devoted to business systems. Still others concentrate on particular applications, such as small business accounting systems.

Find out which dealers offer the most extensive service and support programs, and most reasonable financing terms. A good dealer provides post-sale training on the system and applications programs and good service on equipment. Ask dealers what they have to offer. Do they give training seminars? What about training for software purchased at a later date? Can you get training for all the people on your staff? Can you call for help with specific problems. Ask about the service policy, also. Most microcomputer equipment comes with only a ninety-day warranty. Find out about service both before and after that period. Ask how long a time a machine is typically in the store for service. Does the dealer have an in-house service department? Can you get field service? Do they have a loaner policy during repairs? Once you become dependent on a personal computer, it can be devastating to be without one. Find out what financing terms are available. Many dealers offer reasonable options.

Find out whether the store has satisfied its customers. Always ask for the names of customers to contact for references. If you don't get them, leave. Sometimes you can get a quick idea of a dealer's integrity and helpfulness just by listening to people in the store. If you spot a customer who has come back with a problem or for additional assistance, pay careful attention. It's important to find out how the store deals with customers after the big sale. Talk to them about post-sale support and service. How much training did they get? How good was the service?

Determine whether the store has had experience with your type of application. You may consider yours to be unique, but it probably isn't. The dealer may have had experience with other users with very similar applications. I would strongly suggest, however, that you confine your discussion with dealers to generic functions (word processing, spreadsheet preparation) rather than specific tasks. This will eliminate the tendency to talk in the jargon of your field, making it easier for the dealer to understand what it is you want to do.

Find out if the business has a stable history. I think the first computer store opened in 1977. Needless to say, some stores didn't last very long. I live in the heart of the microcomputer industry and I've seen several stores go in and out of business. If it happens here, it can happen anywhere. If a store has been around for several years, chances are it is doing something right.

Choose a store located near you. The farther you are from your dealer, the less likely you are to call for help and the more difficult it will be to get service. The premium you pay for buying from a dealer goes for the support and service you hope to receive. It makes little sense to buy from a dealer too far away for you to take advantage of this investment.

Buying from a Consultant

Being a consultant, I am partial to this approach. But I must admit that qualified, reliable consultants are extremely rare. Good ones provide more service to consumers than do dealers, in that they build custom systems (at least I do) using components from a variety of manufacturers and tune the systems for maximum performance. Consultants interview their clients, formulate a budget, and select hardware and software based on their knowledge of what a client needs, an assessment of available products, and their own personal biases.

A consultant should spend a fair amount of time with you both before and after the sale. As a result, you should be able to get a state-of-the-art system that performs well and is flexible. I can't speak for all consultants, but I feel a strong sense of craftsmanship about the systems I build. I try to make each one better than the last.

There can be disadvantages, however, to using consultants. They are hard to find, and harder still to evaluate. They normally do not have system components in stock, so all parts of your system will have to be ordered. It's sometimes more difficult to get recourse against a consultant. They generally are not willing to take equipment back if you change your mind. Also, many require some advance payment before building a system. Most of what I've said about the integrity and helpfulness of dealers also applies to consultants. But I'd emphasize even more the importance of talking to the previous and current clients of consultants.

If you are buying a custom system, you should expect custom service. The consultant should set the system up in advance and run it for at least forty-eight hours to detect and eliminate initial problems. The system should be set up at your home or office and you should be given detailed instructions on how to work with it.

Consultants vary in their pricing policies. Expect to pay at least list price for your components plus a system-integration fee. Some consultants give a firm fixed price for the entire system; others add a fixed fee to the equipment cost. Whatever the pricing system, I certainly wouldn't pay a consultant the total price in advance. I'd recommend paying about 50 to 60 percent down (to cover the cost of the hardware) and the rest on delivery and/or acceptance.

T.A.N.S.T.A.A.F.L.

These are my final words of wisdom on buying hardware: There Ain't No Such Thing As A Free Lunch! When you get ready to buy, remember that your time and sanity are both worth something. Cutting corners will probably cost you in the long run. If you don't feel thoroughly familiar with the technology, get some expert help. Expert help is in short supply, but it is there and you can find it—if you've done your homework by reading books and magazines and talking to computer users—so you know what to look for.

18

gros from pp. 176 to 178. "

Buying Software

Buying software is more difficult and frustrating than buying hardware. Software products are less well described than hardware products and tend to be more complex, making evaluation and comparison extremely difficult. Shopping for software is challenging for the novice, who has no basis for comparing programs and doesn't know which features are important when comparing programs that perform a similar function.

When buying software for your new system there are several rules you should keep in mind. The first is that you should purchase machine-independent software if at all possible. Software, not hardware, will be your major investment. Hardware changes rapidly—expect that most of your hardware will be obsolete in two or three years. Good software, on the other hand, can stay with you for years. It takes far longer to learn to use software effectively than it does to learn about hardware.

Buy for long-term use. Once you become comfortable with your computer, your computer literacy and your uses will expand. If you make software decisions based on initial impressions and while you are still a computer novice, you may soon outgrow

176

Illustrations 27-31 Portable Computers

Illustration 27

The Osborne 1 has two 5.25-inch floppy-disk drives and a small display (5-inch with 24 lines of 52 characters each). The new Osborne Executive series has a larger display. *(photo courtesy of Osborne)*

Illustration 28

The Pied Piper Communicator I is one of the lighter portables (12 pounds). It has a single 5.25-inch floppy-disk drive with a capacity of 320 kilobytes, and uses a Z 80 microprocessor. It can be connected to a monitor or to a television set. *(photo courtesy of Pied Piper)*

Illustration 29

The Otrona Attache is a high-end portable with two double-density 5.25-inch drives and a Z80. The display shows 24 lines of 80 characters. *(photo courtesy of Otrona)*

Illustration 30

The Compaq is an IBM-compatible portable that uses the INTEL 8088 microprocessor and two 5.25-inch drives. It has a full-size display. *(photo courtesy of Compaq)*

Illustration 31

The Grid COMPASS is described as an executive work station, although it is smaller and lighter than most portables. It has a flat screen display and makes extensive use of bubble memory. A floppy-disk/hard-disk unit is available to augment the magnetic bubble storage. *(photo courtesy of Grid Systems)*

Illustration 32   A Hard-Disk Drive

The top has been removed from this Shugart SA600 hard-disk drive so you can get a better look at the disk (top), the read/write head (center, resting on the disk), and the head-positioning mechanism (the triangular device in the center). Normally all three of these elements are sealed in a chamber filled with an inert gas to prevent entry of dust and other contaminants. The spindle motor is located to the lower left. This 5.25-inch drive has three platters (disks) and can store up to 10 million characters. *(photo courtesy of Shugart)*

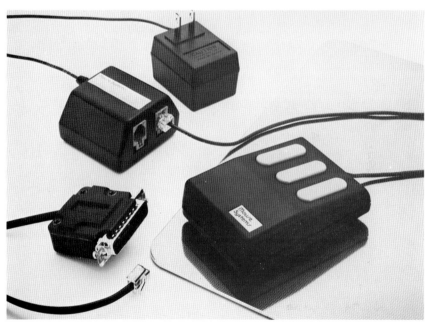

Illustration 33   A Mouse

The mouse is a sensor device that controls cursor movement and sends commands to the computer. Long popular with programmers and designers, these devices are now becoming available on personal computers. This mouse is an independent peripheral and communicates with the computer via an RS232 interface. Note the control buttons on the top surface of the mouse. *(photo courtesy of Mouse Systems)*

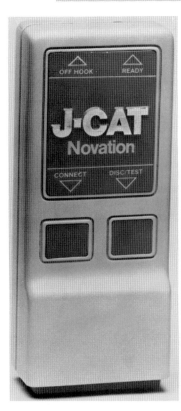

Illustrations 34-36

Modems connect computers to telephone lines. They can be packaged separately and interface with a computer through an RS232 serial port, or they can be placed on a printed circuit board that plugs directly into a computer.

Illustration 34 (top)

The Hayes SmartModem communicates at either 300 or 1200 baud and provides both autodial and autoanswer. *(photo courtesy of Hayes Microcomputer Products, Inc.)*

Illustration 35 (center)

Novation Smart-Cat modems provide 300 baud (Model 103) and 300/1200 baud (Model 103/212) communications via telephone lines. *(photo courtesy of Novation)*

Illustration 36 (left)

The Novation J-CAT is one of the smallest external modem devices currently available. *(photo courtesy of Novation)*

Ilustration 37   An External Clock/Calendar

The Hayes Stack external clock/calendar device can be used with any computer. It sends the day, date, and time to the computer over an RS232 interface. A battery device provides backup against power failure. *(photo courtesy of Hayes Microcomputer Products, Inc.)*

Illustration 38   A Multi-Processor Computer Family

OSM, one of the pioneers in multiprocessor systems, offers a range of machines. The OSM design dedicates a CPU and main memory to each individual user. The users share the external memory and peripherals. *(photo courtesy of OSM)*

Illustration 39   Computer Magazines

Computer magazines and periodicals are one of the best sources of product information about personal computers. Because new products are announced so often, it is impossible to keep books up-to-date. Computer magazines seem to multiply almost as fast as computer equipment. Here are some examples of those currently available. During 1983 at least one new magazine was announced each month. *(photo by the author)*

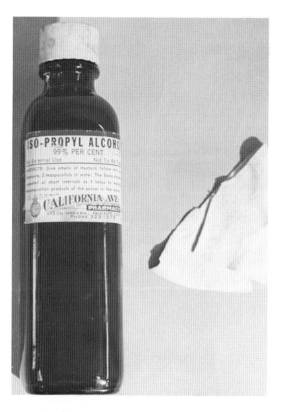

Illustrations 40-42
Cleaning the Disk Drive

I recommend cleaning your floppy disk drives every month to keep them operating properly. Here are three approaches to cleaning them.

Illustration 40

If you can get to the read/write heads of your floppy disk drive, clean them manually using a cleaning solution (either freon or denatured alcohol) and a lint-free swab. I find a small piece of chamois is ideal. Saturate the swab with the cleaning solution and gently rub it across the head surface. If you have a double-sided drive, you will have to clean both the top and bottom heads. The head mountings are quite delicate so be extremely careful when cleaning them. *(photo by the author)*

Illustration 41

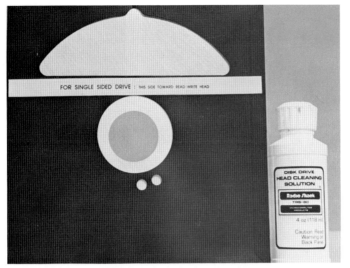

This cleaning kit makes cleaning a little simpler. It uses a cleaning disk which is stored in a protective envelope and looks like a floppy disk. First, turn on the drive. Next, moisten the cleaning disk with cleaning solution from the bottle. Next, insert the cleaning disk in the drive and close the door. Then, load the read/write heads so they will be pressed against the cleaning disk. For the A drive, you can do this by hitting the reset button on the computer. For the B drive, you must first boot the system (with a system disk in the A drive), then tell the computer to read the B directory (with the cleaning disk inserted in the B drive). *(photo by the author)*

Illustration 42

This cleaning kit uses disposable, premoistened cleaning diskettes. The cleaning disk is removed from its sealed pouch and placed in a protective envelope for insertion in the drive. It is then used as described in illustration 41. *(photo by the author)*

Illustration 43   A Basic Computer Troubleshooting Tool Kit

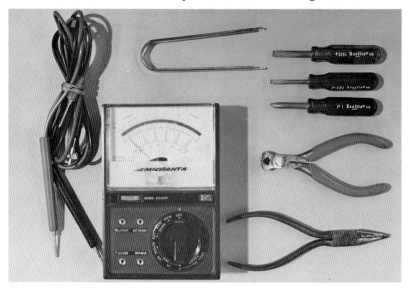

Here are most of the tools you'll need to troubleshoot any microcomputer. At the center is an inexpensive multimeter that you can use to check voltages and continuity of cables. The cables below the multimeter connect it to the circuit you wish to test. Next to the multimeter is a chip puller, used to remove integrated circuits from their sockets. You will also need large and small flat-bladed screwdrivers, a small phillips head screwdriver, a pair of wire cutters, and a pair of needle-nosed pliers. *(photo by the author)*

Illustration 44   The Ribbon Cable

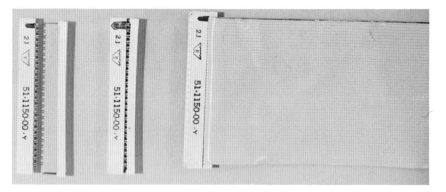

The ribbon cable is one of the most frequent causes of computer error (after the user and the floppy disk). There are two sources of problems—the ribbon and the connector. The diagonal line on this ribbon indicates a break in the insulation and a potential problem. Notice how the connector clamps onto the ribbon. To check the connector, hold it in one hand and pull the ribbon away from it. If you see the brass of the connector teeth, chances are the connector may not be making proper contact with the ribbon. Squeeze it together with a pair of pliers (padded to avoid damaging the connector) to improve the contact. *(photo by the author)*

your software. Try to look ahead. Extra features and flexibility may seem useless now, but in the future you may wish you had bought them.

Good documentation is essential. It should include discussions of how the program works and how to install it, a tutorial to help you learn to use the program, a listing of commands by function, a diagnostic or trouble-shooting section, and applications examples.

Investigate the reliability of the software houses that have published programs you are interested in. After all, software houses come and go. Simple programs are not a problem. But if you have found a complex program that you think you will be using for years, you had best make sure that the originating software house will be around when you need them for support and assistance. Find out how long the house has been in business and what other programs are offered. Investigate their consulting and updating policies. Find out how many copies of the program have already been sold. Give the company a call. When you are talking about laying out hundreds of dollars, a phone call is not out of order.

Talk to other users. Find people who are using the software you are considering. Ask them how they like it. Find out what problems they have had—both with the software and with support. Dealers are another source of information, but remember they make their living selling software. A better source would be to join a local computer club or users group. You can also check out reviews in various publications.

Try the software before you buy it. Most advertisements are exercises in creative packaging—they imply and promise far more than they deliver. The best way to find out if a program is right for you is to try it. This will take some time. Plan on spending a couple of hours so you have time to go over the manual and get some hands-on experience. Sometimes dealers will let you test drive programs. Often you can find another user who has the program and is willing to give you some time.

Some software companies offer trial programs. Ashton-Tate has a very clever one for DBASE II, a data-base management program. DBASE II comes with two sealed disks. One is a sample, which you can use for a test drive. You can play with the program, see how it works, and try some applications. (It will allow only 15 records.) If you don't like it, you return the package with the unopened second disk, which contains the complete program, and you get a refund. Open the program disk and you keep it. A couple of even braver software houses will send you packages on approval, trusting your honesty. I hope the houses are doing well. A California company will rent you software, and you can apply rental fees toward purchases. They are currently involved in lawsuits with several software publishers.

Check out the back-up policy. Some software houses (primarily those supplying Apple software) are so concerned with piracy that they build protection routines into their program disks so they cannot be copied. They then offer back-up disks for a modest fee (from five to ten dollars). I sympathize with the piracy problem, but I feel it is essential to have a number of back-up disks. The floppy disk is the most fragile part of a microcomputer system. As you become dependent on your software, you will have to have multiple back-up copies immediately at hand. I don't recommend buying copy-protected software.

If you are going to depend on software, buy it. Software piracy occurs in a number of ways: A single organization or individual may buy a software package and make multiple copies of it to run on several machines. An individual may get a copy of a pirated software program and, liking it, continue to use it. A computer club may have a stop-and-copy program for members to share their favorite software. Or, a "grey" vendor duplicates and sells illegal copies.

Pirated software is a fact of life. Playing with pirated copies probably won't do yourself or the software house any harm. Remember, however, that once you start to use a program, the support and updates are well worth the initial cost of the software.

19

Potpourri of Buying Tips

Here are a few other random things you should know when getting ready to buy a system.

Tax Deductions

If you are buying a personal computer to use in your work, you will probably be able to write it off as a business expense. You may want to check with a tax adviser. If you qualify, you have several choices in taking this deduction.

The easiest way is to treat your computer purchase as a direct expense. Currently you can deduct a maximum of $5,000 in business-equipment expenditures. This should cover most, if not all, the cost of a personal computer system. Another approach is to depreciate your equipment over a period of years. Given the rapid technological changes in the personal computer field, you can probably justify a three-year depreciation period. But again, check with your financial or tax adviser. If you depreciate the equipment over a long period of time, you may also be eligible for an investment tax credit.

Purchasing a personal computer is a capital investment aimed at improving your productivity. As such, it definitely offers tax advantages. These tax advantages reduce the effective cost of the computer and make the investment even more attractive. And, don't forget to use your personal computer when you prepare your taxes.

Financing

Not long ago, it was extremely difficult to finance a personal computer, but that appears to be changing. Many banks are now ready and willing to finance computer purchases and some dealers offer financing programs.

You might want to consider other alternatives that require less of a financial commitment. Given the rapid advances in the computer field, leasing may provide protection against technological obsolescence. But you should remember that hardware, which is all you're likely to be able to lease, represents only a portion of your system cost. You might want to rent a system. Several firms in my area offer short-term (six-month maximum) rental contracts.

Maintenance and Service

Maintenance and service are often sore points in the personal computer business. Most hardware comes with ninety-day warranties. After that you're on your own. Some dealers and consultants offer more generous terms. Find out what kind of warranty your equipment has before you buy.

It's been my experience that few dealers are interested in or capable of servicing the equipment they sell. There are exceptions; but they are exceptional. Few manufacturers perform their own service. Most contract with large technical service organizations to provide local service. It is possible to get an extended service contract, but it is expensive. Figure on spending each year at least 15 percent of the retail price of your equipment for a service contract. If you feel a contract is essential, find out who will perform the service, where the service will be performed (on site or at the shop), the guaranteed response time to a service request, and if loaner equipment is available in case your equipment cannot be restored to working condition quickly.

Currently there are few independent computer repairmen, but there will be more. Most repairmen specialize, working on only a narrow range of equipment. I think the best way to deal with the service problem is to handle it yourself.

You should be aware that the weakest parts of a computer system are the mechanical ones—the disk drive and the printer. By and large, the electronic components of your system will be reliable once they're properly broken in. Most of the electronic problems I've encountered have occurred during the "infant mortality" period. This is why many consultants and dealers insist on "burning in" their computers. They do this by leaving them on for periods ranging from 48 to 400 hours. If an electronic device is operating correctly after a thorough burn-in, chances are it will remain relatively trouble-free.

This is not to say that you won't have problems with your personal computer; you will. However, it has been my experience that most problems are either the result of an operator error or have a very simple cause. If you are willing to spend the time, you will probably soon be able to solve 80 to 90 percent of your problems by yourself.

Used Equipment

Although personal computers are a recent phenomenon, they are already being recycled in the marketplace. It is possible to get an extremely good deal, if you know what you are doing. Some of my friends actually prefer used electronic equipment, arguing that the longer it has gone without failure, the greater the probability it will continue to do so. The catch, of course, is that you have no service and no support. This almost totally precludes used equipment for the personal computer novice. You might do all right if you can find an experienced person to help you, but you should still expect to be pretty much on your own.

Once you are experienced, the rules of the game change. Then, used equipment can be a real bargain. Where I live we have events known as the computer swap meets. If half the stories my colleagues tell me are true, incredible bargains are to be had for the taking—caveat emptor, of course. (This may be the electronic version of the big fish story. I have never seen any of those great bargains.)

Insurance

Insuring personal computers is also new. If you are buying personal computers for use in your business, chances are your regular business insurance can be extended to cover them against typical hazards such as fire and theft. If you are not using your computer to support your work, and if it is kept at home, then you can probably extend your home insurance to cover it. Your computer system may be the single most expensive system in your house. If your computer costs more than $1,000, I recommend you ask your insurance agent to write a detailed description of your system (including the cost of each component) into your insurance and add the necessary coverage. If you use your computer to support your work, but you keep it at home, you should be particularly careful. Some home insurance policies do not protect business property kept at home. Ask your insurance agent.

I recently reviewed the prospectus for a local firm that has begun writing insurance policies specifically for personal computers. In addition to protecting against theft, this policy also covered against work loss caused by computer failure. This certainly sounds like an interesting concept and could be very valuable to those of us who depend on personal computers. If you are interested in this type of policy, again, I recommend you check with your local insurance agent.

SECTION VI

Using Your Personal Computer

This section is for those of you who have a personal computer. If you have just brought yours home, you will find instructions for putting the system together and for learning how it works. I've also included a standard operating procedure that covers tools, implementation, and preventive maintenance and a more detailed trouble-shooting kit. The latter has been extensively tested and is the cumulative result of years of both embarrassing and traumatic experiences.

Because today's systems are remarkably reliable and trouble free many computer problems can be attributed to stupid mistakes. Good design and rigid quality control cannot protect you against silly errors, bad storage media, and life's little glitches. This section should get you past most of these and even prepare you to cope with a major system crash. May you never have to refer to those pages.

20

crypt 7/1984

Starting Out

This chapter walks you through a few initial sessions with your new personal computer. It covers the components, physical connections, initial disk operations, and a first bout with a program. You should have the following at hand:

- a personal computer system consisting of a computer, a terminal, an external memory system (floppy disk drive), and a printer
- user manuals for each of the hardware components
- an operating system
- the user manual for the operating system or, better yet, a second-source "how to" publication that explains how to use it
- some operating system utilities, including a formatting program, a system generation program, a directory program, and a statistics program and disk-to-disk copy program
- instructions on how to use the utilities
- a couple of simple computer games to get you comfortable with the keyboard

- an applications program—either a word processing program or a financial analysis program—for your first learning effort
- the user manual for the applications program and, if possible, an appropriate second-source tutorial or training manual
- a package of blank disks for use with your system
- some stick-on labels and a pen or pencil
- a minimum of two hours of free time

The Walk-around

Let's start with a quick tour to become familiar with your system. Your dealer or consultant should have done this when you purchased your system. If so, the repetition will be good for you. If not, this step becomes even more important.

To begin, take a look at how your system is packaged. Ignore the printer for the moment and focus on the other components. Following the descriptions in Chapter 9, decide whether your system is an intelligent terminal, an intelligent terminal with external drives, an integrated system, a modular system, a component system, or a portable computer.

The Terminal

Let's take a closer look at your keyboard. It's designed like a typewriter keyboard, but there are some essential differences. On the left side of the keyboard you should find the CONTROL (CTRL) and Escape (ESC) keys. The CTRL key is usually located two keys to the left of the letter ''A'' key and the ESC key is generally located next to the number ''1'' key. These two keys send control signals to the computer and are generally used in combination with other keys.

The ALPHA LOCK key is also located on the left side of the keyboard, between CTRL and A (the position of the shift lock on a typewriter). ALPHA LOCK is similar to a shift lock in that it tells the keyboard to send uppercase letters; however, you must still use the shift key (below ALPHA LOCK on the left) to send the characters shown on the upper part of the number and punctuation keys on the keyboard.

You should be aware of two keys on the right side of the keyboard: the RETURN (RET) and the DELETE (DEL) keys. RETURN usually signifies the end of a complete thought or command when sending instructions to the computer, the completion of a paragraph when composing text, or the end of a statement when programming. You *do not* automatically use a return at the end of each line as you do on a typewriter. The DELETE key erases the character to the left of the cursor on the display. When running applications programs or programming, you can use DELETE to immediately correct errors made while typing entering information on the keyboard.

Your keyboard may have keys to control the movement of the cursor. These keys are generally positioned on the right side and have arrows on them to indicate in what way they move the cursor. You may also have a numeric pad located to the right of the keyboard, with keys for the numbers zero to nine—".", ",", "-"— and ENTER laid out as on a calculator keypad. Numeric keypads allow for the rapid entry of numbers. ENTER is the same as RETURN.

You may also have a series of function keys on your keyboard. These are generally located at the top or left of the keyboard and will probably be marked with an "F" and a subscript number. These keys are used with programs which have been customized to work with your system.

Your display screen should look like a blank tv set. If you turn on the display, terminal, or system, you will see what the cursor looks like. Then turn the system off for the moment. You probably won't be able to see a cursor with a Type 4 system until all the modules are connected.

The Disk Drive

The disk drive is usually a box with slots into which the floppy disks are inserted. These slots may be covered by doors or by rotating levers which hold the disk in the drive. A small ready light on the front of the drive indicates when it is working. If you have two or more drives, they have been labeled for you. The main drive—the one the computer first looks at when it is turned on—is labeled "drive A." Usually, it is the most convenient drive—the one on top or to the left.

The Computer

Next, look at the mechanisms that process the information. What they are and where they are located varies with each type of system. If you have an intelligent terminal (with or without external drives), the computer is located on a printed circuit board inside the terminal unit. An integrated system has the computer in the drive enclosure—it may be a single board computer or a bus with plug-in boards. Because these three arrangements are so densely packaged, I don't recommend opening them unless you really need to do so. If you have a modular system, you may be able to open up the back of the computer module to see the horizontal main circuit board on the bottom of the module and the sockets which receive add-on boards.

If you have a component system your computer will be in a separate box which you can open. Make certain the computer is turned off and unplugged before you open it. Most of these systems use a bus. Inside the box is a series of parallel, multi-connector sockets spaced about an inch apart; you will find printed circuit boards plugged into several of these sockets, which are part of a bus system. There will probably be at least four circuit boards: one each for the CPU, the memory, the floppy disk controller, and the peripheral controller. The boards should be spaced across the sockets to allow maximum distance between them. This way air flow is maximized to cool the computer. Flat, ribbon cables connect some of the boards to jacks at the back of the computer. The width of these cables indicates their function. The widest cables (50 to 35 conductor) are used with disk drives. Narrower cables (25 conductor) are generally used to connect the system to terminal and printers. Portable computers are packaged even more tightly than intelligent terminals, and I don't recommend opening them.

While you are looking over the system components, look at the connecting jacks and cables attached to each, paying particular attention to the shape and size of the various connectors. Look for labels which indicate the purpose of each jack. Note the ON/OFF and RESET switches—most systems put them on the back. You'll be using both these switches often, so remember where they are.

Connecting the Cables

Now that you have identified what kind of package you have and its various components, let's connect the system. If your dealer or consultant has already done this for you, you might want to read along anyway, just to better understand your system.

The Printer Cable

Let's start with the printer, which has either a serial or parallel interface. Serial interfaces generally use DP25 connectors (a trapezoidal shaped plug with a top row of 13 pins and a bottom row of 12) and a round cable. Parallel interfaces may also use a DP25 connector and round cable, but may also use a flat ribbon cable with a special 35-connector plug. Intelligent terminals and portable computers usually have clearly marked printer jacks. Integrated and component systems may have several connectors on the back, so make certain the printer port is clearly marked. Modular systems connect to printers via jacks or via special interface boards that plug into the pseudobus.

Use the adhesive labels to clearly mark the printer jack and cable. Make certain you can tell which way to insert the plug. Some jacks are polarized or keyed so you can't put them in upside down. If yours isn't, then color code it by marking both the jack and the plug on one side with colored nail polish.

The Disk Drive Cable

Next, mark the disk drive cable(s), if you have separate drives. These flat ribbon cables should not be more than six feet long. Eight-inch maxidrives use 50 conductor cables, 5.25-inch minidrives use 35 conductor cables. Both types have flat, dual row pin jacks and plugs that connect them to the computer. The drive cables may be permanently connected at the drive or they may have jacks at that end. Drive cables are usually polarized. But, if they are not, it's simple to determine whether they are plugged in correctly. Each drive has an indicator light. When you turn on the system, if both drive indicator lights come on (most of you will have two-drive systems), then the cable is plugged in upside down. *Do not touch the plugs while the system is on.* If so, reverse the disk drive cable to its correct position. Now mark the disk drive cable with nail polish so you will know which way to insert it. Label the drive cables and jacks.

The Terminal, Monitor, and Keyboard Cables

Separate terminals are connected to the computer by a round cable and a DB25 jack. Mark both the cable and the jack. Make certain to differentiate between the printer and the terminal jacks. Coaxial cables connect monitors found in modular systems to the computer. Although it is easy to distinguish this cable and connector from the others, label them anyway. Separate keyboards are connected to the terminal or computer by either a coiled cord or a four-conductor modular plug such as those used with telephones, or with a flat ribbon cable and two-row multipin connector. These are generally unique and can't be confused with anything else, but go ahead and label them anyway.

Starting Up and Booting the System

You must load the operating system into the main memory of your computer before you can begin to use it. The operating system is stored in external memory, and the process of initially loading it into the computer is called a *cold boot*. The cold boot process begins by reading a small program called a bootstrap loader from a computer ROM. The bootstrap loader instructs the computer to read the first portion of the operating system from its storage location on the floppy disk. This portion loads the rest of the operating system into the computer. An operating system prompt (A>) indicates that the computer is ready for operation and is looking at the "A" drive.

The boot follows one of three procedures. Some computers start the boot process automatically when they are turned on and a disk is inserted into the A drive. Others require you to insert a disk in the A drive and then tell the computer to boot—often by typing the letter "B" followed by a RETURN. In other systems, generally component ones, you insert the disk in the A drive and press the RESET switch. Most hard disk systems boot from a floppy disk, but some boot automatically from the hard disk.

Before booting, make certain you are inserting the disk into the A drive corectly. Hold the disk so your thumb is on the label. The disk is inserted with the label to the back and toward the drive door—either up or to the left. Now close the drive door and tell the computer to boot. If you don't get the prompt A>, try again. If you still have problems, check that the disk is properly inserted, that all system components are plugged in and have been turned on, and that they are all properly connected. If problems persist, call your dealer.

Sometimes it also becomes necessary to do a cold boot after you have started the system. This is called *reboot* and is done when you have had a software failure of some type and your computer is "locked up" and won't respond to any commands. You can then restart the system with a cold boot by pressing the RESET button (CP/M) or simultaneously pressing the CONTROL, ALT and DEL keys (IBM PC and MS-DOS). Rebooting will erase any information in the computer, so you will loose whatever file you were working on when the computer locked. Use a cold boot only as a last resort, after you have exhausted all other remedies.

CP/M uses a *warm boot* to check the status of disks loaded in the drives and reload a portion of the operating system back into main memory. (Some programs require so much main memory that they overwrite portions of the operating system during execution.) To do a warm boot you simultaneously depress the CONTROL and "C" keys.

Simple Commands

Now let's explore some easy tasks you can perform with your operating system commands and utilities.

Directory Program

For your first utility, let's call up the directory program, which shows you what files are on the disk. For CP/M, MS-DOS, and the IBM PC, type in "dir" followed by a RETURN to show this is the end of the command. If you have an Apple, type "catalog" and hit RETURN. The computer should respond by showing on the display the names of the files stored on your program disk. The Apple, IBM PC and MS-DOS will also show how much space each file occupies on the disk.

File names for CP/M, MS-DOS, and the IBM PC may include a three-character file type, such as "COM." If you have a CP/M system, you should see listings for "STAT.COM" and "PIP.COM." With an IBM PC or MS-DOS, you see "CHKDSK.COM" and "COPY.COM." You will be using these operating system utility programs in a few minutes.

Disk Statistics

Now let's try a disk statistics program. This should give you the amount of storage space left on the disk. In CP/M, just type "STAT" followed by RETURN. In MS-DOS and with the IBM PC, type "CHKDSK" and RETURN. (Remember, we saw these programs listed in the previous step.) The file type COM indicates that these are programs that are ready for execution. All you do to start them is type the name of the program and press RETURN.

Disk Back-up

Now let's move to your first computer task: making a back-up copy of your system disk. The disk to be copied is called the source disk, the back-up disk is designated the copy disk. Remember, the disk is the most fragile part of your system—it behooves you to make at least one back-up copy of each of your important disks. Before you use a new program you should make at least one copy of it; then use the copy and store the original disk in a safe place.

There are two ways to do a disk back-up: through a file-to-file or a disk-to-disk copy program. The disk-to-disk copy program is easier and quicker but is system specific. File-to-file programs take more steps but provide more control of the copy process.

Disk-to-Disk Copy Programs

Using a disk-to-disk copy program is simple: you call up the program, put the source disk in drive A, a blank disk in drive B, and instruct the program to start copying. The copy process will take about a minute.

CP/M does not have a generic disk-to-disk copy program, but one should come with your system—it will probably have the word "copy" in its name. The Apple uses a program called "COPYA." The IBM PC and MS-DOS use a generic program called "COPYDISK."

File-to-File Copy Programs

Making back-up disks with a file-to-file copy program requires three steps: formatting a blank disk, loading the operating system on the disk, and copying the files onto the copy disk. Each step requires a different program.

Formatting the Disk

To format a disk you will need a program disk containing the operating system, and the formatter program and a blank disk. If you have an 8-inch system, remember to cover the write-protect notch before formatting the disk. A formatter program prepares new disks for use by writing sectors on them. The program will be named "FORMAT" (Apple, IBM, MS-DOS, some CP/M systems), "INIT" (some CP/M systems), or similar name. It will be stored on your program disk. When you have identified the formatting program, call it up by typing its name. *Do not include the period and the suffix.* (If the program name is INIT.COM, type in INIT. The program will now load, and the computer should display a program menu on the screen. These menus are generally system specific, but they will probably ask the following kinds of questions:

- the location of the disk to be formatted (drive A or B)
- the format density (single or double)

- the number of sides (single or double)
- the sector size
- the number of tracks

At this point, the program disk should be in drive A and drive B should be empty. Put the blank disk in drive B and close the door. Now *open* the door for drive A to prevent accidental formatting (and thereby erasure) of your program disk. If you have a problem, close the door to drive A and hit the RETURN key. The program should then continue.

Now respond to each question on the menu, using the conservative responses shown below. Your system may also allow a default value whereby you can ignore questions by hitting the RETURN key. We won't be using that now; instead, answer that the disk to be formatted is in the B drive; that you will be using the lowest density value, a single side, and the smallest sector size; and that all tracks are to be formatted. When you have completed responding to the menu, the program should start formatting the disk on drive B. If you couldn't open the door on drive A before, do it now. You will be able to hear the other drive working; there will be a click as the read/write head moves from track to track.

When the formatting is complete, the computer will detect the open drive door and will put the formatting program on hold. Close the drive A door and hit the RETURN key. The program should now exit and return control to the operating system, or it should prompt you on how to do so.

Copying the Operating System

Next, you must copy the operating system onto the disk. Most operating systems reserve the outermost disk tracks for the operating system and do not allow them to be used for general storage. It's a good idea to put the operating system on every disk. If you have an Apple, an IBM PC, or an MS-DOS, the operating system can be loaded automatically during formatting. In CP/M copying the operating system requires a special system generation program. CP/M comes with one called SYSGEN; yours may use one with a slightly different name. These programs read the operating system off your source disk and then copy it to your copy disk.

Call the program just as you did the formatting program. If you can't find it, check the documentation for your operating system. The program should be self-prompting. Remember, your system disk is on drive A and has the operating system on it. The copy disk is on drive B. Follow the directions.

As soon as you have copied the operating system, test your work. Switch the disks; the system source disk should now be in drive B, the copy disk (formatted and empty except for the operating system) should be in drive A. Now reboot the system by pressing the REST switch (Apple and CP/M) or by simultaneously pressing CONTROL, ALT, and DEL (IBM PC and MS-DOS). If the computer responds with a prompt (A>), chances are the system copy was successful. If not, repeat the system copy sequence until you are successful. Then switch the disks back again so the source disk is on drive A and the copy disk is on drive B. Do a warm boot and continue with the instructions below.

Copying the Files

The final step involves reading a file from the source disk into memory and then transferring it to the copy disk. To do this we will use your file copy utility (PIP.COM in CP/M, COPY.COM in MS-DOS (and the IBM PC), FID in AppleDOS). FID is self-prompting so I won't cover it here. The following discussion should get you through both PIP and COPY.

The generic command for PIP is

PIP B: = A:filename.ext[V]

followed by a RETURN. "PIP" calls the program; the rest of the command tells PIP what to do. "B:" indicates the copy drive; "A:" indicates the source drive; "filename.ext" represents the name of the file to be copied (and the optional three-character extension); "[V]" tells the program to verify that the file has been copied correctly. Try it by copying PIP from drive A to drive B. The command is

PIP B: = A:PIP.COM[V]

Type it in exactly as shown, including the spacing and punctuation. If you make a mistake, the program will not execute the command. If you type it correctly, the computer should send back a new prompt (A>) when the file has been copied. Otherwise you will get an error message and a prompt.

COPY has a slightly different command format. The generic command is COPY/V source, destination. Source is the name of the source file, destination is where you want the copy to go. The /V tells the program to verify the copied file—it can be located anyplace in the command line after the word COPY. To copy the program COPY from drive A to drive B you would type

COPY/V COPY.COM B:

This instructs the computer to load the copy program and then copy the file COPY.COM from drive A to drive B. Try it.

Global identifiers make it easy to copy more than one file at a time. The CP/M command

PIP B: = A:*.* [V]

tells the computer to copy every file on drive A to drive B.

PIP B: = A:*.COM[V]

will copy every file with a "COM" extent. The same commands in MS–DOS would be

COPY/V *.* B

and

COPY/V *.COM B:

When you use global identifiers, both COPY and PIP will list the name of each file as it is copied.

Using global identifiers, copy the contents of your source disk to your copy disk. Again, in CP/M, type

PIP B: = a:*.*[V]

In MS–DOS, type

COPY/ *.* B:

The program should list each file as it is copied and finish by giving you a system prompt. If not, try again.

Advice on Copying

Disk-to-disk copy programs are much faster and easier than the three-step duplication process described above. Since they copy every track, you don't have to format the copy disk in advance, nor do you have to use a system generation program to load the operating system. This means you have to call only one program instead of three to make a complete copy. On the other hand, disk-to-disk programs are more rigid—you have to copy the whole disk, not selective files, and they erase everything currently stored on the copy disk. Another disadvantage is that you don't get the compression and reorganization of a file-by-file copy. On a new disk, your files are saved in sequential order from the outside tracks in. Because the operating system must go back to the directory track for the address of every block in a file, you get quicker access to those files stored at the outer edges of the disk (and closer to the directory). When you copy a disk using PIP, you can control the way the files are stored on it and can move your more important, frequently-used files to the outside tracks. With a disk-to-disk copy program, the inevitable inefficiencies that built up on a disk through the creation, use, and erasure of files are duplicated exactly on the copy disk.

I recommend using disk-to-disk copy programs to back up program disk and working files. System disks (the ones you use to hold programs when you are working with them) are generally best copied using PIP.

Applications Programs

You are now ready to tackle an applications program. For your first attempt, I suggest either a word processing or a spreadsheet program, depending on which is more familiar to you. I strongly urge you not start with programming. It is something well worth learning to do, but I think you will get more satisfaction from first using a well-designed applications program.

The first step is to copy the applications program disk. Because you will be using this disk as a system disk, you should go through the three-step copy process. First format a new disk, then put the operating system on it. Then copy your file copy and statistics programs onto it. Take your original system disk out of drive A and insert the newly-formatted disk. Do a warm boot to read the directory. Now remove your applications program source disk from the protective envelope. Make certain that the disk is write-protected before inserting it into drive B. Now use your copy program to copy files from the applications source disk to your new system disk. Don't forget to verify the copy routine. When you have copied the applications programs to the new source disk, remove the applications disk from the drive, replace it in the protective envelope, and put it in a safe place. You will not be using it again unless you lose all copies or unless it must be returned to the publisher to get an updated version of the program.

The next step is to install the applications program on your system. During the copy process, you probably noticed that the program consisted of several files. One of these files probably holds the installation program. Most sophisticated applications programs have a relatively automated, menu-driven installation procedure. Upon command this program (which is generally called INSTALL) will load and will begin asking you questions about what kind of terminal and printer you have. Enter the codes describing your terminal and printer, following program instructions. Other questions usually have a default value (press the RETURN key, with no subsequent response). When in doubt, the best solution is to go with the default value.

You will have to decide the best method for learning to use the applications program. For your first one you might want to avail yourself of a dealer-sponsored class or individual tutorial. Packaged tutorials are available in print, audiotape, and videotape. You should be able to use the program on your own in 3 or 4 hours, but expect to spend 20 to 40 hours before you are completely comfortable with it. Concentrate on mastering one program before you move on to a second one. Once you have learned the first one, subsequent ones will seem easier.

Starting Out Your Computer

Burn In

Your computer system is a mix of both electronic and mechanical components. Over the long run the mechanical components (disk drive and printer) are the most likely to fail since the moving parts will receive constant wear. Unlike mechanical components, the electronic components (computer and terminal) are most likely to fall victim to "infant mortality" caused by failure of integrated circuits. Experienced system builders protect against electrical component failure by ''burning in'' their computers. They do this by leaving them running under power for an extended length of time. This gives any weak chip plenty of time to fail. You can reduce the risk of electronic failure by doing the same thing. This will give you time to get any problems fixed while your system is still under warranty—remember, most personal computer systems come with only a 90-day warranty.

Burn-in is simple—just leave your computer and terminal running constantly for the first month. If your system still runs well after 700 hours, chances are you won't have any electrical problems. Use the system whenever you want—just don't turn off the computer and terminal when you finish. Remember to remove floppy disks from the disk drive to prevent wear and to keep unauthorized people from playing with the system during burn-in. Also, when not using the system turn the brightness control on your terminal or display all the way *down* so nothing shows on the screen. This will prevent ''burning'' characters into the phosphors on the screen. Boot the system every couple of days and run a hardware test program to make certain everything is working properly. If your machine does not have automatic systems diagnostics, get one from an independent vendor and use it to check out the CPU, main memory, and terminal. (Hardware diagnostics programs are discussed in Chapter 21.) If you find a problem, immediately call your dealer.

Burn-in is a very powerful check against component failure. Manufacturers test their machines, but most can't afford an extended burn-in period. By doing it yourself, you can gain considerable piece of mind at very little cost.

Check Your Power

Power fluctuations are a common cause of computer problems. Flickering lights nearly always indicate power problems. They are most likely to flicker when your power system is suddenly subjected to a heavy load, such as a garbage disposal, refrigerator, or vacuum cleaner.

If you think you may have a power problem, get it checked out immediately. Ask your power company or your dealer to temporarily install a power line monitor to analyze your power system. Most electricians should also be able to perform this analysis. If you find a problem, take steps to solve it as soon as possible before it affects your computer. You will need some kind of power conditioner for protection. Surge and spike protectors are the cheapest ($50 to $100) but protect against only brief power fluctuations. A power stabilizer ($200 to $500) will even out consistently bad power. An emergency power device provides a battery backup system that automatically kicks in during a power failure. Talk to your dealer, electrician, or power company to determine the type of conditioner to meet your needs. All are readily available and very easy to install.

Good, clean power is essential to the health of your computer. The initial cost of a power conditioner may seem high, but protection against just one system crash can more than repay your investment.

21 *Cryp 7/1984*

A Standard Operating Procedure for Personal Computers

It's a good idea to develop a standard operating procedure (SOP) to guide you in using your personal computer properly. If you learn your SOP while learning to use your computer, it will help you to build good work habits and prevent future disasters. Take it from one who didn't; the time to learn good work habits is while you are learning to use your computer, not after-the-fact. This chapter contains the SOP I give my clients. It's based on my own experience and that of other computer users I've observed. I've included some preventive maintenance features. I'm not saying this SOP will protect you from every computer disaster known to mankind; it won't. It will teach you habits that will reduce the risks of computer accidents and significantly decrease the cost of inevitable hardware and software failures.

Preparing Your System

Know Your Hardware

The first step is to make sure you know all the components in your system and how they are connected. I covered most of this information in the previous chapter. Make certain you mark all cables so you can disconnect and reconnect components without error. If your computer has a bus, label all the boards plugged into it and mark their position on the bus.

Buy Top-quality Floppy Disks

As I have said before, your main investment in your personal comuter system is time—the time you spend learning how to use it, selecting and learning software, and creating data files and programs. The fruits of your labor are stored on your floppy disks, and it behooves you to protect them. They are both the most valuable and the most vulnerable part of your system. It's stupid to save a couple of dollars by buying low-quality disks. A single disk failure can ruin hours of work. Top-quality disks are less error-prone than cheaper ones. I recommend either Dysan or Maxell disks—I've found both brands to be quite error-free.

Protect Your Floppy Disks

Even the best quality disk will fail unless you treat it properly. There are a number of things you can do to protect and prolong the life of your disks. One of the most important is to handle them properly. Don't touch the exposed media or bend the disk. Whenever a disk is not in a drive, it should be stored in its protective sleeve. When labeling a disk, always fill in the label before putting it on. If you must write on a labeled disk, use a soft tip pen and write very gently. If you want to relabel a disk, take off the old label first.

Disks are best stored vertically. You can keep them in the box they come in, one of the fancy commercial disk-storage boxes, a looseleaf binder with special sleeves, or special file folders. Once you have developed a storage system, use it. Don't leave disks lying around on tables, terminals, or computers, where they can be bent or something can be placed or spilled on them. Because the mylar base of the diskette is sensitive to heat they should not be placed on any warm surface or in the sun. (Remember, computers and terminals throw off heat. The tops of both devices are too warm for floppies.)

Floppies are sensitive to magnetic fields, of course, and should not be exposed to them. Obviously you shouldn't store them next

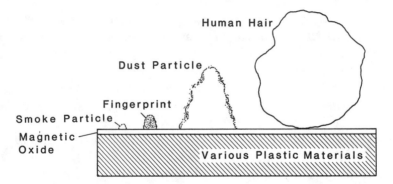

FIGURE 21–1. Disk Contaminants. The floppy disk is the most vulnerable part of any computer system. This scale drawing shows the thickness of the magnetic coating compared to common contaminants. *(drawing by Rashida Basrai)*

to the ten pound magnet you used last summer to retrieve your outboard from the bottom of the lake, but other sources of magnetism are more subtle. Many hand tools, particularly screwdrivers, are magnetized. The speakers used in radios and audio systems contain large, powerful magnets.

Separate Programs from Data Files

I think it is best to keep applications programs and data files on separate disks. This provides flexibility for back-up procedures and selective updates, and efficiency in disk storage. By now you should know that I consider two disk drives mandatory. Drive A, the main or default drive, is the drive the operating system goes to for both cold and warm boots. I run the disk containing the programs and operating system on the A drive and the disk containing data files on the B drive. If you have a hard disk, use it to keep your most frequently-used programs and current data files, but I still recommend segregating programs and data on the floppy disks you use to augment and back up the hard disc.

Back Up Your Floppy Disks

I can't stress this enough! Back up your files. If you have a floppy disk system, you need two back-up routines, one for program disks and one for data disks.

I organize system disks by function. I have disks for word processing, for financial analysis, for file programs, and for system maintenance. Some have common programs, because I often need several programs to support a single function. My word processing disk, for example, has a word processing program (Word-Star), a spreadsheet program (CalcStar), two spelling programs (SpellGuard and The Word Plus), an outline thesaurus (Random House Electronic Thesaurus), and a number of basic utility programs (file copy, disk copy, disk statistics, etc.) Together, these programs take up 600 to 900K of storage.

I keep my program disks very full and am very careful about the positioning of programs on the diskette, keeping the most frequently used files to the outside of the diskette so they can be accessed more quickly. Once I have a program disk set up properly, I rarely change it.

I make several back-up copies of program disks. That way if I have any problems with one, I can immediately replace it with another. I recopy these disks at the beginning of each month to make certain that the spelling program dictionaries are up-to-date. It really isn't necessary to back up more frequently, because the information on these disks does not change very much.

Data disks change more rapidly. In fact, every time you use a data file, you will probably change it. To protect yourself against loss you must back them up frequently—at least once a day when you are using them.

I recommend a three-copy back-up system that rotates the disks over a three-day period. On the first day, use disk A. At the end of the day, make two back-up copies, disks B and C. On the second day, use disk B and make new back-up copies on disks A and C. On the third day, use disk C, copying it to disks A and B. Then repeat the sequence.

Why make three copies? Because you are never certain if problems are caused by a system failure (either hardware or software) or an operator error. If the error was yours, the second copy should work, but if there was a system error, you could lose the second copy. The third copy is your reserve—you keep it safe until you are certain your system is operating properly again. When you use a back-up copy, take precautions. Before you insert it in the drive, make certain that it is write-protected. Don't use the back-up copy directly—start by making another copy. This may seem tedious, but it could save you a lot of frustration.

Back Up Your Hard Disk

If you have a hard-disk drive, you will need a slightly different back-up procedure. You should still organize your program disks by function. You will probably want to keep infrequently-used programs on floppies and load them only when needed.

Because Winchesters have much greater capacity than floppies, you should avoid making complete copies of all the data on your hard disk. Instead, you should make three copies of data files only as you change them. Organize your back-up data diskettes by topic or project.

Build a Library of Support Utilities

Utility programs help you organize and maintain your system and your files. You will need at least eight of them to support your work. Some will come with your operating system, others must be purchased separately. Directory, statistics, file copy, disk copy, formatting and systems copy utilities were all discussed in Chapter 20. You will need two additional programs. A hardware diagnostics program will help you to check operation of each system component and identify problems. A disk maintenance program checks disks for bad sectors, recovers accidentally-erased files, and restores damaged files. Both of these programs are discussed in more detail later in this chapter.

Using Your System

Don't Let Data Disks Get More Than Half Full

I never let my data disks get more than half full, to allow room for working files. (Working files temporarily store information that won't fit in main memory.) Almost all word processing and some other programs use working files. Once you understand how they are used, you will realize why you need to leave "breathing space" on your data disks. Let's look at word processing.

Word processing working files are the size of your document. If your permanent file requires 100K of disk space, then the program will need at least 100K for the working file. Some word processing programs occasionally create additional working files to support rapid movement through the text. Thus, a 100k document might actually take up as much as 400K of space on the disk (100K for the permanent file and 100K each for three working files.) When you try to save that file, you need still another 100K of space for the new copy of the permanent file. This is carrying the working file load to extremes, but it can happen. Your first clue that you are short of disk space will come when you try to save a file you have worked on for three hours and get the message "insufficient space to save file." I assume by now I've made my point—don't let your data disks get more than half full.

Do Intermediate Saves Every Ten Minutes

An intermediate save is a routine that makes a permanent copy of the working file without affecting work in progress. Remember, the working file is a temporary one. If the power fails or there is a hardware or software breakdown, you can lose your working file. Your best protection is to make a permanent copy of that file every ten minutes. That way, if there is a system crash, all you lose is ten minutes worth of work. Most applications programs and languages have an intermediate save command. For example, WordStar uses ^KS, and CalcStar uses ^S. One of the first commands you should learn in any program is the intermediate save. Get in the habit of doing an intermediate save whenever you leave the computer for a break, to talk on the telephone, or to do something else, as well as every ten minutes when you are working continuously.

Open the Disk Drive Doors During Breaks

Get in the habit of opening the disk drive doors any time you leave the computer. This protects against unauthorized use and reduces wear on the disks. On double-sided drives, the bottom head is loaded whenever the door is closed and the disk is spinning. When you leave, just do an intermediate save and open the doors. When you return, close the doors and continue working.

Keep Your Back-up Disks Safe

Keep back-up disks in different locations. I keep one set of data disks next to the computer, another set in a file cabinet, and the third set in a fireproof safe. If you don't have a safe, keep one set of back-up disks in another location so if there is a fire, you won't lose all copies. Good locations include a garage, a neighbor's house or apartment, or maybe even the trunk of your car. (A six-pack size cooler is perfect for keeping disks in your car. It will hold more than 20 maxifloppies or more than 100 minifloppies and protect them against heat damage.)

Make Weekly Archival Copies of Data Files

Your daily back-up files will be in your regular disk format to give you the greatest amount of storage. But what happens if your computer crashes and requires extensive repairs? You may find a loaner, but what if the only one available can't read your regular format? What happens if you buy a new computer? How will your transfer files form your old format to a new one?

The key to these problems is to maintain a set of files on a *standard format* for your disk drive. For 8-inch drives, record archive files using the single-side, single-density, 128-byte sector format. For 5.25-inch disks, use the IBM PC single-side, single-density format. I strongly recommend that you keep copies of your important program and data files on standard format disk, if your system supports this procedure. You can do this selectively— copy only those files that you have added or changed significantly during the past week.

Review and Catalog Disks Weekly

There are many ways of organizing your disks. One way is sequentially. I do so by project, but this requires a lot of disks. Some people use disk catalog programs. Such programs provide an alphabetized listing that shows where each file is located. This can save diskettes, since the catalog makes it possible to have many unrelated files on the same disk.

You should review your files and disks on a weekly basis and reorganize them as required. It can be frustrating to look for a file when you can't remember on which disk it is located, or the exact name of the file, or have a number of files with the same name. Maintain some kind of record showing which files are located where and what they contain. If you are using your personal computer to work on projects for other people, it is absolutely essential that you document an organizational structure so others can locate information.

Taking Care of Your System

Clean the Hardware Weekly

Personal computer equipment doesn't need much care, but it is a good idea to keep it clean. Once a week I give all my equipment the once-over. Clean the terminal screen. Dust it and wipe off any stains. You can use a commercial cleaner and a soft cloth. Spray the cleaner on the cloth, not directly on the screen. If your screen has a plastic shield, use a plastic cleaner. Simply dust the screen if you have a nylon net over it to cut glare. I use a soft brush to dust off the keyboard. Check that the interface cable is firmly plugged into the socket. Cables are sometimes bolted to the terminal, but I don't recommend this. If I trip over the cable, I'd prefer that it pull out of the plug rather than pull the terminal off the stand. Make certain that the ventilation slots on the terminal are not covered or plugged. Remember, all your components need air flow for cooling. Dust off the surface of the disk and computer housing. Make certain the drive interface and peripheral cables are firmly connected. Make certain the ventilation slots are clear. Dust off the exterior of the printer. Dust out the area below the print head, but only after you turn off the printer and disconnect the power plug. Check the interface cable.

Run a Weekly Hardware Diagnostics Check

My diagnostics program (DIAGNOSTICS II) has a quick routine for verifying that the CPU, timing and main memory, and the disk drive are all in working order. It also has routines to check the terminal and printer. I recommend running these checks once a week. Some personal computer systems have an automatic check on start-up, but it's a good idea to do a more thorough check once a week.

Clean the Read/Write Heads Once a Month

If you use high-quality disks, you shouldn't get much oxide build-up on your read/write heads, but it's best not to take chances. You can get drive cleaning kits for about $20. It takes about 30 seconds to clean each drive. I consider it time well spent. Make certain that the heads load against the cleaning disk.

Visually Inspect Your Disks

Disk wear is insidious in that you don't realize you have a problem until it's too late. A monthly check of your frequently-used disks can save you a lot of trouble.

Take the disk out of the envelope and check the area around the spindle hole. If you see cracks or signs of wear, put a reinforcing ring around the spindle hole. At $25, a reinforcing ring kit is a good investment. I automatically put rings on all my new disks. Some come with rings already installed.

Next, look at the cutout on the bottom (unlabelled side) of the disk. An unworn disk shows a perfectly smooth surface at the cutout. If you can see lines resembling record grooves, your disk is getting worn. You are most likely to see lines on the directory track (track two on 8-inch disks, track four on most 5.25-inch disks, track seventeen on Apple disks). If you see signs of wear I recommend you replace the disk at once. It probably has life left in it, but its days are numbered and I wouldn't trust it.

If you have a disk maintenance program, you should run it on your diskettes every month to check for bad sectors. The program allocates all bad sectors to a dummy file so you won't have to worry about using them accidentally. A few bad sectors shouldn't be much of a problem, but if you find a scratch pattern (sector 5, track 6; sector 5, track 7; etc.), or many bad sectors, you should replace the disk.

Trouble-Shooting Your Personal Computer

Rules for Handling Problems

No matter how careful you are, or how adept you are at using a computer, sooner or later you are going to encounter problems. It's the nature of the beast. While it is impossible to provide solutions to all the problems you may face, here are five rules which should help you deal with a large percentage of them.

Rule 1: Buy Smart!

Get off to a good start by having your computer system properly tested and installed. Personal computers are robust machines. Properly installed, they should give you very little trouble. Most major computer problems originate in the hardware or the operating system, and show up very early. A reputable dealer or consultant will assemble and run your system for at least a week before it is delivered to head off any infant-mortality problems. If all your components work well together for a week of heavy use,

210

they should run for a long, long time (barring external problems such as power fluctuations). Buying components and integrating them yourself can be expensive, time consuming, and risky unless you know what you are doing. Accepting components in unopened boxes is equally risky. If you are a novice, insist on predelivery burn-in as part of the terms of the purchase. Also, demand to see how your system operates before you accept delivery.

Rule 2: Don't Panic!

Many novice computer users (and a large percentage of veterans) believe that computers are extremely fragile. As a result, they treat every problem as a disaster of monumental proportions. When something goes wrong, they panic, often exacerbating what was really a very simple problem.

If you have bought smart, chances are you will only have simple problems, which can be solved through common sense. The trick is not to panic so that common sense has time to rise to the occasion. This can take a couple of minutes. If you have a problem, take three deep breaths, lean back, relax, and proceed to the next rule.

Rule 3: Don't Do Anything until You Think It Through.

This is perhaps the most important rule in dealing with computer problems. The trick is to stop and figure out the solution before you take action. Your main concern is to solve the problem without losing whatever unsaved data you have in your working file. Here's an example to show what I mean.

I have a new terminal that locked up on me during the first two weeks I used it; especially when I was working with the text editor. I had not followed my own rule of doing ten-minute saves, so I often had as much as thirty minutes of unsaved input—two to three pages—when the terminal locked up. The first time I tried the reset button on the computer. I immediately lost my unsaved text, of course, and the terminal remained locked. I finally had to turn it off and start all over again. The next time it happened, I began randomly hitting function keys in an attempt to unlock the terminal. It worked once, but I somehow sent a signal to the computer that knocked me out of the text-editor program and I lost all the unsaved text. Finally I remembered Rule 3 and stopped to figure out what was going on.

The problem was that I had been hitting the special-function print key by mistake. The terminal had locked because my printer was not attached to it. The correct solution was simple: Leave the computer on but turn the terminal Off to clear it. That way, I didn't lose any text by turning off the terminal, since my working file was stored in the computer. All I had to do was turn the terminal back on and send a scroll command to the editor program to bring the text back up on the screen. It took me more than a week before I remembered to follow Rule 3. In that time I probably retyped a total of ten pages of text—more than two hours of work— while working out the solution only took about ten minutes.

When you encounter a problem, stop immediately and put your hands in your pockets or behind your back. Move back from the terminal and the computer so you can't touch anything. Now ask yourself the following questions:

1. Exactly what is the problem?
2. What might have caused it?
3. What can I do to resolve the problem?
4. What are the consequences of each solution?
    a. how will it affect the program currently running?
    b. how will it affect unsaved data?
    c. how much time have I invested in the unsaved data?
5. What solution will have the least negative impact?

If the first solution you try doesn't work, go back and ask yourself the questions again.

Rule 4: Consider the Obvious First.

It's amazing how many computer problems are caused by obvious mistakes—those that are common to all mechanical devices, not just computers. To save yourself potential embarassment, quickly answer these questions when you're in a jam:

1. Are all the computer components turned on?
2. Are they getting power—is the plug plugged into the wall socket?

3. Are the components properly connected to one another?

I'd include my own experiences with this rule, but, as you might expect, they tend to be embarrassing and might lessen my credibility. Suffice it to say that nobody is immune to ignoring the obvious, so stop and check. If everything is powered and properly connected, move on to Rule 5.

Rule 5: Consider the Source.

After several years of dealing with personal computers, I have been able to rank by order of diminishing frequency the sources of computer problems. It isn't based on hard data, but I believe it's fairly accurate. The sources are operator mistakes, media wear, damaged and improperly connected cables, and loose sockets.

Operator Errors

More than 50 percent and perhaps as many as 75 percent of all computer problems are caused by operator error. It's easy to make mistakes with both your hardware and software, particularly when you are starting out. However, operator mistakes are not made exclusively by novices. I never cease to be amazed at how I can make the same mistake over and over again, and how ingenious I am about implementing new ones.

THE COMPUTER. The computer is really very robust, and that leaves very little room for operator error unless you work at it. You can cause problems by taking a look at the inside of the computer, if you don't know what you are doing. When a machine malfunctions, we all have the impulse to open it up and take a look. People who have absolutely no understanding of cars open up the hood for a look when their automobiles break down. The assumption is, I guess, that you can spot something grossly wrong, or, perhaps, simply by looking you can make it all better. This seldom works with cars and almost never works with computers. Once you open the computer, the impulse to touch something becomes almost irresistible. It's an impulse that leads to disaster; avoid it. Some of the problems I have encountered on opened computers are disconnected or improperly connected cables, improperly inserted modules, shorted connectors, and improperly installed jumpers.

If you absolutely must open up the computer, at least follow these rules:

1. Turn off and unplug the computer before you open it.
2. Carefully observe and document the position of any component before moving it so you can restore it to its former position.
3. Before inserting plug or module, be certain to line up pins and sockets properly. (Failure to do this is the most frequent cause of postinstallation hardware failures.)
4. Be particularly careful about ribbon cables. The wires in these cables are extremely thin and fragile. Sharp folds and abrasions can easily damage them.
5. Before closing up the computer, check that everything is properly connected.

THE DISK DRIVE. Disk-drive errors are easy to spot. The most common is inserting a floppy disk improperly. The label should always be away from the drive, either facing up or to the left. Always hold your thumb on the label when you are inserting a disk into the drive.

Another common problem is the failure to write-enable the disk. Many 8-inch disks come with a write-protect notch that must be covered with tape before you can write on the disk. On 5.25-inch disks, the notch is uncovered to write-enable the disk.

Failure to initialize or format disks is another common operator error, which results in ambiguous messages.

Warm boots cannot be implemented unless the disk in the main drive contains a copy of the operating system. Because data disks normally run on the second drive, some people forget to put the operating system on them. When they move a data disk to the main drive to make a backup copy and do a warm boot, they get a system error. The best way out of this problem is to put a copy of the operating system on *every* disk you use. Tracks dedicated to the operating system can't be used for anything else anyway, so why not play it safe?

THE TERMINAL. Terminals offer wealth of opportunity for operator errors. Generally, the more sophisticated the terminal, the greater the chance of error. Most errors are the result of hitting

the wrong key, which can either transmit a bad command or signal to the computer, or cause the terminal to behave erratically.

The most benign result of sending a bad code to the computer
is that the command is rejected. The computer sends back a message indicating its perplexity. Or, the program may interpret the
message as an appropriate command and execute it. Unless the
bad code is a major command like ''erase file,'' this error can be
rectified by an appropriate command. The most severe result of a
command error is a software hangup, in which the program
won't do anything or recognize any new command. I'll talk more
about this under software problems.

Errors can also cause the terminal to behave unpredictably. It
may lock up and refuse to send any commands to the computer or
it may suddenly jump into reverse video. The trick is to handle
these errors without sending any signals to the computer. By hitting the off-line key, you can disconnect the terminal from the
computer, and use whatever processing power your terminal has
to solve the problem. Many terminals have reset keys for restoring standard operating parameters. Most allow you to reconfigure
terminal settings by using escape commands. Check your terminal manual for instructions.

A second approach is to turn the terminal off, wait a few seconds, and turn it back on. This automatically resets all the terminal parameters to their original values. This also clears the terminal screen, but has no impact on the computer. You can call back
the display with the appropriate software commands. I have successfully done this with several word processing and financial-
analysis programs without losing any data.

Terminal reset is one emergency procedure you can practice in
advance. Try it with your most frequently used applications program to make certain that it works. Call up the program and create a dummy data file. Then hit the OFFLINE key to see how it
works. When you are off line, you should be able to type into the
terminal without sending any message to the computer. While
off-line, check the reset procedure for your terminal. Also try
turning your terminal off and back on. Practicing these procedures takes a few seconds and can bring enormous peace of mind
if you ever lock up your terminal.

A common way to lock up a terminal and computer is to send
something to the printer when it is disconnected from the system

or turned off. Most systems require a feedback signal from the printer called "a handshake" before material is sent to the printer. If the computer has sent a print command and does not receive this feedback signal, the system locks up.

THE PRINTER. Printer errors, which tend to be fairly simple to correct, include failure to close the cover, change the ribbon, and add or properly install paper. Some printers have a disabling switch which activates when the cover is open and a paper-out sensor. If these errors are corrected and the printer is properly connected, it should work. If it doesn't, you can implement the printer's self-test program to determine whether it is in working order. If the printer passes the self test, then you probably have a communication problem.

Communication problems usually date from when the system is first integrated or the printer is added to your system. These problems tend to be complex and frustrating. Here's one I recently encountered. I was putting together a system for a client. I was familiar with the components, although the printer had recently gone through a model revision. The feedback or handshake line (DTR) had been moved, but I modified that on the communications module of the printer. When I connected the system in my studio, it worked fine, but when I installed it at the client's, the printer wouldn't work. I brought it back and hooked it up to my system, which I set up to duplicate the client's, and lo, it worked.

We finally found the problem. The printer communications package used one line (#21) to turn the printer on and off remotely. A normal signal from the computer over this line kept the printer turned off. When testing the computer in my studio, I had used a nine-connector extension cable between the printer and the computer. The cable did not support line 21 so it filtered out the interaction between the printer and the computer. When I had installed the printer, I had connected it directly to the client's computer, which promptly turned off the printer. Once the problem was identified, the solution was simple. We used a nine-line cable to connect the printer to the computer. This prevented communication over line 21 and the printer worked beautifully.

THE SOFTWARE. Software errors are caused by erroneous commands. Once you have entered the wrong command and pressed the return key, there is really very little you can do except figure out some way to repair whatever damage you have caused. Your only hope is that the command may require some time for processing. In that case you may be able to abort the command by hitting the escape key.

A classic software error is to erase a file by mistake. Fortunately there are ways to compensate. One way, of course, is to maintain back-up files. If you have been methodical, you can probably resurrect the erased file by copying it from your back-up file.

If you don't have a back-up file, you may still be able to recover an erased file. Most operating systems don't actually erase a file when you give the command. What they do is tag the appropriate directory entry to indicate that the blocks and sectors associated with that particular file are now available. This means the operating system can use them next time it needs space for a save. For example, in CP/M, the first byte of the directory entry shows that a file is active. When you erase a file, this lead byte is changed to a unique code. All you have to do to restore the erased file (assuming you haven't used any of the blocks allocated to that file), is change the lead byte. You should stop as soon as you realize you have made an error. Don't use the disk again until you have restored the file. This keeps open the blocks allocated to the file. This restore maneuver is facilitated by any number of programs on the market, most of which are simple to operate.

There is one potential problem that you should be aware of in restoring files. If you have used the same file name several times, you may have multiple file entries in the directory with the same name—one active and several erased. When faced with several directory entries with the same name, how do you decide which one is the most recent version? One solution is to restore the files one by one, renaming each in the process. Then you can use a compare program to identify the differences between the two files. It's a tedious process, but generally less work than rekeying a complete file.

Media Failure

Media failure is the second most frequent source of problems. While magnetic media may seem to be fairly robust, they are actually quite fragile. And, problems are often difficult to detect. For example, a scratch on the storage surface may affect only a few bytes spread across several physically adjacent tracks. The damage caused by such a scratch does not become apparent until you attempt to access the scratched sectors. With a maximum of 1.2 megabytes of storage on a disk, this may not occur for some time. It is quite difficult to associate media failures with specific actions unless they are very obvious. Don't be lulled into bad habits.

Media problems generally result in bad or lost data. The severity of the problem depends on whether the error occurs on the directory, operating system, or data tracks. The most severe problems occur when the directory tracks are damaged. If the operating system can't find a file address, the file can't be accessed, and all data stored on it is usually lost. Unfortunately, the directory tracks get the greatest amount of wear because the operating system must read them every time it accesses a block to either save, read, or erase data. They are rewritten every time you save a file. The user normally can't access directory tracks directly, which makes it very difficult to correct any directory errors.

When directory track failure occurs you can usually see a distinct line on the outer edge of the floppy disk where the magnetic oxide has been worn away. Once the magnetic oxide is worn away there is nothing you can do: The data is lost and the disk is unusable. The only defense against this is to use only the best possible magnetic media and keep the read/write heads on your disk drives clean. Check your disks frequently for signs of wear. When they appear, immediately copy the contents to a new disk.

A less severe form of directory error is caused by bad data in the directory entries. Problems in finding and using files on a disk may be caused by such bad data. It is possible to correct these problems with special editor programs, which allow you to directly manipulate data on the disk.

Errors on the system tracks are somewhat less severe than directory errors. You can always reinstall the system on the disk or, if the tracks are permanently damaged, you can still use the disk in your secondary drive. Errors on the data tracks are generally the least severe. At the most, you will only have to retype the information into the computer. Good back-up procedures can significantly reduce risks in this area.

Although physical damage to the surface of the disk can make portions of it unusable, you may not have to reuse the disk if you make certain that you don't store any data in the damaged sectors. This is usually done by identifying the bad sectors and assigning them to a dummy file so they are not available for storage. There are a number of commercial software packages available which do this.

Bad Cables and Cable Connectors

Cables are the most common source of communication problems between the computer and the disk drive, the terminal, and the printer. If you leave the cables alone once your system is installed and working, chances are they won't cause problems. Once changed or moved, they can provoke difficulties.

One source of error is an improper connection. It's fairly easy to misalign multipin connectors. The more pins, the easier it is. Always make certain that the plug is properly aligned to the pins when connecting cables to system components.

Another source of error is improperly installed connectors. Most ribbon cables use special insulation displacement connectors, which have small brass teeth pressed through the insulation to make contact with the metal conductors. The cable is held against the brass teeth with a cover that locks to the connector. Some cables have a second cover that serves as a cable strain relief.

Pulling on the cable can break the connection between the brass teeth of the connector and the conductor. You can spot this problem by looking at where the connector is joined to the ribbon cable. If the brass teeth show through a gap between the connector and the cable, you may have a bad connection. This can sometimes be fixed by putting the connector in a vise and pressing the cover tight against it. Do this very carefully to avoid damaging the face of the connector. If you still have problems, replace the cable.

Damaged cables can also cause problems. Ribbon cables are very thin and can easily be damaged. Avoid folding them sharply. If the insulation is damaged or you can see the connector wires, replace the cable.

Bad disk-drive cables are the most common hardware problem I have encountered. If you are experiencing frequent disk-read errors on a variety of disks, all of which are in good condition, chances are your problem is a bad cable. Disk-drive cables generally have either 35 to 50 communication lines. Because they are so wide, the insulation displacement connectors are prone to problems. If you suspect the drive cable, the best solution is to replace it. If you plug and unplug your drives frequently, you are a prime candidate for cable problems. I strongly suggest you keep a spare drive cable on hand.

Loose Sockets

Most personal computers manufacturers use sockets to hold integrated circuits on their circuit boards. This makes for easier manufacturing and trouble-shooting, but it introduces a potential source of problems. Sockets rely on mechanical connections between the socket and individual integrated circuits. Dirt, excessive moisture, and expansion and contraction with changing temperatures can interfere with these mechanical connections.

Loose sockets are a common cause of hardware failure, especially of the computer. It's generally impossible to identify which socket is loose. The symptoms are simple—the computer won't work and all diagnostic tests fail. Treatment is equally simple, if you have access to the computer board(s).

First, turn off and unplug the computer. Now, support the board from beneath and press down firmly on each socketed integrated circuit. You should have one finger underneath each socket (on the bottom of the board) as you press the chip down into the socket. If you have a bus system, unplug the board before treating it. If you have a single-board system and you cannot get underneath the board, be extremely careful.

I once watched a technician destroy a single-board computer by failing to handle it properly. He had forgotten to turn off and unplug the computer. The board he was working on was mounted just above the bottom of the box, and he couldn't get his hand under the board to support it while he was pushing down on the chips. When he had worked out to the edge of the board, he pushed so hard that several pins on the underside of the board touched the bottom of the box and shorted. It was very exciting. Smoke poured out from below the board and the computer immediately went dead. I got a new board free of charge.

This is about as far as you can go with common sense trouble-shooting. If you can't find a solution to a problem using these procedures, chances are it's somewhere in the hardware and is going to require expert diagnosis. It may be time to call your dealer, your consultant, or your computer repair service.

Diagnosing Problems

If you wish to continue on your own in diagnosing problems, I've included two approaches that take you beyond the five rules. They entail more risk, so consider the consequences very carefully before you proceed.

Diagnostic Programs

Diagnostic programs are software routines that check out hardware components. The catch is that the specific component must be at least partially functional before it can be diagnosed. There are two types of diagnostics programs: those designed for or built into specific components and generic diagnostics programs.

Built-in Diagnostics

Some computers, printers, and terminals have built-in diagnostic and self-test routines. Some run automatically whenever the component is turned on; others are called up by the user as they are needed. Check out your equipment to see what kinds of diagnostic- and self-tests each component provides. Your operation manuals should describe how to use them.

My computer, for example, has a monitor program in ROM that can be used for simple operations. A very handy one is a memory-test routine that checks the main memory to make certain it is operating properly. It just takes a few seconds. I also have a sophisticated terminal with some simple built-in test routines that can be called up and executed in the offline mode. I can use these to check the baud rate and communications functions. My two-year-old printer has a self-test routine that prints out the full character set on command to verify mechanical functioning. It also sends audio signals to indicate basic problems.

Generic Diagnostics Programs

You can also buy generic diagnostics programs to check out each of your system components. I strongly recommend you get one of these programs, particularly if your components are short on built-in diagnostics. Again, however, there is a catch. Your system has to be working for you to be able to run the program. These programs are most useful for dealing with minor rather than acute problems. I find them to be very helpful in preventive maintenance, tune-ups, and routine checks. I suggest you build periodic diagnostic routines into your standard operational procedure.

The Board Swap

If you have a bus-based system (either a full bus system like the S-100 or an expansion bus system like the Apple or IBM PC) and you know someone who has an identical computer, you can swap boards to identify problems. Here's how you do it. For this discussion, I'll assume that the test is being done at the site of the problem system (the host system) and that it is being tested against a known good system.

You start by bringing the good computer to the site of the host computer. Mark the components so you can distinguish between the two systems. Be certain you mark all the individual boards or modules. Disconnect the host from its peripherals and reconnect them to the good computer. Now go through your start-up routine on the good computer. Make certain that all the peripherals work properly.

If you have problems with a host peripheral here, then it would seem that the component and not the computer is bad. Replace the peripheral with the equivalent component from the known good system and try again. If you can't get the system to run, stop, assemble the known good system, and make certain that it still works correctly. Go for outside help.

If you get the host peripherals to work with the good computer, then the problem is inside the host computer. Disconnect the known good computer and reconnect the host computer. Now start swapping computer boards between the two computers one by one. Go through the start-up routine after each swap until the host computer appears to work properly. Then swap computers. You should now have the known good computer connected to the system. It should have all but one of its own boards. If the known good computer fails to run, chances are that the board from the host computer is bad. Swap machines again and replicate the test just to be sure.

Once you have identified the bad board, you can send it in for repair. Some dealers and repair services will give you a loaner board to keep you going while yours is being repaired. You might also consider getting together with several people who have the same system and purchasing a set of back-up boards. This can be a very inexpensive form of insurance, given that the monthly rate for service contracts is 1.5 percent of the system retail price.

Board back-up is ideal for organizations that utilize multiple personal computers. One set of extra boards should be sufficient to back up as many as twenty personal computers.

Board swapping is a sensible and reliable way to check individual components and modules. One word of warning. Sometimes minute differences in timing will keep known good boards from working in another system. This isn't common, but it does happen and should be taken into consideration when swapping boards.

The Easter Egg Hunt

The day after I had completed the earlier part of this chapter I had a major system crash. My S-100 computer quit working. Totally. I went through the trouble-shooting procedures in this chapter and when I got to the board swap I discovered that all of the boards were damaged. I decided that perhaps this was a message that the trouble-shooting chapter was incomplete, so I began to repair the boards myself following the principles laid down in the rest of this chapter. Since I had already determined that all four boards were bad (CPU, memory, disk controller, and printer controller), I next had to determine what was bad on each board. I did this by conducting what is known in the trade as an Easter Egg Hunt. I started by getting a complete second system to serve as a reference (the known good system). Then I pursued the following objectives.

Verifying the Quality of the Boards

Procedure: I swapped my boards into the reference sys-
                tem, one by one, attempting to boot each time.

Result: The reference system consistently failed to
                boot.

Assessment: All four of my boards were bad.

Identifying Bad Components

Procedure: I replaced all the known good boards in the ref-
                erence system. Next, I took the CPU board and
                swapped one integrated circuit chip with the
                corresponding chip on the known good CPU
                board. I reinserted the known good CPU board
                in the reference system and attempted to boot.
                If the system booted, I marked the chip with a
                green stick-on label, swapped the chips back to
                their home boards, and moved on to the next
                chip. I went through this for each board, being
                careful to insert the chips properly. I marked
                each chip socket and chip to show how they
                should be connected. When I found a bad chip,
                I marked it with a small red label. It took an
                hour to do each board.

Result: When I had completed this procedure, I had
                tested each chip on each board. All chips
                marked with red labels were identified as sus-
                pect.

Assessment: I found ten bad chips on the CPU board and
                one bad chip on each of the other boards.

Replacing Bad Chips

Procedure: I wrote down the numbers of each of the bad
                chips. On my system the numbers are printed
                on the circuit boards, which made the job eas-
                ier. I called a number of electronics supply

houses until I found one that had the chips I needed, and went down to buy them.

This is easy where I am, but may be more difficult if you are not close to a major city. An alternative is to get a copy of a major personal computer magazine (e.g., *Byte*) with ads listing integrated circuits for sale. All the chips I needed were fairly common ones and were listed in the ads I saw. They were also fairly cheap—most cost about one dollar.

After obtaining the new chips, I replaced the bad ones on my boards. I marked the new chips as I inserted them so I could identify them later. Once the chips had been replaced, I conducted a board-by-board swap with the reference system to check out each board again.

Result: All four boards were returned to working order.

Assessment: I was lucky—I was able to restore all four boards by replacing the integrated circuits. My total investment in replacing the boards was eight hours of time and twenty dollars in parts. All these repairs took no more than a chip remover, some small stick-on labels, and some common sense. My problems might have been more severe—I could have damaged the components that are soldered to the board.

Checking the Power Supply

The first steps were sufficient to fix the computer modules, but I still didn't know if the motherboard they plug into and the power supply were all right. These were next on the test procedure. I used a multimeter for this test. You can buy a cheap one from Radio Shack for ten to twenty dollars. They are very handy and I recommend you get one.

Procedure: To test the motherboard and power supply, I first turned on my system without the boards inserted to see if the fan and the reset button worked. They did. Next, I checked the voltages where the power supply connects to the motherboard. I looked at the documentation that came with my computer to find out what the supply voltages were and to distinguish between the wires. Typical of all S-100 systems, mine has four wires—+8, +16, −16 and ground. (The numbers refer to DC voltage.) I set the multimeter to test for DC voltage and connected the leads to the meter (black to common or ground, and red to positive). To measure the positive voltages I turned on the power supply and pressed the metal tip of the black probe to the negative or ground wire and the metal tip of the red probe first to the +8 wire and then to the +16 wire. Both read well above the required voltage (actually they read +12 and +20). To read the negative voltage (−16) I reversed the leads—red to the ground wire, black to the −16 wire—again, OK.

I then had to make certain that the power was actually traveling down the bus. I started with the +8=volt supply. On an S-100 system, the ground is carried on two opposing pins—50 and 100 (they are at the extreme right side of the socket as you look down the motherboard toward the back). The +8 is carried at the opposite end of the socket—on pins 1 and 51. I put the black probe on pin 50 of one socket and systematically pressed the red probe against pins 1 and 51 of each socket on the board. (The trick is to be very careful where you put the red probe and not to short two adjacent pins together.)

Next, I checked the +16 supply, which is on pin 2. I had to be more careful here, because the +16 voltage is on the opposite side of the socket at pin 52 and I didn't want to short these two pins together. Finally I reversed the leads, pressing the red lead against a ground pin and using the black lead to check pin 52 on each socket to verify the −16 voltage.

Results: I found +8 volts available on every socket on pins 1 and 50. Unfortunately the +16 and −16 volts were only available on the last socket—the one closest to the power supply.

Assessment: There was a short circuit on the motherboard.

Repairing the Motherboard

Procedure: I turned off the computer and disconnected the power cord. Next, I removed the screws connecting the wires bringing the power from the power supply to the motherboard and the screws holding the motherboard to the bottom of the computer box and carefully turned the motherboard over. When I looked at the circuit lines carrying the +16 and −16 volts from the last to the next-to-the-last socket, I found that both had been burned through.

I took some fine, insulated wire (#28) and soldered one end to pin 2 on the back socket and the other end to pin 2 on the next to the back socket to "jump" the +16 voltage around the break in the circuit. I soldered a second jumper between pin 52 on the back socket and pin 52 on the next to the back socket to restore the −16 voltage supply. (I made certain that very little of the bare portion of the jumper wire was exposed to prevent an accidental short to an adjacent pin. I used high quality electronics solder and made a good connection. I checked that no solder had accidently dropped or spread onto the board to create a short circuit between pins.

Before replacing the motherboard, I tested it again to make certain that the patch was good. This time I did a power-off test. I set the multimeter to read resistance (R x 1) and check for a good connection by touching the two metal probes together. If you have a good connection, (no resistance in the circuit) the needle on the multimeter will swing all the way over to the right.

Next, I checked the +16 circuit by placing one probe on the connection between the +16 wire and the motherboard and the other successively on pin 2 of each socket. Since all these pins are connected, if the circuit is good, the meter should read zero resistance at each pin. After checking the +16 circuit, I checked the −16 one, placing one probe at the wire connection and the other on pin 52 of each circuit. This check does not have to be a very precise one. If the circuit is good, the needle on the meter will swing from its rest position on the left toward zero resistance at the right. Once you see the needle swing, you can move on to the next pin.

Result: An unbroken circuit was established between the supplying +16 wire and each pin 2 and between the −16 wire and each pin 52.

Assessment: The jumpers had restored the circuits.

Reinstalling and Testing the Motherboard

Next, I had to reinstall the motherboard—a tricky maneuver because all the sockets have to be lined up properly to be able to insert the circuit boards.

Procedure: I reinstalled the motherboard loosely, reattaching the power supply wires. I then inserted circuit boards at each end of the motherboard to line it up. When they were firmly in place, I tightened the screws holding down the motherboard. Next, I removed the two boards, leaving all sockets empty, reconnected the power cord, and turned on the box, looking for signs of smoke—none appeared. Next I went through a check of the power supply.

Result: There was +8 voltage available at every pin 1 and 50; +16 available at every pin 2, and −16 available at every pin 52.

Assessment: The jumpers worked—there was adequate power to every socket.

Putting the Computer Back Together

Now that I had functioning boards and mainframe, it was time to assemble and test them together.

Procedure: I reassembled the computer by inserting the boards into the appropriate sockets. (I always leave a blank socket between boards to maximize cooling.) Next, I reconnected the boards to the internal cables in the computer and connected the terminal, disk drive, and printer to the computer. I connected the computer to the power, turned everything on, and attempted to boot.

Result: The computer worked, after spending one hour checking the mainframe and using three inches of #28 insulated wire and one inch of solder.

Assessment: By following simple, common-sense procedures, I was able to identify the faults and repair my computer without assistance.

Total time:	seven hours
Equipment:	chip puller
	small flat-blade screwdriver
	small phillips screwdriver
	soldering iron
	small needlenose pliers
	wire cutters
	insulation stripper
	multimeter
Supplies:	thin insulated wire
	solder
	miscellaneous integrated circuits

cut ¶ 7 chpt. 22

It is possible to do a significant amount of repair work yourself, just by using common sense, a few simple tools, and a pragmatic procedure. If I had had my computer professionally repaired, it would have cost me several hundred dollars, and I would have been without my computer for several days. I saved both time and money by doing it myself. The tool kit that I have assembled cost me less than fifty dollars.

Remember that if you go beyond board swapping in diagnosing your computer, be very careful and consider all possibilities before you act. If I had inserted my newly repaired circuit boards without checking the mainframe and motherboard, I might have damaged the boards again. Don't take shortcuts. Stop and think before every step.

Disasters happen to everyone—even to those who allegedly know what they are doing. The key to surviving them is to not panic. Take a pragmatic, systematic approach: Identify, isolate, and solve the problem; then, reassemble the system. Do not act on assumptions; test them out. Good Luck!

SECTION VII

MOVING ON

23

A Personal Computer Renaissance

In *Design for Survival* Victor Papanek (one of my favorite designers) tells a story that he attributes to R. Buckminister Fuller:

> In the past two decades, two important papers were presented to learned societies, one on anthropology and the other on biology. And both researchers were working completely independently. But it happened by chance that I saw both papers. The biological one was looking into all the biological species that have become extinct. The anthropological one was looking into all the human tribes that have become extinct. Both researchers were trying to find a commonality of causes for extinction. Both of them found the same cause independently—extinction is a consequence of overspecialization. As you get more and more specialized, you inbreed specialization. It's organic. As you do, you outbreed general adaptability.
>
> So here we have the warning that specialization is a way to extinction, and our whole society is thus organized.

We live in a society of specialized professions. But when we specialize, we narrow our focus, become less self-reliant, and lose our ability to cope in society except in our own narrow area.

Why do we specialize? One answer is that specialization provides short-term security in an increasingly complex world. Another is that there is simply too much information available; we are overwhelmed by information. A third is that we have become lazy and complacent. Why favor long-term growth at the expense of short-term profits?

Why, indeed? Ask the steel industry, the shoe industry, the auto industry. Ask the domestic companies that used to build television sets. What do all these industries have in common? They didn't keep up with the technology. They got complacent and lazy. They failed to keep up with changes in the marketplace, maximizing short-term profits at the expense of survival. They specialized by default.

As a society, we have all specialized by default. In doing so, we have come dangerously close to losing the very quality that has been responsible for our success: The ability to confront and overcome an infinite variety of problems. Lazarus Long, the hero of Robert Heinlein's *Methuselah's Children* and *Time Enough for Love*, probably said it best:

> A human being should be able to change a diaper, plan an invasion, butcher a hog, conn a ship, design a building, write a sonnet, balance accounts, build a wall, set a bone, comfort the dying, take orders, give orders, cooperate, act alone, solve equations, analyze a new problem, pitch manure, program a computer, cook a tasty meal, fight efficiently, die gallantly. Specialization is for insects.

I am totally opposed to specialization. I grew up in a microculture that stressed survival skills. During the twenty years I spent in education and the more than fifteen years of organized observation of and research on organizations, I have seen the effects of specialization on our society and I want no part of them.

When I started this book I defined the computer as a general-purpose information tool, but it's really more than that. It's the tool by which we can reverse our headlong race toward specialization and dependence and find the path to generalization and self-reliance. It's the key to a new renaissance. As Marshall McLuhan said, "The medium *is* the message."

The medium of this new renaissance is the personal computer, and the message is "work smart." What does it mean to work smart?

Working smart is a philosophy of work that emphasizes general skills, prior preparation, and organization. It doesn't rely on personal computers, but it helps you to take full advantage of them.

Working smart involves using tools to amplify your skills and power. When you dig a ditch, you use a shovel to focus and extend the power of your arms and legs. Personal computers help you to focus and extend the power of your mind.

Working smart means drawing on past work to deal with present problems. Previous problems and solutions can be electronically filed and cross-indexed so relevant information can be identified quickly and applied to current problems.

Working smart means avoiding excessive specialization that narrows perspective and filters out new ideas. Specialization is a product of information overload. Personal computers are tools that help you to organize, manage and use information, rather than be overwhelmed by it.

Working smart means developing generic problem-solving skills—learning to break problems down into components, develop alternative solutions, and then pick the one most appropriate to the circumstances.

Working smart means stopping to plan before you act. Craftsmen who work in multiples (create multiple copies of a single item) often spend more time in setup than production. Setup is the creative part of the process—designing the production procedures and creating the special tools and jigs that support it. Setups are important in working with personal computers, too. You can develop software tools and procedures that will help you do repetitive tasks quickly and easily. A setup takes more time than producing a single item or performing a task one time, but once done, it allows you to perform successive iterations much more quickly.

Working smart means working iteratively—developing a basic solution for a problem and then tuning it to get the best possible solution. It means rewriting again and again, rather than being satisfied with a first draft. It means working through all possible permutations of assumptions in exploring models. It means exploring alternative solutions and picking the best one. Personal computers make the iterative approach viable.

Working smart does not mean getting replaced by machines. It does not mean abdicating responsibility to computers. It does not mean being programmed to serve a machine. It does mean using the personal computer to extend your own capabilities by allowing it to take over routine, time-consuming tasks, leaving you more time for thinking and creative work.

Above all, working smart means greater emphasis on individual responsibility and productivity. It means greater freedom to go your own way, unconstrained by the performance of others.

Why don't you start working smart? Get involved. Explore this new technology and find what it can do for you. Get a personal computer. Learn to use it as a tool to facilitate and improve your work and to make you more productive. Explore new ways to make it work for you. If you are willing to invest both the money and the intellectual effort, I'm sure you will reap a handsome return. You will also get a new perspective on yourself and on the standards by which you judge work quality.

Don't keep your experience to yourself. Spread the word. Share the vision. I'm inviting you to join a growing movement—a magnificent conspiracy. The term isn't mine, it was coined by Spider Robinson:

> I consider myself a member of a magnificent conspiracy, and I am attempting to recruit anyone I can—you, if you're not busy. There's a whole lot of us, more than you might think, and our stated purpose is to save the world.
>
> This requires a conspiracy to smuggle knowledge, to disseminate some simple truths that no one taught us in school. Basic keys to how the Universe works, which are not so much suppressed as buried in misinformation and derision.
>
> For instance: If there's one thing I absorbed through the skin from better than ninety percent of the teachers I ever had, virtually all adults who spoke with me, and all the entertainment media I was ever exposed to, if there's one thing my upbringing prepared me to accept as *certain*, it is the proposition that work of any kind is a drag. That the smart man avoids work, that the dummies are the ones who *work* for a living, that leisure is the proper pursuit of the clever and the powerful.
>
> Isn't that incredible? It took me better than a quarter century to learn, the hard way, that hard work at something you want to be doing is the most fun that you can have out of bed (and that working at something you don't want to be doing is a logical impossibility—that we are all self-employed). To learn that the dummies are the ones who think it possible to cheat the boss or the customers without cheating themselves; to learn that the smart man finds ways to make everything he does be work; to learn that "leisure" time is truly pleasurable (indeed tolerable) only to the extent that it is subcon-

scious grazing for information with which to infuse newer, better work.

They told me often, for instance, that "marriage is hard work"—but somehow the way they said it made that sound like a disadvantage.

How could I have been so basically misinformed for so many years about the way reality is put together? Why did I have to *deduce*, from three decades worth of memories (breaking my back helping my neighbor David get his hay in before the rain, dodging pitchforks in pitch darkness on top of a truckload of hay; literally writing myself into unconsciousness to meet the deadline for the *Stardance* novel; shoveling out my outhouse in the summertime), that the definition of "riches" is "abundant, meaningful work"?

Why didn't anybody *tell* me?

> —Spider Robinson, "TIDBIT: foreword to 'The Magnificent Conspiracy,'" *Antinomy*, New York, Dell Publishing Co., 1980.

Changing your attitude toward work will take effort. Niccolo Machiavelli acknowledged in *The Prince* that change never comes easily.

> We must bear in mind, then, that there is nothing more difficult and dangerous, or more doubtful of success, than an attempt to introduce a new order of things into any state. For the innovator has for enemies all those who derived advantages from the old order of things while those who expect to be benefited by the new institutions will be but lukewarm defenders. This difference arises in part from fear of their adversaries who were favored by the existing laws, and partly from the incredulity of men who have no faith in anything new that is not the result of well-established experience. Hence it is that, whenever the opponents of the new order of things have the opportunity to attack it, they will do so with the zeal of partisans, while the others defend it but feebly, so that it is dangerous to rely upon the latter.

Machiavelli's words are particularly appropriate because they are based on his experience of living during a period of dramatic change. The Renaissance provided the intellectual, cultural, and organizational foundations for today's society.

Now we are entering a neorenaissance. A new order of things is coming and it is going to make the violent social upheavals of Machiavelli's day seem like child's play. You can help control and direct that change, if you choose to get involved. Or you can sit passively and become more specialized through inaction, move closer and closer to cultural extinction. The choice is yours. I've made my choice—and I'm inviting you to join the personal computer renaissance. You can start by working smart.

A Personal Computer Glossary

(goes from pg 239 to 285 = 46 pgs.)

— A — *(28 words begin with A)*

abort: An orderly termination of a program, which returns control of the computer to the operator or to the operating system.

access time: The time required to read a specific word of information in memory storage.

accumulator: A special purpose register to the CPU that stores a word of information for arithmetic or logical operations performed by the ALU.

acknowledge: A control signal that indicates that information has been received. The acknowledge (ACK) signal is generally used as part of a handshake protocol.

acoustic coupler: A device that connects a computer (or terminal) to a telephone line by converting the computer's digital signals to the telephone's analog signals and vice versa.

A/D (Analog to Digital): Conversion of analog signals to digital ones to be processed by a computer.

(7) **address:** The position of a specific storage location in memory, indicated by a number.

(8) **address bus:** A set of communications channels that transmits main-memory locations between computer components. The size of the address bus determines the amount of main memory which the computer can control. Most 8-bit microprocessors, for example, use a 16-channel address bus, which allows them to control 2^{16} (65, 536 or 64K) locations by bytes. The newer 16-bit microprocessors have larger address buses and can control more main memory.

(9) **ALGOL (ALGOrithmic Language):** An early high-level language used by computer scientists, primarily for teaching. ALGOL was used on main frame computers and is best known as a forerunner of Pascal.

(10) **algorithm:** A solution to a specific problem, generally expressed as a series of steps.

(11) **alphanumeric:** An adjective denoting the ability to handle both alphabetical and numerical characters.

(12) **ALU (Arithmetic Logical Unit:** The portion of the CPU that performs arithmetical and logical operations. At a minimum, ALUs can add and subtract (negative addition), compare, and do AND and OR operations.

(13) **analog:** A signal having a continuous range of voltage or current values, in contrast to a digital signal, which has two discrete values, zero and one.

(14) **AND:** A logical operation requiring that two or more conditions be met before some specified action is taken. If A = 0 AND B = 0, THEN C = 1, ELSE C = 0. In this statement both A and B must equal 0 before C is set equal to 1; otherwise, C is set to 0.

(15) **ANSI:** American National Standards Institute.

(16) **APL (A Programming Language):** An interactive, high-level language used for algorithmic programming. APL has a unique set of operators and requires a special keyboard.

(17) **append:** To attach to the end of something (as in to append the new information to the end of the file.)

(18) **AppleDOS:** The disk operating systems used with Apple microcomputers.

(19) **architecture:** Pertaining to the electronic design and structure of a particular system component.

(20) **array:** A multidimensional table used to organize and store a large number of information "chunks," accessed by the array name and address. This two-dimensional array is named Table 1:

	A	B	C	D
1	1	2	3	4
2	5	6	7	8
3	9	10	11	12
4	13	14	15	16

To reference information, you use the name of the array and the row and column address—TABLE 1 (A,2) = 5; TABLE 1 (D,4) = 12.

Arrays are used for most numerical processing, financial spreadsheet programs, and relational data base.

(21) **ASCII (American Standard Code for Information Interchange):** The most common code for representing characters. The ASCII code uses seven bits to represent a total of 128 characters.

(22) **ASCII keyboard:** A keyboard which generates all 128 ASCII characters.

(23) **ASR (Automatic Send Receive):** A description of a computer terminal that can record information and transmit it automatically or automatically receive information. This requires some type of information storage device.

(24) **assemble:** The process of creating a machine code file (file of binary commands that can be directly executed by the computer) from an assembly language file.

(25) **assembler:** A computer software program that converts assembly language (a machine-specific, low-level, mnemonic language used for writing very efficient code) into machine language (binary object code).

(26) **assembly language:** A machine-specific, low-level, mnemonic language used to write extremely efficient software programs. Assembly language code has a one-to-one correspondence to machine instructions. Each assembly language phrase represents a specific machine code instruction.

A (cont) — *B - starts*

See assembler above. Here are a couple of lines of assembly language code for the Z80.

    100 MVI A,83
    101 OUT 84

asynchronous: A term used to describe devices which do not operate synchronously in relation to some common timing device.

auto answer: A term indicating that a modem (a device that connects a terminal or computer to telephone lines) can automatically establish a connection with another station when called.

B - (29 words) with B)

background program: A multi-tasking program that is executed when the CPU is not busy with a priority task.

backplane: A series of parallel bus sockets used to connect computer system modules together. (Also called a motherboard.)

back-up: The process of making a duplicate copy of a program, data file or a physical storage medium (such as a floppy disk) to protect against loss or damage.

bank: A logical unit of memory. With most 8-bit computers, memory can be banked in units of 16k bytes.

bank select: A method of memory management in which the CPU can be directed to address specific banks of main memory. This provides a means of expanding a machine's memory beyond the capacity of the address bus. (The CPU can be directed to one bank of memory, then switched to another.)

BASIC (Beginners All purpose Symbolic Instruction Code): A popular language initially developed for teaching, but widely used for general microcomputer applications because it is very easy to learn and use. Because there are a number of BASIC dialects, compatibility between different dialects is often a problem. Many hardware manufacturers, such as Apple and North Star, provide versions of BASIC which are specific to their machine. The most generic BASICs are those designed for execution on the CP/M operating system. These include BASIC80, CBASIC, and SBASIC.

BASIC80 (also MBASIC): An interpreted BASIC from Microsoft. MicroSoft also sells a compiler which can be used to translate a program written in BASIC80 for more efficient execution.

— B (cont)

⑧ **batch processing:** A noninteractive method of computing. Once a program has been submitted for execution, the user cannot submit additional input.

⑨ **baud:** A measure of the speed at which information is transmitted. Although baud actually refers to the number of signal pulses per second, it is popularly interpreted as the number of bits per second.

⑩ **Baudot:** A 5-bit code used to represent characters, primarily for teletype and telex transmission.

⑪ **BDOS (Basic Disk Operating System):** The portion of the CP/M operating system that handles disk operations.

⑫ **benchmark program:** A standardized program used to compare the execution speed of different computers.

⑬ **berg jumper:** A nonmechanical switch that provides options on circuit boards. The jumper consists of a set of pins that can be shorted together using metal lined plastic caps to select different options. The advantage to this approach is that the settings are easier to see and more reliable than with mechanical switches.

⑭ **bidirectional printing:** A technique in which consecutive lines are printed in alternate directions (left to right, then right to left) to reduce carriage-return delays. Bidirectional printing is about 30 percent faster than unidirectional printing.

⑮ **binary:** A method of representing numbers as the sum of powers of two using a sequence of zeros and ones. For example:

$$1110 \text{ (binary)} = 1(2^3) + 1(2^2) + 1(2^1) + 0(2^0) = 8+4+2+0$$
$$= 14 \text{ (decimal)}$$

⑯ **BIOS (Basic Input Output System):** The portion of the CP/M operating system that interfaces with specific hardware. The BIOS is written by the system manufacturer (rather than Digital Research) and provides the interface to the computer, the disk drives, the terminal, the printer, and other peripherals.

⑰ **bit:** A binary digit, the basic unit of information storage for digital computers. A bit has one of two values, zero or one.

⑱ **block:** The logical unit of information storage on external memory devices (such as disks or tapes). Information is moved between the computer and the memory device in blocks. Blocks are generally composed of smaller units called records, which are, in turn, composed of words.

(19) **boot:** The process of starting up a computer using a bootstrap loader program. CP/M, MS-DOS and some other operating systems define two levels of start up. A cold boot loads the complete operating system, together with the formatting data and disk directories in the disk drives. A warm boot loads only a portion of the operating system, together with the formatting information and disk directories.

(20) **bootstrap:** A small set of instructions that load the operating system into a computer when you first start it up. Normally stored in ROM, the bootstrap is immediately accessible when the computer is powered on. It clears memory and establishes connection with input/output devices.

(21) **BPI (Bits Per Inch):** A measure of the density at which information is stored on magnetic media such as tapes and disks.

(22) **branch:** A computer programming instruction that transfers program control to some other part of the program (rather than the next sequential instruction).

(23) **bubble memory:** A semiconductor memory technology that stores information in tiny magnetic bubbles. Bubble memory has a slower access speed than RAM and has been touted as a candidate for bridging the memory gap between high speed RAM and the lower speed disk memory devices. Bubble memory is being used primarily in applications (mostly military electronics) for which mechanical memory (rotating-disk) devices are impractical.

(24) **buffer:** An intermediate, temporary storage device or location.

(25) **bug:** An error in a computer program. Debugging is the art of identifying and eliminating errors from computer programs.

(26) **bundling:** Selling the hardware and software components together at a single price.

(27) **bus:** A series of communication channels used to pass signals with common functions. Computers use buses to pass data, storage or memory addresses, control signals, and power between components.

Although all computers have a bus structure of some kind, the term bus is generally used to refer to computers designed so components can be plugged into the bus via sockets. Some systems (like the S-100 bus) put all the components on socketed cards which are plugged into the bus. The S-100 bus has 100 communication lines and will support a variety of microprocessors, including the 8080, Z80, 8085, 8088, 8086, and 68000. Other bus systems include the STD bus and the MULTI bus which are used for industrial computers.

Another design approach puts most of the computer components on a single board, but also provides sockets so additional components can be plugged into the bus to expand the capabilities on the basic computer. This approach, called a pseudobus, is used by Apple computers and the IBM PC.

28. **bus extender:** A device that plugs into a bus socket and provides additional sockets, much like the three-plug adapter expands the electrical socket in your home.

29. **byte:** A group of eight bits. Also, the unit of storage required to represent a character in computer memory.

C (10 words that begin with C)

1. **C:** A high level computer language developed at Bell Labs and used to write the Unix operating system, which is highly regarded by programmers and is one of the operating system contenders for the 16-bit microprocessor.

2. **cache:** A high-speed memory buffer located either between the CPU and RAM or between RAM and the external memory devices. The cache improves CPU performance by providing faster access to information than is possible when that information is stored in external memory.

3. **CAD (Computer Aided Design):** An applications area for computers in which the computer is used to support the design process. CAD generally requires specialized, dedicated computer hardware and software and sophisticated peripherals to both provide input to the design process and to reproduce the designs themselves.

4. **CAI (Computer Aided Instruction):** An applications area for computers in which the computer runs software designed to teach specific skills or information. The software is designed to be highly interactive and to utilize feedback and responses from the user to determine how the instructional material should be presented.

5. **CAM (Computer Aided Manufacturing):** An applications area for computers in which the computer is used to control the operation of one or more machines.

capacitor: An electronic component which stores an electrical charge.

card: A printed circuit board or module that has been designed to plug into a bus socket.

card cage: A rack used to hold cards that have been plugged into a series of sockets (called a backplane or a motherboard) to access a bus.

carriage: The moving portion of a typewriter or printer. A typewriter carriage includes the platen and all paper movement parts. A lever on the left side of a manual typewriter advances the paper and returns the carriage so the next line can by typed. The IBM Selectric typewriter altered the design by fixing the paper control mechanism and transferring the printing element to the moving carriage. Microcomputer character printers always have the printing mechanism on a moving carriage.

Carriage Return (CR): The typewriter or terminal key that initiates the movement of the carriage back to the left-hand margin. This operation may also be designated by a return key.

cartridge: A plastic package containing two reels of ¼ inch or ½ inch magnetic tape, which is used as a sequential data-storage device. Cartridge tapes are generally used to back-up hard- or Winchester-disk drives.

cassette: A tape storage device similar to a cartridge, but using ⅛ inch tape. Used for storage of both audio and digital signals. Cassette storage devices were popular in the early days of microcomputers (before floppy-disk drives became economical) and are still found on some low-priced personal computer and hobby machines. Digital quality cassettes (rather than audio cassettes) should be used when storing digital information.

catalog: A list of the files stored on one or more units of a particular storage medium (such as a floppy disk).

CBASIC: A popular intermediate-compiler BASIC dialect for 8080, 8085, and Z80 machines. CBASIC is a very popular business-program language because it offers high-precision numerical variables. The current version is known as CBASIC2. CBASIC was developed by Compiler Systems, which has since been purchased by Digital Research.

CCD (Charge Coupled Device): A semiconductor memory technology that stores information by moving changes through a series of sequential capacitors, much like a bucket brigade moves water from one pail to another. Slower than RAM, CCD is a candidate for bridging the memory gap between RAM and external memory devices. CCDs are also used to store visual images in television cameras.

CCP (Command Control Processor): The part of the CP/M operating system that interfaces with the user.

chaining: A technique for executing programs that exceed the memory capacity of the computer. The program is broken into a series of smaller programs (to fit in the computer), which are executed sequentially.

channel: An electronic connection that passes signals between two elements, much as a wire transmits currents.

character: A letter, digit, or other graphic symbol. A character in computerese refers to the information that can be stored in one byte.

character generator: A ROM-based device that converts character codes into dot patterns to represent the character. Used in terminals and dot-matrix printers.

character set: The repertoire of characters which computer, printer, or terminal uses for displaying or processing information.

character string: A vector (one-dimensional array) of characters.

chip: A small rectangular piece of silicon that has been processed to form an integrated circuit. These circuits are mounted into a plastic body with metal legs that connect the silicon chip into a more complex unit. The term is also used to refer to these packaged integrated circuits.

chunk: A conceptual unit of information.

circuit board: A thin plastic board into which are mounted individual electronic components—diodes, resistors, capacitors, and integrated circuits—and connective paths so that the components can perform specific functions. A conductive surface is deposited on the plastic board and then selectively removed, except for the channels connecting the components.

clock: A circuit that transmits a regular timing pulse to trigger and synchronize the execution of instructions in the computer. Microprocessor clocks typically operate at one to eight Mhz (millions of cycles per second).

C (cont)

(27) **clock frequency or rate:** The measure of the speed at which the clock emits pulses. The clock frequency is given in Mhz (megahertz—millions of cycles per second.)

(28) **close:** A programming file operation. When a file is closed, it passes from program control and is usually stored on an external memory device.

(29) **CMOS (Complementary Metallic Oxide Semiconductor):** A type of integrated circuit characterized by very low power consumption. CMOS devices are frequently used in portable devices and for constant memory applications in which power is provided by a battery when the system is turned off.

(30) **coaxial cable:** A type of transmission wire composed of a central conductor covered with insulation, a second conductor wrapped around the insulation, and a final layer of external insulation and shield.

(31) **COBOL (COmmon Business Oriented Language):** A high-level language available for microcomputers, using English-like structure designed for self-documentation. COBOL rose to popularity as a business language for use on mainframe computers.

(32) **code:** A set of programming instructions or statement. Lines of code (individual program statements) are often used to measure programmer productivity. Also used to refer to a set of symbolic information representations. ASCII codes, for example, provide representations of 128 different characters using seven bits of information.

(33) **CODEC (COder-DECoder):** A chip used in analog-digital signal translation.

(34) **cold boot:** A bootstrap loading sequence in which the entire operating system is loaded into the computer.

(35) **command:** An instruction to the computer.

(36) **comment:** A nonfunctional programming statement for documentation. These statements appear in the program listings, but are ignored by interpreters and compilers when the program is executed.

(37) **compiler:** A translation program that converts a program written in a high-level language into machine code so it can be executed by the computer. At their most elementary level, computers can only understand instructions in binary machine code (a series of 0s and 1s). All programs

and data must be converted to binary form before they can be processed by the computer. A compiler translates an entire program and saves it for later executions. The program is originally written in high-level language called source code. Compilers translate source code either directly to machine code or to an intermediate level "object code" which is saved and run through a second compiler at execution time to translate from the object to machine code. Any time a change is made to a compiled program, the change must be made in the source code and the source code recompiled to create new machine code. Because they translate the entire program, compilers are very efficient.

computer: A general purpose information processing device consisting of a central processing unit (CPU), memory, input and output (I/O) facilities, a power supply, and a cabinet.

computer system: A total information-processing package consisting of a computer and other necessary support peripherals such as external memory, terminals, and printers (called the hardware) together with the programs (software) required to direct the hardware to do useful work.

concatenate: A process of sequentially joining independent files to form a single file.

concurrent CP/M-86: See CP/M.

conditional: A type of computer language operator that makes a logical test to direct the flow of program control using parameters generated during program execution.

conditional statement: A class of computer programming instructions that are executed only when certain specific requirements are met. For example: IF A > B then C = 0 will set C equal to 0 only when A is greater than B.

console: The primary device for entering commands to a computer. Mainframes and minicomputers generally have dedicated control consoles. Some microcomputers also have dedicated consoles but most modern machines use general-purpose terminals as consoles.

constant: A fixed value in a program. For example, the mathematical term pi is a constant. It always has the value of 3.1416.

continuous form: Unseparated sheets of paper used on computer printers. The paper comes in a continuous format with sprocket holes on each side so that the paper is accurately positioned as it moves through the printer. Perforations across the paper allow it to be separated into individual sheets after printing. Some continuous forms also have perforations along the sides so the sprocket holes can be removed, leaving a relatively smooth edge on all four sides. Continuous forms come in a variety of sizes which are determined by the size of the individual sheet after it has been separated from the form. Some companies now offer a high-grade continuous form with a very smooth edge. The detached sheets are similar to quality stationary. Continuous-form printing is faster than single-sheet printing. Continuous-form paper is packaged fan-folded flat along the perforations.

Control (CTRL): A command key found on the left side in the middle row of the terminal keyboard, used to differentiate between commands and text. It is used like a shift key, in conjunction with other keys. It is represented on the screen as ^. The ASCII code contains codes for control character combinations, just like it does for capital letters. Thus, ASCII has different codes for C (shift c) and ^c (control c).

control bus: A bus that transmits control signals between various computer modules. Some of the typical control signals include the clock pulses, and commands to read, write, interrupt, and acknowledge.

control character: A keyboard character used as a specific command to a particular program.

controller: A computer module that provides an interface between the CPU and a peripheral device such as a floppy disk drive. Many controllers contain dedicated microprocessors that actually relieve the CPU of much of the work involved in managing the peripheral. Floppy disk controllers, for example, are highly complex and contain a microprocessor chip that is considerably more sophisticated and expensive than the typical CPU.

control unit: A portion of the CPU responsible for fetching and decoding instructions. It contains a register for storing instructions and a program counter for keeping track of them. It manages the control bus and generates the control signals sent along the bus.

conversational: An adjective describing programs or systems that engage the user in a two-way dialogue. The conversation may originate with the program or system (in which case the user responds to queries or prompts) or it may originate with the user (in which case the system responds to user statements). In the latter case, the computer provides feedback for each statement after it has been interpreted and executed.

cpypw7/1984   e (cont.)

(53) **core:** A small magnetic washer used to store information. Prior to the invention of semiconductor RAM, cores were the primary high-speed memory devices. Each core stores one bit of information by being magnetized in one direction or the other. They are strung together in a three-dimensional grid and packaged very closely together. The primary advantage to cores is that they don't lose their memory when the machine is turned off. The disadvantages are that they are very expensive to produce and operate, and they take up more space than RAM to store data. As a result, semiconductor RAM has placed cores for most memory applications.

(54) **counter:** A hardware or software register that incrementally keeps track of operations. It adds "one" to its contents every time an operation takes place.

(55) **CP/M (Control Program for Microcomputers):** A popular operating system for microcomputers developed by Gary Kildall in the early 1970s. Originally designed for the eight-bit family (8080, Z 80, 8085) it has been modified to run on the 8086 and 68000 16-bit microprocessors. (The eight-bit version is now known as CP/M-80, the 16-bit versions as CP/M-86 and CP/M-68.) CP/M is distributed by Digital Research, a company founded by Kildall. Concurrent CP/M-86 is a multi-tasking version of CP/M-86, which will simultaneously run several applications programs. The latest version of Concurrent CP/M-86 will run much of the software designed to run under PC-DOS (the standard operating system for the IBM-PC) and its generic twin, MS-DOS.

(56) **CP/M Users Group (CPMUG):** A non-profit organization which distributes public domain software to run on the CP/M operating system. The software is distributed in volumes on floppy disks. There are currently more than 90 volumes of software available. For more information write:

The CP/M Users Group
1651 Third Avenue
New York, NY 10028

(57) **CP/NET (Control Program for Networks):** A program developed by Digital Research to connect a number of independent microcomputers running CP/M (or MP/M, the multi-user version) in a local network.

(58) **CPS (Characters Per Second):** A measure of printer speed that predates the use of hertz to measure cycles per second.

(59) **CPU (Command Processing Unit):** The central intelligence of the computer that processes and executes program instructions. The CPU in-

cludes an Arithmetic Logic Unit (ALU), a controller, and a series of registers that store data, instructions, and addresses and serve as an instruction counter.

crash: A jargon term for system failure. The system failure may be a result of hardware (equipment problems) or software errors.

CRC (Cyclic Redundancy Check): A method of checking data transmission or storage errors using an algorithm based on a binary polynomial. The algorithm is used to calculate a variable from the stored data that is then compared against a cyclic redundancy check character. If the two values match, the data are assumed to be good. Many disk test utility programs provide cyclic redundancy checks.

CROMIX: A machine-specific, Unix-like operating system developed by Cromemco.

cross-assembler: An assembler program which runs on one computer to produce machine code for a different computer.

crosstalk: Interference between two signals.

CRT (Cathode Ray Tube): The electron tube used to display pictures on a television set and to display characters and pictures on a computer terminal. CRT usually refers to any VDT (Video Display Terminal).

crystal: A quartz object that emits piezoelectric vibrations. Used to control frequencies and to generate timing signals for electronic watches and computers.

CTS (Clear To Send): A control line in the EIA standard RS-232C interface used for asynchronous serial data transmission. A clear-to-send signal indicates that data may be transmitted over the interface.

current loop: A simple two-line circuit for transmitting data between two devices. Characters are sent along one line through control of the current flow, while the other line serves as a return. Current loops are used with low speed printers and teletypes.

cursor: A special character used to denote position on a video display. During input, the cursor indicates where the next character will be placed on the screen. On some terminals the cursor is moved by the computer to indicate some particular piece of information on the screen. The cursor is usually represented on the screen as an underline character or a solid block, and may appear either as a steady character or flash on and off. Terminal and program designers have a number of different techniques for user control of cursors. Some use special keys marked by arrows (up, down, left, right). Others use control codes generated by the CTRL key in combination with regular character keys. Other devices include a joystick, touchpad (moving a finger across the pad moves the cursor), and a mouse—a device with vertical and horizontal wheels that is merely moved across a hard surface in the direction one wishes the cursor to go.

cycle time: The time required for a component (such as memory) to complete its internal operation in response to a single instruction and be available for use again.

D/A (Digital to Analog): A term used to describe the conversion of information from digital coding (the way it is stored in the computer) to analog signals to be used to control external devices such as speakers and motors.

daisy wheel printer: An impact printer in which characters are stored on the ends of spokes of a rimless wheel (hence its name). The wheel is attached to a carriage that moves across the paper. When the carriage moves to the position where a character is to appear, the wheel is rotated until the appropriate character is in position. A solenoid hammer then strikes the petal and forces the character against a ribbon, transferring an impression to the paper. Daisy wheel printers produce fully formed characters (as opposed to characters made up of a series of dots) and are used for high-grade, letter-quality printing.

data: Organized information. In computers, the term refers to the information that is processed by (and produced by) programs. Thus, computers generally deal with two types of information: programs (which tell the computer what to do) and data (the input to and output from the programs).

data acquisition: The operation of acquiring information using external sensors such as thermocouples. Such data are generally collected in analog form and converted to digital form by an A/D converter for the computer.

data base: A systematically structured collection of data organized for easy input, access, retrieval, and update. Data bases can contain either numerical data or information coded as text.

— D —(cont)

data bus: A set of communication channels that moves data between computer elements. Data is carried in parallel, so the bus requires as many lines as there are bits in the word. Thus a typical eight-bit computer requires a data bus with eight lines.

data file: A collection of information stored in external memory under a unique name so it can be accessed by the computer.

data set: A modem device that converts digital signals from a computer to analog signals to be transmitted over standard telephone lines.

data tablet: An input device used to digitize hand-drawn information for computer input. The data tablet consists of a sensitized surface and a stylus. When the stylus is moved across the surface of the tablet, sensors continuously translate the stylus position into digital coordinates which are sent to the computer.

data transfer rate: A measure of the speed at which information can be moved between two devices (such as a disk drive and memory). Data transfer rates are usually measured in bits per second (BPS).

DBMS (Data Base Management System): A program that creates, maintains, and uses data bases. Some of the DBMS routines define how the data is entered and stored in the machine. Others implement the access and updating of the data. Still other routines generate reports to describe the contents of the data base.

DDT (Dynamic Debugging Tool): A program used to write, analyze, and correct programs written in assembly language.

debugger: A program for identifying and correcting software problems. Sophisticated debuggers allow one to trace the flow of information and control as the program is being executed. DDT is a well known debugger.

default parameter or value: An option provided by the program or system in lieu of user input. Programs typically offer users a set of values and request that one be selected. If the user does not select a value, the program resorts to the default value.

descender: That portion of a character that drops below the base line. The characters *g,j, p,g,* and *y* all have descenders. Some character generators do not have sufficient resolution to permit descenders, and are, thus, difficult to read.

(16) **diagnostics:** A set of software utility programs used to identify hardware and media problems.

(17) **digital:** The quality of having discrete states (as opposed to continuous states). The basic digital element is the bit, which has one of two states, on or off, or values, zero or one.

(18) **DIP (Dual Inline Package):** A standard method of packaging integrated circuits. A DIP has a plastic body on which the integrated circuit is located and two rows of pins or legs which carry signals to and from the circuit. The width of the DIP is determined by the size of the integrated circuit.

(19) **DIP switches:** A set of small binary switches packaged on a DIP. DIP switches provide users with options on the circuit board that do not require its physical modification.

(20) **directory:** The table of contents for a file system that includes a description of the name, location, and size of each of the files so they can be easily accessed.

(21) **disk:** A magnetic-mechanical data-storage medium, which is round and flat (like a phonograph record) and coated with oxide that can be selectively magnetized to record data. The disk rotates on a drive past a magnetized read/write head that records information on the disk or reads from it. Data is stored on disks in concentric circles called tracks (like the grooves on a phonograph record). The read/write head moves across the surface of the disk to access different tracks.

(22) **disk controller:** A specialized computer module that connects a disk data-storage system to a CPU. *Command Processing Unit.)*

(23) **diskette:** See **floppy disk.**

(24) **disk file:** A collection of related information stored under a single name on a disk storage system.

(25) **display:** An output device that temporarily shows visual information from a computer by using some form of electronic medium such as a cathode ray tube.

(26) **DMA (Direct Memory Access):** A method of high-speed data transfer between memory and some peripheral device without going through the CPU. Some displays use DMA techniques to directly display the contents of a portion of the computer memory.

(27) **DMAC (Direct Memory Access Controller):** A chip used to automate DMA transfers.

(28) **documentation:** A document which describes and explains how to use a piece of hardware or software. One of the long-standing major complaints of personal computer users, documentation is often a key factor in determining how quickly you learn to use a new component or program. Hardware documentation should include: a description of what the device is and how it works, a schematic diagram, and instructions on how to install, use, and troubleshoot the component. Software documentation should include: a description of what the program is and how it works, installation instructions, a tutorial to help you use the program, a ''crib sheet'' which provides an abbreviated explanation of all the program commands, and troubleshooting instructions. All documentation should provide a means of getting help—either a telephone number or an address.

(29) **Do-loop:** A high-level programming-language construct that directs the computer to continue executing a particular set of instructions until a specified condition is met.

(30) **DOS (Disk Operating System):** A computer program designed for use with disk drive-based systems, which manages the operation of the entire system. It controls the operation of the computer itself, communication with peripherals, and the management of disk files.

(31) **dot matrix printer:** A printer that forms its characters with a set of dots organized in a matrix. They are activated by a character generator. The quality of the characters is dependent on the size and number of the dots, the dot patterns, and the number of passes the print head makes across the paper. Characters can be formed by an impact process, heat, or static discharge. Impact printers (the most common) form characters using thin wires that are struck by solenoid and bound forward, hitting a ribbon and transferring the dot image to paper.

(32) **double density:** Descriptive of technique for increasing the number of characters stored on magnetic media.

(33) **double-density:** Records 6816 bits per inch, while single-density records at 3408 bits per inch.

(34) **double precision:** Descriptive of a technique for increasing the accuracy of stored number by using twice as many bits to represent numbers. Double precision is particularly important with scientific notation, in

which numbers are represented as decimal fractions and the powers of ten to which the fractions must be raised. For example, 123 might be represented as 1.23×10^2 or 1.23×100. The reason double precision is important is that the size of the decimal fraction in scientific notation is limited by the word size. If the number is very large, the last digits are dropped and accuracy is lost. For example, 1,234,567,890 might be represented by 1.234567×10^9 which would actually be 1,234,567,000. This is an error of 0.008 percent. It may not seem like much, but in some cases any error is unacceptable. Doubling the precision allows more numbers to the right of the decimal point and reduces error.

double-sided disk: A disk on which data can be stored on both surfaces.

down time: Computerese for time lost due to hardware or software failure.

DRAM (Dynamic Random-Access Memory): A RAM design that stores information as charges on metallic oxide capacitors. It provides very dense, low-cost memory, but must be constantly refreshed, as the charge "leaks" from the circuit. DRAM is currently used to measure the state of the art in integrated circuit design. In the past, DRAM were considered more error prone than the more costly and less dense static RAM. Currently DRAM is used for most microcomputer internal memory.

drive: An electromechanical device that spins and "plays" disks in response to computer signals. Loaded by solenoids, its read/write head moves across the surface of the disk to either read or write from it.

drum: A magnetically-coated electromechanical data-storage device that rotates at high speed past a series of read/write heads. Used for high-speed external memory in mainframe computers, the drum is faster than a disk drive. It is uncommon in microcomputers.

DSR (Data Set Ready): A control line on the EIA Standard RS-232 asynchronous serial interface that signals when the receiving device is ready to receive data.

DTR (Data Terminal Ready): A control line on the EIA Standard RS-232 interface that signals when a data terminal is ready to send information.

dual intensity: A video display technique that provides two levels of illumination for displayed characters.

(43) **dual processors:** A term used to describe computer systems with two CPU's. Dual processors are used to increase performance by dedicating one processor to perform specific operations, to allow the user to run multiple operating systems (for example, using both a 6502 and a Z80 processor so you can use both Apple DOS and CP/M), and to increase reliability by using one processor to "backup" the operation of the other.

(44) **dumb terminal:** A low-cost data terminal that lacks internal buffers and sophisticated editing and display features. The "low end" of CRT terminals.

(45) **dummy variable:** An interim storage value or location. The traditional meaning refers to a value that is inserted into an equation or computation for test purposes and is later replaced by the actual variable. The term also refers to an intermediate storage location for the holding of information that is not desired as an answer, but is needed to perform other calculations.

(46) **dump:** An operation in which the contents of one memory level are transferred to another. The contents of CPU registers can be dumped to main memory. The contents of main memory can be dumped to a disk, a display, or a printer.

(47) **duplex:** A term referring to techniques for providing communications channels between two devices. Full duplex allows both units to simultaneously send and receive information. Half duplex allows only one unit to send information at a time.

(48) **dynamic memory allocation:** A memory management technique in which limited main memory is shared among multiple tasks or users using some operating system algorithm.

E (16 words)

(1) **EBCDIC (Extended Binary Coded Decimal Interchange Code):** The eight-bit character code used by IBM. It represents the same characters as ASCII, but the two codes are not compatible. ASCII is currently the predominant character code for microcomputers.

(2) **editor:** A computer program designed for inputting and modifying text strings and inputing and program code. A text editor is a specialized editor program designed to facilitate the production of documents (as opposed to programs or data files).

~~*- E (cont)*~~

EIA RS-232C (Electronic Industries Association Recommended Standard 232, revision C): A standard interface for serial asynchronous communications. This is not as "standard" as it seems. The standard refers to the type of connector (DB-25, a trapezoidal connector with a top row of 13 pins and a bottom row of 12 pins), the fact that information is transmitted serially—one bit at a time—over the line, and the minimum voltages required to make a signal.

emulation: Real-time simulation. An emulator program makes computer A mimic the instruction set and performance of computer B so that computer A can execute programs designed for computer B. For example, a program which tells a 16-bit 68000 computer to emulate the operation of a Z80 so it can run Z80 software.

END: A program statement signifying end of program.

EOF: (End of File): A special indicator used to mark the end of a file.

EPROM (Erasable Programmable Read Only Memory): A form of Read Only Memory (ROM) that can be erased and reused. Some EPROM can be erased by sending a specific electronic signal. Others are erased by exposing the integrated circuit, which rests under a quartz window, to hard ultraviolet light. A special device loads programs into the EPROM.

ESC (ESCape): A control character on a standard ASCII keyboard. It is used by itself or in combination with other characters to send specific messages to the CPU. The ASCII character set contains a number of escape codes.

Ethernet: A local-network system designed by Xerox.

even parity: A character coding technique to check errors. Since the ASCII code requires only seven bits, the eighth bit (the parity bit) is used as a check bit. It is used to make certain that the sum of all eight bits in the byte is even (hence, even parity). If the sum of the seven character bits is even, the eighth bit remains zero; but if the sum is off, the eighth bit is changed to one so the total sum will be even. When the byte of information is received, the parity bit (eighth bit) is checked. If it is zero, but the sum of the remaining seven bits is odd (or vice versa), a parity error is called.

execute: In computerese, the action by a computer of performing an instruction or a series of instructions (a program).

- E - (cont) F starts

(12) **execution time:** The time required for a computer to execute a single instruction. This includes the time required to fetch the instruction, decode it, and execute it.

(13) **exerciser:** A system or program designed to test for malfunctions in either main or external memory.

(14) **expansion board (bus extender):** A modified motherboard that is connected into the main board to increase the number of components or modules that can be added to a computer.

(15) **expansion bus:** A pseudobus that allows functions to be added to a single board computer. It represents a design compromise between a fully modular approach and a single-board computer.

(16) **external memory:** A generic term that refers to any memory device not directly addressed by the CPU (not part of main memory). External memory devices include cache memories, disk drives, and cassette drives.

F - (24 words)

(1) **fan-fold paper:** Continuous form paper, joined along and folded on perforations in a zigzag fashion so it can be easily fed into a printer.

(2) **FCB (File Control Block):** A 33-byte portion of main memory used by CP/M to hold information describing a file currently in use.

(3) **fetch:** The process of reading the contents of a specific memory location into the CPU.

(4) **field:** A set of adjacent words used to record a single chunk of information.

(5) **FIFO (First In, First Out):** A computer algorithm in which information is processed in the order it is received.

(6) **file:** An organized collection of related information stored under a single name.

(7) **file-management system:** A program or collection of programs designed to facilitate the creation and management of files.

(8) **firmware:** A software program stored in ROM and immediately accessible by the computer.

⑨ **fixed-head disk:** A high-speed disk-storage system that has one read/write head for each track.

⑩ **flip flop:** An electronic binary switch circuit. A flip flop is fixed in a specific state (zero or one) until reset or power is removed from the circuits. Flip flops are used in static memory circuits. They are considered highly reliable. Unlike dynamic memories they do not require constant refreshment to retain their state.

⑪ **flippy:** A double sided floppy disk designed for use in a single-sided drive. To access the second side, the disk is removed, flipped over, and reinserted into the drive. When the disk is flipped, tracks on the flip side are recorded in the opposite direction from those on the initial side. This means that flippies cannot be read by double-sided drives.

⑫ **floating point:** A method of representing numbers in the computer using scientific notation in which a number is entered as the product of a decimal fraction times a power of ten. This provides more rapid mathematical processing and the use of numbers greater than the absolute value that can be stored in the computer word size. For example, an eight-bit word can store values from 0 to 256 (2^8). If you want to store negative numbers as well, then one of the eight bits must be used to indicate sign, leaving seven bits for a maximum value of 128 (2^7). With floating point notation, a portion of the word is used to store the decimal fraction, the rest to store the exponent of 10. For example, 70,000 might be stored as 7.0 and 4 (7×10^4).

⑬ **floating-point package:** A software package designed to support floating-point mathematics. Often used with a special processor designed for this function.

⑭ **floating-point processor:** A CPU designed for floating-point arithmetic. These processors are often offered as add-on equipment for microcomputers dedicated to extensive numerical work.

⑮ **floppy disk (diskette):** A disk-storage medium made of mylar that is so thin that the disk must be permanently bound inside a rigid cardboard jacket so it can be rotated without deforming. Floppy disks rotate quite slowly (300 to 360 rpm). The read/write head actually rests on the magnetic surface during reading and writing. Because this contact scrapes magnetic oxide from the surface of the disk, the inside of the envelope is lined with a special napped material that continuously cleans the surface. The disks come in three sizes: maxi (8 inches in diameter), mini (5.25 inches in diameter) and micro (3 or 3.5 inches in diameter). The floppy disk is the most popular external-storage medium for microcomputers.

flow chart: A symbolic representation of a program using special shapes to indicate different types of operations. It is used to diagram the flow of control while writing a program.

foreground program: The primary program is a multitasking environment—the task that has the highest execution priority.

format: The process of organizing information for display or storage. Also refers to the process of preparing soft-sectored diskettes for use on a system.

formatter: A program used to prepare disks or tapes for storage and establishing specifications, data directories, and file control marks.

Forth: A complex, low-level language that uses what is called threaded code and reverse Polish notation for writing formulas. A threaded language is one in which each statement is made up of calls to other statements. Forth starts with a set of basic operators (called words), which are combined to form more complex words. The language is completely dynamic and expands as new words are defined. This is an extremely powerful language, but is considered fairly difficult to learn.

FORTRAN (FORmula TRANslator): One of the first general-purpose high-level languages, popular in scientific computing. It is a compiler language and is most common on mainframes and minis, although it is available for micros.

front-end processor: The processor dedicated to user or process interface and interaction. It reduces the main processor's interface burden so it can work more efficiently. Some timesharing applications use smart or intelligent terminals to serve as front-end processors to provide continuity of support to the user.

front panel: A microcomputer console that facilitates direct interaction with the computer. A front panel provides switches and displays, which allow you to write data to specific storage locations and to read data stored in main memory.

full duplex: A communication mode in which data can be transmitted and received simultaneously.

gap: The space buffer between two records or sections of information stored on magnetic memory used to adjust for format fluctuations caused by variations in drive speed.

GIGO (Garbage In, Garbage Out): A computerese phrase that recognizes that output quality is determined by input quality.

glitch: A power or signal fluctuation that can cause great harm to the delicate electronic circuits and magnetic media of a microcomputer.

global variable: A program variable that can be used throughout a software program, as opposed to a local variable that can be used only within the program segment within which it is defined.

GOTO or GO TO: A branching command used in high-level languages.

GPIB (General Purpose Interface Bus): The common name used for the IEEE standard 488-1975 interface bus, which is used to connect analog devices to a computer.

GT (Greater Than): A logical expression in programming. Sometimes represented by >.

H (Hexadecimal): Suffix used to indicate hexadecimal or base-sixteen numbers.

half-duplex: A communications mode in which data can be sent in only one direction at a time.

handshaking: A data communications synchronization technique used to transfer data between two devices. A minimum of three channels are needed to handshake: one for ground, one for the data signal, and one for the handshake signal. The receiver toggles (turns on) the ready-to-receive signal (DTR), which tells the transmitter to send data. When the receiver cannot take any more data, perhaps because its buffer is full, it turns off the signal and the transmitter stops sending data.

hard copy: Computerese for computer output printed on paper.

hard disk: A disk using a rigid substratum covered with magnetic oxide. Being rigid, it can rotate at high speed without deforming, allowing faster data-transfer rates than floppy disks. Although there are different types of hard disks, the term usually refers to Winchester disk. Winchester drives take one or more fixed, rigid disks and have read/write heads that float a few microns (millionths of an inch) above the magnetic surface, suspended by a moving curtain of air created by the motion of the disks. The disks and read/write heads are sealed into a dust-protected capsule. Compared to floppies, hard disks have a greater storage capacity since the rigidity of the disc surface allows for a larger number of tracks per inch. The term "Winchester" comes from the fact that the first hard drive to use this technology was the IBM 3030—3030 being a popular caliber for Winchester lever action repeating rifles. Although hard disks are more expensive than floppies, Winchesters offer cheaper storage on a cost-per-bit basis. There are two drawbacks to this technology. One is that a sudden power failure can damage the disk surface if the heads drop before the disk stops rotating (called a head crash). The other is that because the disks are permanently fixed, they must be backed up with another storage device—usually cartridge tapes or floppies.

hard sectoring: A formatting technique for disks in which each track is permanently divided into segments which are mechanically indexed by holes in the disk.

hardware: The physical components of a computer system, including the computer, the external memory system, the terminal, and the printer.

hardwired: The provision of a function using hardware rather than software.

head: A magnetic device that reads or writes information on magnetic media. Sometimes referred to as a read/write head.

head crash: A system malfunction in which the heads of a hard disk drop onto the surface of the disk while it is still moving, resulting in surface damage. Generally caused by a sudden loss of power.

Hertz: A measure of frequency, named after Heinrich Hertz. One Hertz (Hz) represents one frequency change per second.

hexadecimal: A numbering system with sixteen as its base. Very common in microcomputers because it can record a single byte with just two symbols. The characters used are zero through nine, and A,B,C,D,E, and F. FF = 255 in decimal or 11111111 in binary.

H (cont)   ·I· starts

(13) **hierarchical:** A technique for organizing information in vertical levels. Each element is identified in terms of its relationship to one or more elements in the level above it.

(14) **high-level language:** A programming language that is relatively understandable (English-like) and has a powerful instruction set. High-level languages must be translated onto machine language for execution using either a compiler or an interpreter.

(15) **high resolution:** A term used to describe video display systems and printers that can display images in great detail and with a high degree of accuracy.

(16) **housekeeping:** Computerese for administrative functions required for efficient system operation and task-oriented processing.

I (26 words)

(1) **IC:** See integrated circuit.

(2) **IEEE (Institute of Electrical and Electronic Engineers):** A professional organization which plays a major role in determining electronic standards.

(3) **IEEE 488 (Institute of Electrical and Electronic Engineers standard 488):** A standard for general-purpose interfaces used to connect analog devices to a computer.

(4) **IEEE 696:** The standard S-100 bus.

(5) **IF, THEN, ELSE:** A series of logical commands used in high-level languages to control program flow depending on the truth of a logical statement. IF the statement is true, the THEN statement is executed. If not, the ELSE statement is executed.

(6) **impact printer:** A printer that generates characters by striking a ribbon with a character impression against the paper.

(7) **index hole:** A hole in a floppy disk that indicates the beginning of the first sector or a track. The index hole is read by a light that shines through the hole in the disk envelope onto a light sensitive cell. The light is blocked by the rotating disk until the index hole appears and lets the light fall on the cell, triggering the drive control circuits.

initialize: The act of setting up conditions for basic operations. In programming, one initializes storage locations by setting them equal to some value (usually zero). Initialization programs format floppy disks so that the operating system can write information on them.

ink jet printer: A printer that creates characters by squirting tiny droplets of ink against paper. Deflection magnets controlled by the printer direct the drops of ink to the proper position on the page.

input: Computerese for information that controls a program or is processed by the program.

instruction: The basic element of a computer program. The instruction is a command to the computer to perform a specific operation. The program is an organized set of instructions designed to be performed in a particular sequence.

instruction set: The basic set of operations (instructions) that are performed by the CPU. Typical instruction sets for eight-bit microcomputers contain 70 to 150 instructions. They are performed internally by registers located in the CPU.

integer math: Mathematics performed on integer (whole) numbers only and producing integer numbers as results.

integrated circuit (IC): A circuit fabricated on a single chip of silicon.

intelligent terminal: A terminal that contains a computer, memory, and some form of external memory and is capable of independent operation. Some computers come packaged as an intelligent terminal, including the North Star Advantage and the Zenith Z-89/90. The intelligent terminal packages all the basic system elements except the printer into a single unit.

interactive: The quality of real-time, two-way dialogue. Used to describe a computer system designed to carry on such dialogue with the user.

interface: The hardware and/or software required to connect a peripheral to a computer system or to connect one computer system to another.

intermediate compiler: A software program that translates a high-level computer language into an intermediate-level code and saves it. At exe-

"internet"

cution time, the intermediate-level code is processed through a second compiler and converted into machine code.

interpreter: A software program for translating high-level language programs one statement at a time into machine language. Unlike a compiler, an interpreter allows immediate modification of a program.

interpretive language: A conversational computer language which uses an interpreter and can provide feedback on each statement as it is made.

interrupt: A signal sent from an I/O device or peripheral requesting immediate service. This causes the CPU to save what it is working on, handle the problem, and return to what it was working on before the interruption.

input/output (I/O): Used to describe devices or communication channels used to move information into and out of the computer.

I/O bound: A condition that exists when the speed at which a computer can execute a program is determined by the speed with which data can be moved into and out of the main memory.

I/O port: A data channel that connects peripherals to a computer for data input and/or output.

I/O processor: A special purpose computer dedicated to managing input and output operations.

iterative: Characterized by repetition.

JCL (Job Control Language): A special language that provides the operating system with the information needed to execute a specific program.

job: Computerese for a package consisting of a program and data that have been submitted to the computer for execution.

joystick: A device used to control two-dimensional movement; sometimes used as a cursor control mechanism for video display terminals.

jump: A programming instruction that stops the sequential processing of instructions and transfers control to some other point in the program. Typically, jumps are used in conjunction with some type of conditional statement. (See IF, THEN, ELSE.)

(5) **jumper selectable:** Descriptive of a condition of being able to select a function by physically connecting or disconnecting jumper wires on a circuit board.

(6) **justify:** To align text against a right and left margin.

K   (9 words)

(1) **K:** Abbreviation for kilo or thousands. In computer context, K refers to 2^{10} or 1,024. Thus a 65K-byte memory actually contains 65,536 bytes.

(2) **Kansas City standard:** A standard interface for connecting cassette recording devices to computers using the EIA RS-232 standard interface.

(3) **KB (Kilobyte):** 1,024 bytes.

(4) **keyboard:** A device for coding and inputting data through the depression of keys that are connected to a code generator. A computer keyboard provides the capability to enter, at the least, all standard characters (all twenty-six letter in upper and lower case, all digits, and punctuation marks), and encode any ASCII character.

(5) **keypad:** A special-purpose keyboard, generally having a limited number of keys. For example, a numeric key pad will generally have keys for 0–9, .,-, and "enter."

(6) **keyword:** A high information word or operative word in a title, abstract, or file, which can be used out of context to help describe, label, and access the data. Keywords are used to index documents and to search for specific locations in text.

(7) **kilobaud:** One thousand bits per second.

(8) **kludge:** Computerese for an inelegant or sloppy solution to a problem.

(9) **KSR (Keyboard Send Receive):** A description of an I/O device with a keyboard that can send and receive data.

L   (22 words)

(1) **Large Scale Integration:** See LSI.

(2) **LE (Less Than or Equal To):** A programming conditional, also represented by $<=$.

(3) **learning curve:** A performance profile that shows improvement as a function of time.

L (cont)

LED (Light Emitting Diode): An electronic device that permits current to flow in only one direction and emits light when the current flows through it. LEDs are frequently used in computers as feedback devices.

letter quality: Adjective used to describe printers that produce the kind of high-quality hard copy that you would want to have in an important business letter. Letter-quality printers generally use impact technology to create fully formed characters using die-cast type. Some extremely sophisticated dot matrix printers and ink jet printers can produce hard copy approaching, but not equal to, letter quality.

LF (line feed): A control key found on many terminals which is used to advance on line, much like the "index" key on an IBM selectric typewriter. Although the line feed key appears on many terminals, its function has been almost totally replaced by the RETURN key.

LIFO (Last In, First Out): A processing rule that specifies the last information received is the first information processed.

light pen: A stylus that sends signals to the computer by movement against a CRT screen. When placed against the screen, the stylus is tracked by the computer. Light pens are used to input data to the computer and to select options from data menus presented on the CRT screen.

line printer: A high-speed device that prints an entire line of text at one time. (One line is usually 80 or 132 characters long.)

line surge: A sharp fluctuation in the AC power-line voltage that can damage computer circuits and magnetic media.

LISP (LISt Processing language): A high-level interpretive language that is used extensively in artificial intelligence work.

listing: A hard (printed) copy of a computer program.

load: The process of moving data or program instructions into position for execution. Also used for the operation of moving a disk-drive read/write head in position to move data to or from the disk.

loader: An operating-system utility program that moves a program to be executed into main memory.

local network: A communications system that passes information between independent computers and peripherals located within close geo-

L (cont)   *M - starts*

graphic proximity. The advantage to networking is that it allows computer independence, yet permits machines to communicate with each other and share expensive peripherals.

logical expression: A program statement that includes a logical test. The results of that text determine the direction of the program flow.

logical operator: A programming language construct which tests the truth of relational propositions and uses the results of the test to direct program flow. A typical test might look like this:

    IF(A.EQ.B) THEN C = 1, ELSE C = 0

This tests to see if the value stored as variable A is equal (EQ) to the value stored as variable B. If the two values are equal, then the statement is true and C is set equal to 1. If the statement is false, then C is set equal to 0. The logical operator in this statement is ''EQ''.

loop: A set of instructions that are designed to be repeated.

loop counter: A register that counts the number of times a loop is executed.

LPM (Lines Per Minute): A measure of printer speed.

LSI (Large Scale Integration): A semiconductor fabrication technique in which thousands of circuits are placed on a single silicon chip.

LT (Less Than): A program conditional also represented by <.

M (47 words)

machine language: A binary-code language, of instructions and data that can be directly executed by a CPU.

machine readable: An adjective indicating that the information has been properly coded so that it can be read directly into a computer.

magnetic media: A material used to store information by magnetizing particles in an oxide coating. Magnetic media include cards (used by the IBM magnetic-card Selectric typewriter), tapes, disks, hard disks, and drums.

magnetic tape: A sequential data-storage medium used for large files and archives.

mainframe: A large computer that requires a conditioned environment, manipulates large words (thirty-two or sixty-four bits), accommodates multiple users, and is extremely expensive. Also sometimes used to refer to the cabinet in which a modular computer system is fitted. A modular mainframe consists of a power supply and a motherboard into which the computer modules are plugged.

main memory: The internal memory of the computer; generally RAM. The amount of main memory a computer can control is limited by the size of the address bus. Main memory is usually volatile—its contents are lost when the computer is shut down.

main program: A term used to indicate the set of instructions having primary control in a complex, modular computer program. Such a program is composed of a series of independent modules called subroutines and subprograms. The main program is responsible for overall program control and for calling the respective subprograms as they are required. This programming approach is very popular in high-level, modular languages such as BASIC and FORTRAN.

mass storage: External, slower memory that is not directly controlled by the CPU, but by a controller. Typical mass storage devices for microcomputers include floppy disks, hard disks, and cassette tapes.

MB (Megabyte): A measure of storage capacity in one million bytes; 1,024 × 1.024 bytes or total of 1,048,576 bytes.

mechanical memory: A term used to describe external memory devices such as disks and drums, which depend on mechanical movement, in contrast to RAM and ROM, which are solid state and have no moving parts.

media: The material on which information is stored. Computer media include paper (punch cards and tape), magnetic materials (cards, tapes, floppy disks, hard disks), and optical materials (very new, but providing the greatest storage density).

memory: A storage area for binary data and programs.

memory bank: A block of memory locations with contiguous addresses.

memory management: A system for allocating memory in a multiprogram environment using a combination of hardware and software.

(15) **memory map:** A symbolic representation of how memory is allocated.

(16) **memory-mapped I/O:** An I/O technique in which peripheral devices are addressed as memory locations.

(17) **memory-mapped video:** A display technique in which the display shows the contents of a portion of main memory. Memory-mapped displays are very fast and are quite useful for graphics because a portion of the display can be changed by altering the contents of the appropriate memory locations. The disadvantage is that the display uses memory that could otherwise be used for program execution.

(18) **menu:** A set of options displayed by a program to a user.

(19) **merge:** The process of combining two ordered files of information so as to preserve the initial ordering of the resulting file.

(20) **Mhz (MegaHertz):** A measure in terms of a million cycles per second.

(21) **micro:** Prefix meaning one millionth part of. Also used to mean very small.

(22) **microcomputer:** A small computer using a microprocessor (CPU on a single chip), which does not require special environmental conditioning. A microcomputer includes several components including a power supply, the CPU, memory, and I/O interfaces.

(23) **microjustification:** A printing technique that provides justified right margins by inserting small spaces between words and characters. This results in a more even appearance than simply inserting spaces between words.

(24) **micron:** One millionth of a meter.

(25) **microprocessor:** A complete CPU on a single chip. It includes an Arithmetic Logic Unit (ALU), an Control Unit (CU), and internal registers to support the ALU and CU.

(26) **microsecond:** A millionth of a second, abbreviated uS or uSec.

(27) **milli:** Prefix meaning one thousandth part of.

(28) **millisecond:** A thousandth of a second, abbreviated ms or msec.

(29) **minidisk:** A 5.25 inch floppy disk.

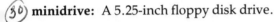

(30) **minidrive:** A 5.25-inch floppy disk drive.

(31) **mnemonic:** A symbolic representation of a command in assembly language or operations code.

(32) **MODEM (MOdulator-DEModulator):** An interface device between a computer or terminal and a telephone line. It contains A/D and D/A converters that translate digital into analog signals.

(33) **module:** A function-specific computer circuit board.

(34) **monitor:** A low-level operating program that can be used to control operation of the CPU at a very basic level. Also a high-resolution display screen.

(35) **MOS (Metallic Oxide Semiconductor):** A semiconductor fabrication technique used to create high-density integrated circuits.

(36) **motherboard:** A series of parallel bus sockets into which computer system modules are plugged.

(37) **mouse:** A small device that fits in the palm of the hand and is used to control cursor movement on a screen. Wheels on the bottom of the mouse sense motion in two dimensions. The rotation of the wheels is converted into signals that are transmitted to the terminal or computer by a cable connecting the two units. Sometimes the mouse also has push buttons that can be used to send additional signals.

(38) **moving-head disk drive:** A type of drive in which a single read/write head moves across the surface of the disk to access individual tracks. This is the most common form of disk drive for microcomputers.

(39) **MP/M (Multi-programming control Program for Microprocessors):** A multiprogramming version of the Digital Research CP/M operating system. It allows multiple programs to be run simultaneously on a computer.

(40) **MD-DOS:** A disk operating system for the INTEL 8088 and 8086 microprocessors, currently (mid-1983) the dominant 16-bit operating system. MS-DOS was first developed by Seattle Microcomputer, which sold it to MicroSoft, which sells it in generic form. PC-DOS, the operating system that comes with the IBM PC, was developed by MicroSoft and is very similar to MS-DOS, although PC-DOS has some machine-specific code which makes it difficult to run PC-DOS programs on some MS-DOS systems.

MS-DOS is considered more user friendly, but somewhat less powerful than CP/M. It is rapidly becoming the de facto standard operating system for 16-bit computers, due to the incredible market success of the IBM PC. The latest version of MS-DOS (2.0) incorporates the hierarchical file directory structure of UNIX.

MTBF (Mean Time Between Failures): A reliability measure indicating the average length of time between system failures.

MTTR (Mean Time to Repair): A performance measure indicating the average time required to repair a device.

MULTI bus: A microcomputer bus system used primarily for high-level industrial control. It supports a variety of CPUs.

multiplex: Descriptive of a technique for sending multiple signals over a single communications channel.

multiprogramming: Another name for time sharing—a computer management technique that allows the computer to deal with several programs simultaneously.

multitasking: An adjective used to describe operating systems that allow the user to execute more than one program at once.

multiuser: An adjective used to describe operating systems that permit several users to simultaneously share access to a single computer.

N (10 words)

NAND (Not AND): A logical operator.

nano: Prefix indicating one billionth part of.

nanosecond: A billionth of a second.

NE (Not Equal to): A conditional operator, also shown as < >.

network: A set of communication channels that connects a set of computers. Also, a technique for organizing information in a data base.

nibble: Four bits, or half a byte.

noise: Random signals or interference.

nonvolatile: Descriptive of a type of memory that does not lose its information when power is removed. ROM is a nonvolatile memory; RAM is a volatile memory.

NOT: The logical negative operator.

number crunching: Arithmetic-intensive processing.

OASIS: A time-sharing operating system for eight-bit (8080, Z 80, 8085) and sixteen-bit (8086) microcomputers from Phase One Systems.

object code: The output of a compiler (or translator). The object code may be either directly executed by the CPU when it is loaded (absolute object code) or it may require an additional translation before it can be loaded and executed.

OCR (Optical Character Recognition): A process for automatically converting text on paper into machine-readable code by "reading" the characters with an optical scanning device and sending the appropriate computer code for each character.

odd parity: A data transmission checking scheme in which the eighth bit in a byte is used to ensure that the sum of all the bits in the byte is odd so it can be checked for errors.

OEM (Original Equipment Manufacturer): A computer company which buys hardware and software components from other manufacturers and combines them into complete systems.

off line: Disconnected from the computer.

operating system: The software program that organizes and manages the hardware resources of the system. The operating system handles communication with peripherals, job scheduling, interaction with the user, file handling, and other tasks.

operation: A discrete machine action, such as carrying out an instruction or a statement.

operation code: The assembly-language verbs that tell the machine what to do.

Operator: The principal user of a computer system. Also used to refer to arithmetic and logical software functions which perform actions on variables under program control.

optimization: Tuning hardware or software to maximize performance.

output: The information the computer produces as a result of executing a program.

overlay: A memory management technique in which the same memory locations are shared by different program routines.

over strike: An operation in which an impact printer strikes each character twice to give a darker impression.

P   (32 words)

packet switching network: A network of computers that communicate by moving blocks of information of a fixed length to specific recipients.

parallel: Descriptive of a data transmission technique that moves all the bits in a word simultaneously.

parameter: A definable characteristic of a system or program.

parity: An error-detecting technique that uses the eighth bit in a word to make the sum of all eight bits consistently odd or even. The ASCII code prescribes seven bits to designate 128 characters and the eighth bit may be used for a parity check.

parity bit: A check bit used with some data transmission devices to verify that a byte has been properly transmitted. The ASCII character code uses seven bits to represent 128 characters. The eighth bit can be used as a parity bit. The parity bit becomes either zero or one depending on the type of parity check (even or odd) so that the sum of all eight bits is either even or odd.

parity error: A condition that exists when the sum of all eight bits in a transmitted byte does not agree with the parity check. If the parity is even and the sum of the eight bits is odd, then there is a parity error, indicating that one of the eight bits has been improperly transmitted.

Pascal: A high-level structured programming language developed by Nicholas Wirth and named for the French mathematician Blaise Pascal.

password: A unique sequence of characters used to identify authorized users of a system and protect the system or specific files from unauthorized access.

. P- (cont)

(9) **patch:** A piece of program code temporarily inserted into a program for debugging or modification.

(10) **PC-DOS:** The primary disk operating system for the IBM personal computer. (See MS-DOS.)

(11) **peek:** A program operation which allows one to look at the contents of a particular memory location.

(12) **peripheral:** A device that is connected to and dependent on a computer for operation.

(13) **personal computer:** Generally refers to a personal, low cost, portable computer designed for a variety of applications.

(14) **pico:** One thousandth of a billionth.

(15) **pixel:** The smallest single element of a visual display, usually a single dot.

(16) **PL/I (Programming Language One):** A high-level multipurpose language developed for both numerical and text applications. Available for microcomputers.

(17) **PL/M (Programming Language for Microprocessors):** A high-level language for microprocessors; a dialect of PL/I.

(18) **pointer:** A CPU register that stores memory addresses.

(19) **poke:** A program operation that loads a specified value into a specific memory location. (Can be used to modify a memory mapped display.)

(20) **polling:** A peripheral management technique in which the status of peripherals is sequentially checked.

(21) **port:** A channel used to connect an I/O device to a computer.

(22) **power down:** An orderly shut down of a computer and its peripherals to prevent damage.

(23) **power supply:** The device that converts alternating-current line voltage into the direct-current voltages needed by the computer.

(24) **power up:** The orderly start up of a computer and its peripherals after a power down.

(25) **procedure:** A logically distinct set of program commands that the computer calls up by a single name. Similar to a subroutine or a subprogram.

(26) **program:** A sequence of instructions that cause the computer to perform useful work. Programs can be written in machine language (binary code that can be directly executed), assembly language (symbolic code) that must be translated in machine code before execution, and high-level languages that must be interpreted or compiled before execution.

(27) **program counter:** A CPU register that stores the address of the next instruction to be fetched from memory for computer execution. The program counter is usually incremented automatically each time an instruction is fetched.

(28) **PROM (Programmed Read Only Memory):** A ROM that is programmed after manufacture. Some PROMs can be reprogrammed with special hardware or software.

(29) **proportionate spacing:** A printing technique in which the amount of space allowed each character is determined by the width of the character.

(30) **protected field:** A display technique in which specific areas of the display cannot be modified by the user at the keyboard.

(31) **protocol:** A set of rules governing the exchange of information.

(32) **pseudobus:** A computer design that places all the connective devices of the computer components on a single board, but provides sockets for plugging modules into the bus to add additional capabilities. Apple computers and the IBM PC use a pseudobus design.

Q — (4 words)

(1) **Q-bus:** A bus structure used by Digital Equipment Corporation for its LSI-11 computers.

(2) **quad density:** Describes the storage density of a disk medium. Quad density is a technique used with 5.25 inch disks to provide four times the storage of single-density disks.

(3) **queue:** A data structure used to organize tasks according to a first in, first out rule.

(4) **QWERTY:** The traditional typewriter keyboard layout, represented by the six upper left letters.

— R — *(handwritten: — R — starts)*   *(handwritten: (18 words))*

rack mountable: Adjective for equipment designed to be installed in a standard nineteen inch metal cabinet called a rack.

RAM (Random Access Memory): Read/write memory.

record: A set of data elements (or fields) that share a common bond. A record is the basic element of a file or a data base.

refresh: The operation required to maintain information stored in dynamic memory (DRAM).

register: One word of very fast memory that is used for temporary storage of information while the CPU performs operations on it.

relational: An organizational technique for developing a data base as a large matrix.

return: A high-level programming instruction used to return program control from a subroutine to the main program. Also used as an abbreviation for "carriage return."

reverse Polish notation: A structured method for writing mathematical formulas in the order in which they are to be evaluated.

reverse video: A visual display technique that reverses the usual display so that dark characters are shown against a light background.

rollover: The quality of a keyboard that allows one to type very rapidly, hitting keys almost simultaneously, yet still coding the characters in the order struck.

ROM (Read Only Memory): A nonvolatile memory storage device that can be written to only once and thereafter cannot be changed. Used to store machine-specific instructions such as a monitor program.

RPG (Report Program Generator): A business oriented programming language designed for use with data bases.

RS-232C: The Electronic Industries Association Recommended Standard for serial communications.

run: Execution of a program on a computer.

(handwritten: S — (37 words))

SBASIC: A version of BASIC that features structured organization somewhat similar to that of Pascal.

scientific notation: A method of writing numbers as a decimal fraction and the power of ten by which the fraction must be multiplied to put the decimal in the proper place: 123,000 is written as 1.23 5 (1.23 × 10^5 or 1.23 × 100,000.

screen: The visual display element of a terminal or monitor. Also used to designate the contents of the screen.

screen generator: A program used to define visual displays that are to be presented on a video display terminal (VDT).

scrolling: A technique of using the CRT screen as a window to a file by moving the window horizontally or vertically to look at files larger than the screen. A typical screen holds 1,920 characters—24 lines of 80 characters each.

sector: A contiguous portion of a disk track. Tracks are divided into sectors to make storage more efficient and rapid. (If the tracks were not sectored, data could be stored only in one-track units.)

seek time: The time required to move a disk read/write head to a specific track.

semiconductor: A material that can be manipulated to control the passage of electrons through it.

sequential access: A storage method that allows one to access individual elements only in a fixed order. Magnetic tape is a sequential access medium.

sequential file: A file in which elements are stored sequentially.

serial: A data transmission technique in which elements (such as bits) are transmitted sequentially, one at a time.

single-board computer: A computer design that places the corrective device of all the computer elements—CPU, main memory, and I/O controllers—on a single printed circuit board.

single precision: A method of storing numbers which uses one word. One word of storage limits the size of numbers that can accurately be represented, causing small errors to creep in during calculations involving large numbers. For greater accuracy, numbers can be stored using two words of storage as double precision numbers. (See scientific notation)

single sided: A disk storage technique in which data is stored on only one side of the disk.

single step: To execute a program one instruction at a time. Used to debug programs.

Smalltalk: A teaching language and software system developed at the Xerox Palo Research Center. Very visually oriented and easy to use. Designed to make the computer more of a creative medium.

smart terminal: A terminal that has a buffer so it can store a certain amount of information and some processing capabilities. Smart terminals are particularly useful for timesharing because they can provide a high-quality interface to the user for limited periods of time.

smoke test: A checkout given to new equipment. You turn it on and see if smoke appears (indicating overheating)—a source of endless frustration to builders of electronic kits.

SNOBOL (StriNg Oriented symBOlic Language): A high level programming language used for the manipulation of character strings and text.

soft sectored: A disk format in which the sectoring is done under software control.

software: Instructions and programs that tell the hardware what to do.

software package: An off-the-shelf computer program designed to fill a specific need such as word processing or financial analysis. The package usually contains not only the program (usually stored on a floppy disk), but also documentation, and (by extension) support and upgrades.

solenoid: A device that converts electrical current into linear motion. The solenoid consists of a hollow coil and a magnetized core. The electrical current magnetizes the coil and forces it to move in a linear direction.

S-100: A common microcomputer bus that uses one hundred channels. Standardized as IEEE 696, the S-100 bus was designed primarily for the 8080 CPU, but also supports the Z 80, 8085, and some 16-bit CPUs.

source code: A program written in a high-level language before it has been run through a compiler or interpreter.

spikes: Sharp, temporary fluctuations in signals or voltage.

S (Conts)

(27) **split screen:** A display technique in which the screen is divided into two or more windows to display independent data.

(28) **SPOOL (Simultaneous Peripheral Operations On-Line):** A programming technique that allows the computer to maintain I/O operations with a slow peripheral device (such as a printer) while simultaneously executing another program.

(29) **statement:** A syntactically complete instruction in a high-level language.

(30) **static memory (SRAM):** A metallic-oxide semiconductor memory technology that uses a flip-flop storage circuit to store information. Simpler and more stable than dynamic RAM, it does not lose its charge until power is removed and does not require refresh. Flip-flop circuits are about four times as complex as the capacitor circuits used in dynamic RAM, and SRAM as a rule costs about twice as much as the same amount of DRAM.

(31) **STD bus:** A low-level industrial process control bus developed by Pro-Log. The STD bus can be used with a variety of 8-bit microprocessors. It uses small (4.5 by 6.5 inch) modules that are generally function-specific.

(32) **stepper motor:** A motor that rotates a fixed amount each time it receives a signal pulse. Stepper motors are often used to move the read/write heads on floppy-disk drives.

(33) **string:** An ordered sequence of data elements, such as characters.

(34) **structured language:** A high-level computer language that stresses a logical flow of control and extensive self-documentation. Pascal, ALGOL, and C are popular structured languages.

(35) **structured programming:** A set of programming techniques designed to improve the readability and reliability of programs by increasing programmer discipline.

(36) **subroutine:** A discrete program segment, identified by a name that is called by the main program when needed.

(37) **swapping:** A memory-management technique in which the program and data code are nominally stored on external memory, transferred into main memory when needed, and then transferred back out to external memory when they are no longer needed.

T (starts)

- T - (15 words)

teletype: A slow peripheral device for electronic data transfer. Not particularly amenable to microcomputers because of its slow speed.

terminal: A peripheral device through which a user can communicate with a computer. It has a keyboard to input data and some type of display for showing input messages and responses from the machine.

thimble printer: A variation of the daisy wheel printer in which the spokes are bent up at an angle of approximately seventy-five degrees and two characters are placed on each spoke. The thimble rotates in a horizontal plane and the carriage moves up and down to position the proper character in front of the solenoid. The thimble holds 128 characters.

threaded: A style of programming in which instructions are composed of calls to other simpler instructions.

throughput: A measure of the execution efficiency of the system. Generally given in instructions executed per second.

timesharing: A computer management technique in which the CPU is simultaneously shared by a number of users, each receiving the computer's total attention for a small portion of the available time.

toggle: A switch that initiates a program action. Also the act of initiating the action by manipulating the switch.

touchpad: A flat pad used to control cursor movement. The pad senses the movement of a finger on the pad and sends signals that move the cursor in the direction the finger moves.

TPA (Transparent Program Area): The portion of main memory that CP/M leaves for use by programs.

TPI (Tracks Per Inch): A measure of the storage density of disks.

track: A concentric circle on a disk or drum surface on which data is stored. An 8" floppy disk has 77 tracks. A 5.25 inch floppy diskette may have 35, 40, 80 or 100 tracks, depending on the drive manufacturer.

tractor feed: A method of moving continuous-form, fan-fold paper through a printer. The tractor has sprocket wheels that engage perforations in the edge of the paper and move the paper past the print mechanism.

A PERSONAL COMPUTER GLOSSARY

transaction: A dialogue between a computer and a user for a specific purpose.

TRS DOS: The family of disk operating systems used by Radio Shack (TRS-80) computers.

TURBODOS: A CP/M compatible disk operating system that has been designed to maximize program execution speed.

URL > Uniform Resource Location - Basically the address of any Gopher - FTP Telnet or WWW site. (3 words)

unbundling: Pricing hardware and software components of a system separately.

UNIX: A minicomputer operating system developed at Bell Telephone Labs that provides a very productive environment for programmers. A number of firms have developed Unix-like operating systems for the new generation of sixteen-bit microprocessors.

utilities: Operating-system-specific software programs used to perform routine tasks such as debugging, formatting disks, and copying files and disks.

V — (4 words)

variable: A named program entity that can assume one or more values during program execution.

VDT (Video Display Terminal): A computer peripheral used to communicate with a computer. The VDT incorporates a display screen, keyboard, controller and communications interface. Also referred to as a CRT (Cathode Ray Tube) terminal.

vector: A one-dimensional array; a means of storing related data items in a single dimension so they can be accessed under a common name.

volatile memory: Memory that loses its contents when the power is turned off.

W — (6 words)

warm boot: A disk operating system function that reads the directories and format information from disks and reloads portions of the operating system. In CP/M a warm boot reloads the Command Control Processor (CCP) into memory. CCP is not required when the computer is processing applications programs, and its memory locations are occasionally used by those programs. A warm boot reloads the CCP when execution of these programs has been completed.

Winchester disk: See hard disk.

window: A portion of a screen. Some word processing programs allow the screen to be segmented into a number of individually controlled areas. These areas are called windows.

word: The unit of information that is manipulated by the CPU. Microprocessors today use eight-bit and sixteen-bit words.

word processor: A special purpose computer dedicated to processing documents.

write protect: A method of preventing new information from being written onto magnetic media. Floppy disks have small notches which are "read" by LEDs in the drive. On 8-inch disks the notches are left open to write protect the disk. On 5.25-inch disks the notches are covered to protect the disk.

— X — (1 word)

XENIX: A version of Unix for 16-bit microcomputers developed by MicroSoft.

— End —

Index

ge fund pg. 287 to 297...

A B

B - C

Read only memory (ROM), 46
Read/write heads, cleaning, 209
Reboot, 191
Recording information on disks, 64–65
Registers, 38–40
Repairmen, 181
Replace operations, word processor, 135–136
Reset key, 51
Resolution, monitor, 99
Restoring files, 217
RETURN (RET) key, 50, 187
Robinson, Spider, 236–237
Role-playing games, 151
Rotation time, 66
Rounding off, 141

S

SBASIC, 125
Screen surfaces, 53
Scrolling, 58
Search commands, word processor, 135
Sectoring, 62, 64–65
Seek time, 66
Seeking, 63, 66
Selectric:
  adapter, 76
  printers, 76
  -type keyboards, 51, 56
Serial interfaces, 82, 189
Serial ports, 47
Serial printers, 71–86
Service, 180–181
Settle time, 65
Sharp portable systems, 91
Single-board computer, 37, 38
Single-user architecture, 106
16–bit chips, 41–44, 159
Smart terminals, 54–55, 58

Sockets, loose, 220–221
Soft sectoring, 64–65
Software, 101–152
  applications programs: *see* Applications programs
  buying, 176–178
  directories, 163–165
  languages, 101, 120–129
  operating systems: *see* Operating systems
  operator errors and, 216–217
  packaging of, 61
  piracy, 178
  utilities, 101, 103, 113–119, 205
  work applications, 15–23
Software houses, 177
Solid-state switches, 50
S-100 bus, 44
Source, The, 21, 115
Source disk, 192
Sources of problems, 213–221
Special business programs, 150
Specialization, 233–235
Specific business support packages, 148–149
Spelling programs, 16, 26, 61, 137–138
Spooling, 110–111
Spreadsheet programs, 139, 140, 141
SS-50 bus, 44
Stack pointer, 39
Standard operating procedure, 201–209
Standards, 157–158
STAT, 114, 116
Static RAMS, 45–46
Statistics programs, 22, 114, 116, 150, 192